'This book is an invaluable resource to therapeutic practitioners wanting to understand more about working with domestic abuse. The book draws on an impressive wealth of practice experience and research evidence. Grounded in a trauma-informed, person-centred and relationship-focused lens, Jeannette and contributing authors engage deeply with the complexity of working with this client group, offering practical strategies, self-reflection exercises, and theoretical insights that will support therapists to develop their practice and understand more about domestic abuse.'

Tanya Beetham, PhD, *is a lecturer in Psychology and Counselling at The Open University. She is a counsellor/psychotherapist with research expertise in domestic abuse.*

'This book is a well-researched and accessibly written guide to working with domestic abuse, which addresses a range of theoretical and professional perspectives. Readers are encouraged to discern whether they are suited to domestic abuse as a specialism and to this approach to the work. A valuable resource for any practitioner.'

Nikki Dhillon Keane *is the author of the BACP guidance* Working with Domestic Abuse in the Counselling Professions *and* Domestic Abuse in Church Communities *(rpbooks.co.uk) and founder of Safe in Faith and cofounder of the Faith and VAWG Coalition.*

Working with Client Experiences of Domestic Abuse

This edited volume shares relevant theory and practical strategies to support counsellors to work effectively with those who have experienced domestic abuse.

The effect of relational and other abuses can impact an individual's ability to engage with family, friends, counsellors, or other professionals trying to support them due to a reduced ability to trust and the impact of complex trauma. Helping someone to recover requires specific knowledge and skills, not usually part of a standard professional training programme. This book acts as a training handbook, providing an overview of what clients need at different stages of recovery. It contains chapters written by staff who deliver counselling and mental health training and provides their insight into the specific issues that clients may present, providing constructive and accessible suggestions for practice, together with a chapter on counsellor self-care. The reflections/exercises in each chapter will help the reader to assess their competency.

Working with Client Experiences of Domestic Abuse will be of interest to mental health professionals, counselling training courses, and domestic violence services, who wish to incorporate counselling as part of their service offer.

Jeannette Roddy has been a practicing counsellor/psychotherapist and researcher in domestic abuse counselling for over 10 years. She became a university academic in 2014, teaching and supervising counselling students in practice and research, and developing a domestic abuse counselling service. In 2022, she left academia to set up Dactari, which specialises in delivering domestic abuse counselling, training and research.

Working with Client Experiences of Domestic Abuse

A Handbook for Counsellors, Psychotherapists, and Other Mental Health Professionals

Edited by Jeannette Roddy

LONDON AND NEW YORK

Designed cover image: © Getty Images

First published 2023
by Routledge
4 Park Square, Milton Park, Abingdon, Oxon OX14 4RN

and by Routledge
605 Third Avenue, New York, NY 10158

Routledge is an imprint of the Taylor & Francis Group, an informa business

British Library Cataloguing-in-Publication Data
A catalogue record for this book is available from the British Library

Library of Congress Cataloguing-in-Publication Data
Names: Roddy, Jeannette K., 1961- editor.
Title: Working with client experiences of domestic abuse : a handbook for counsellors, psychotherapists, and other mental health professionals / edited by Jeannette Roddy.
Description: Abingdon, Oxon ; New York, NY : Routledge, 2023. | Includes bibliographical references and index. |
Identifiers: LCCN 2022061800 (print) | LCCN 2022061801 (ebook) |
ISBN 9781032181790 (hbk) | ISBN 9781032181783 (pbk) |
ISBN 9781003253266 (ebk)
Subjects: LCSH: Family violence. | Family psychotherapy. | Counseling.
Classification: LCC HV6626 .W665 2023 (print) | LCC HV6626 (ebook) |
DDC 362.82/92--dc23/eng/20230321
LC record available at https://lccn.loc.gov/2022061800
LC ebook record available at https://lccn.loc.gov/2022061801

ISBN: 978-1-032-18179-0 (hbk)
ISBN: 978-1-032-18178-3 (pbk)
ISBN: 978-1-003-25326-6 (ebk)

DOI: 10.4324/9781003253266

Typeset in Times New Roman
by MPS Limited, Dehradun

Contents

Note to Readers

The therapy model proposed in this book allows flexibility in working with a client, who has experienced domestic abuse, in a counselling situation. It highlights a counselling process and a range of issues that may need to be addressed at each stage, together with some hints and tips about how to do so. The approach is based on primary research and has been tested at the University of Salford Counselling Research Clinic, to good effect. However, the counselling profession continues to evolve, and this book presents only a snapshot of knowledge at the time of writing. Please note that no technique or practice recommendation is guaranteed as safe with every client or within every situation. The book provides information for qualified counsellors or mental health professionals that can be used within their own professional capacity and judgement. It is not a substitute for formal training or supervision in this area of work. The book can be used as a text within formal counselling training where the training organisation can provide appropriate supervision and personal development for the students. Neither the publisher nor the authors can guarantee the effectiveness or appropriateness of any specific approach suggested in this book in every respect.

The URLs used in this book were live at the time of writing and referred to existing websites. The publisher and authors are not responsible for any content that appears on third-party websites.

Contributing Authors

Elaine Beaumont, University of Salford, UK, Dr Elaine Beaumont is a psychotherapist and lecturer at the University of Salford. She works with a range of organisations and charities primarily working with people who have experienced trauma (http://www.beaumontpsychotherapy.co.uk/index.asp). Elaine is the co-author of the bestselling books: *The Kindness Workbook, The Compassionate Mind Workbook*, and *The Self-Compassion App*.

Keelan Donohue, Psychotherapist, UK, Keelan A. Donohue is a BACP registered psychotherapist from Greater Manchester. He is currently committed to Specialist Mental Health Mentoring for University students, alongside working with other counselling services. With degrees in counselling and psychotherapy and psychology, his specific research interests are in domestic violence and LGBTQ+ related issues.

Linda Dubrow-Marshall, University of Salford, UK, Dr Linda Dubrow-Marshall, PhD, MBACP (Accred.), Counselling and Clinical Psychologist (HCPC) is the co-programme leader of the MSc Psychology of Coercive Control programme at the University of Salford where she is a Senior Lecturer. She has a private practice and is co-founder of the Re-Entry Therapy, Information and Referral Network (RETIRN).

Rod Dubrow-Marshall, University of Salford, UK, Dr Rod Dubrow-Marshall, PhD, MBPsS, is a psychologist and Co-Programme Leader for the MSc Psychology of Coercive Control at the University of Salford. Rod has researched the psychology of coercive influence for over 20 years, developed the Totalistic Identity Theory to explain its psychological effects and is co-founder of RETIRN (UK).

Sarah Eccleston, University of Salford, UK, Sarah Eccleston is an experienced Couples Counsellor who trained at the Relate Institute. Sarah has delivered the Respect Programme and worked with both the perpetrators and victims of domestic abuse. She is currently a lecturer at the University of Salford, where she is the Programme Leader for the MSc in Counselling and Psychotherapy.

Celeste Foster, University of Salford, UK, Dr Celeste Foster is a senior adolescent mental health nurse and registered adolescent psychotherapist who has been working in Child and Adolescent Mental Health, since 1995. She is a Senior Lecturer in Mental Health at the University of Salford. Her research involves new models of nursing practice, pupil emotional wellbeing, and interventions for adolescents.

Leigh Gardner, Metanoia Institute, UK, Leigh Gardner has been a counsellor for over 20 years, in secondary schools and private practice. She is currently a Senior Academic Lecturer at the Metanoia Institute as a Senior Academic Lecturer on the BSc (Hons) Person-Centred Pluralistic course. Leigh's learning and research interests are CYP, Expressive Therapies, Multi-Lingualism, Trauma, and Creative Education.

Joanna Omylinska-Thurston, University of Salford, UK, Dr Joanna Omylinska-Thurston is a Counselling Psychologist with IAPT, Greater Manchester Mental Health NHS Trust and a Lecturer in Counselling and Psychotherapy at the University of Salford. She is a co-founder of a new creative psychotherapy model called Arts for the Blue which is currently being tested with different client groups.

Sarah Riding, University of Salford, UK, Sarah Riding is currently a lecturer in Social Work at The University of Salford. She previously worked as a child and family's social worker and a specialist social worker in Child and Adolescent Mental health services. Sarah's research interests focus on childhood and adult trauma and embedding equality and inclusion in social work practice.

Jeannette Roddy, Dactari Ltd, UK, Dr Jeannette Roddy is an accredited counsellor/psychotherapist and CEO of Dactari, a specialist domestic abuse counselling, training, and research organisation (www.dactari.co.uk). Prior to this, whilst working as a Senior Lecturer, she created the successful University of Salford Domestic Abuse Counselling Service, which is based on the model and training described in this book.

Laura Viliardos, University of Salford, UK, Dr Laura Viliardos is a lecturer in Counselling and Psychotherapy at the University of Salford and clinical lead for the University Counselling Centre. She is a qualified counsellor and counselling supervisor. She specialises in domestic abuse and sexual violence support work, with research interests in the experiences of adult male survivors of abuse.

Mark Widdowson, University of Salford, UK, Dr Mark Widdowson is a UKCP registered psychotherapist, an EMDR Europe accredited practitioner, a Teaching and Supervising Transactional Analyst and holder of the European Certificate of Psychotherapy. He is a Senior Lecturer in Counselling and Psychotherapy at the University of Salford and has a private practice in central Manchester working with individuals and couples.

Preface

In the very first participant interview I did for my PhD research, the person concerned made a very strong plea for me to write a book about the findings to encourage other therapists to learn about how to work with domestic abuse after her many experiences of therapy which did not help. A few years later, that book was published, and whilst I had some positive feedback, it was not enough. It did not show people clearly enough what was required, although it alluded to many things.

I felt that what was needed was something based on experience, so that I had confidence that what was proposed would work. In effect, I had to develop a competency framework which could then be translated into a training programme, which could then be used to train counsellors ready to work with domestic abuse clients. To do that, I needed to have a domestic abuse clinic plus support to develop the teaching programme.

By now in my late 50s, I decided to make the move to Salford (over 100 miles away from home) to gain access to a clinic. What I also gained was access to a staff team who were experts in trauma, coercive control, compassion, and working with children and young people. As I started to share my vision of training counsellors and starting a new clinic, the project seemed to take on a life of its own as people were both interested and keen to take part.

Since running the first programme in 2019 when we opened the clinic, we have trained over 50 counsellors and helped hundreds of clients. Feedback from counsellors during their clinical placements and participation in group supervision has given me confidence that we are doing something useful that is worth sharing more widely. We have proved that we can work effectively with domestic abuse clients outside of the framework of frontline domestic abuse services. This provides the opportunity to train other counsellors and private practitioners in the skills and knowledge required for this work. More trained counsellors could alleviate pressure on frontline services and provide a much wider pool of mental health resources for clients who have experienced domestic abuse. This book provides one part of that vision, providing knowledge of what is required. Additional training will provide the skill. This is a "how to" book as we explain what is needed in counselling based on our experiences and research and invite you to explore if this sort of counselling is for you.

Jeannette Roddy

Acknowledgements

There are many contributors who have helped to bring this book into being and deserve my thanks. The research would not have been possible without the resources provided by York St John University, the University of Sunderland, and the University of Salford. Thanks also to Professor Lynne Gabriel, who has supported me from the very start of my PhD, was a collaborator on the Competency Framework for Domestic Violence: the first step in producing this book, and has provided numerous opportunities for me over the years to help to develop my research.

Translating the competency framework into an outline training programme for counsellors was made much easier with the help of my friend and colleague Leigh Gardner, who has never failed to believe that we could make this happen even when I was doubting myself. Linda and Rod Dubrow-Marshall were there to support the creation of the programme and help create the core course material. Elaine Beaumont, Celeste Foster, Maria Kefalogianni and Debbie Lewis helped to add interesting and valuable elements to the initial programme. This has developed as people have left and others joined. The support of everyone has been invaluable.

All these book chapters were written by the current teaching team, fitted in with many other commitments. Everyone has taught on the programme on a voluntary basis believing in what we were doing. I am enormously grateful for their generosity in time and expertise.

We could not have done this without the volunteer counsellors who undertook six days of training and 12 months of counselling as volunteers, or the hundreds of clients we have worked with, who have provided data, referred friends and colleagues to the service, and inspired our counsellors to continue this work.

More recently, I have left the University of Salford and set up a new company, Dactari, specialising in domestic abuse counselling, training, and research, with the help of counsellors and colleagues from the University of Salford. My thanks to Amy Armitage, Gordon Worswick, Karen Nolan and Sarah Bagshaw, who are also involved with Dactari, for their helpful review of the manuscript before going to press.

Finally, I must mention my husband of 32 years, who has supported my work from starting my PhD research through to living away from home at Salford. He has been there to encourage me when everything seemed to be going wrong, to celebrate when things have gone well, and to smile when friends have asked why I have such an interest in domestic abuse! I know how lucky I am to have him, and it is good to be home with him once more.

Thank you all for your support, help and hard work, and for your encouragement and belief in the possibilities for improving counselling for those who have experienced domestic abuse.

Chapter 1

Introduction

Jeannette Roddy

This chapter positions the rest of the book in relation to current thinking and practice within a domestic abuse context. The key objectives for the chapter are to:

1 Understand what domestic abuse is, its prevalence and effect on human beings
2 Provide a brief history of our developing understanding of how to work with individuals from a counselling perspective
3 Highlight challenges with existing counselling models of practice
4 Explore research outcomes from a client perspective to improve counselling practice
5 Identify how this book matches the domestic violence counselling competency framework
6 Provide an outline of the book content

Fifteen years ago, as I began my counselling training, I was lucky to gain a placement at a local Women's Aid agency as a volunteer counsellor. At that time, in 2007, domestic violence support was focused on women and my training informed me that one in four women would be affected by domestic violence in their lifetime. Today, statistics show that human relationships are still fraught with difficulty, suggesting not only one in four women but also one in five men experience domestic abuse in their lifetime (ONS, 2021). The introduction of a legal definition of domestic abuse in the 2021 Domestic Abuse Act has changed things, as this acknowledges that abuse could happen to anyone, whatever their situation within the family, or current or previous partnerships. Although the statistics appear broadly unchanged in 15 years, it remains shocking to consider that over 13 million people in the United Kingdom today will experience abuse at the hands of their families and/or intimate partners at some time in their lives.

Back in 2007, there was growing recognition of the mental health consequences of domestic abuse. Research was showing high prevalence of depression, suicidal ideation, and PTSD in women who had experienced domestic violence (Golding, 1999; Herman, 1992; Humphreys & Thiara, 2003). Since then, there

DOI: 10.4324/9781003253266-1

have been more studies completed confirming significant levels of mental health difficulties (Ferrari et al., 2016; McManus et al., 2022). Now, however, some studies show that men too can experience mental health consequences from an abusive relationship (Hines & Douglas, 2009, 2011, 2015).

Despite the acknowledgement of the mental health difficulties of this client group, little research has been conducted into what might be helpful in recovering from such an experience. A recent meta-analysis of 33 trials from across the world (Hameed et al., 2020), which used a range of different approaches, research questions, support worker roles, and number of sessions, concluded that psychological therapies for women do not appear to cause any harm, probably reduce depression and may reduce anxiety symptoms, but it was not clear they reduced the effects of trauma. The study called for further research in this area, particularly with trauma interventions, and for more rigorous trials to produce better data, echoing the call for more rigorous data collection identified much earlier (Ramsay et al., 2005). It appears that, from a policy perspective, little progress has been made on mental health treatment in the last 15 years, due to inadequate data.

There are many reasons why these rigorous studies are hard to complete. There is still little agreement on the purpose of therapy in domestic abuse, whether it is to reduce symptoms of depression and anxiety, for example, or to reduce symptoms of trauma, or to increase decision making ability, personal safety, or well-being. Given that most therapies offered are 10–20 sessions long, it is important to decide what the therapy will focus on when conducting a trial. Of course, there must also be clear focus on the selected research question, which is where the first problem arises. Of the many aspects of life that are affected when people experience domestic abuse, which ones should be selected for improvement. The second problem is, given that this client group do experience serious mental health difficulties, what selection criteria can be identified for the trial: will it be all potential clients, or just those who are moderately unwell. Thirdly, given the anxiety/depression/trauma presented may be dependent to some extent on the client's history and clients may have had one or multiple abusive relationships, which can impact the therapy process, what history is acceptable for inclusion in the trial. In addition, there are issues around whether people have had therapy before and whether that was successful or not, which might impact on outcomes, as well as whether one defined therapy will really meet the needs of a hugely complex client group.

Although many therapies have been offered and only mild to moderate efficacy shown (Hameed et al., 2020), the method or approach to the work tends not to be published in detail, perhaps as it is not seen to be robust enough. This means that the potential for practitioner learning from the research is lost. Many domestic abuse counselling services have created their own models of practice from their experience which work well in their environment and some offer limited training. Many of the practice-oriented texts for domestic abuse counselling are also based on practitioner experience (Dutton, 1992; Sanderson, 2008; Walker, 1994) and all offer useful insight into how to work with women who have experienced domestic abuse. However, what appears to be missing is a practical and successful model of practice, based on research, which also meets the criteria for rigour and does not only address the needs of women.

This book does not quite meet that definition, but it does offer an interesting alternative. It provides a description of an approach to domestic abuse counselling that is based on client research (Roddy, 2014). The model is based on research with both female and male participants (Roddy and Keech, 2019) and so is applicable to a wide range of clients. This research was then used to develop a competency framework for counsellors working in the field (Roddy & Gabriel, 2019). The competencies identified included the personal characteristics of the therapist, plus the knowledge and skills required to work with the clients. This formed the basis for a training programme for therapists, trialled at the University of Salford. The training course, focusing on the knowledge and skills required, was written and delivered by a team of lecturers from the university, based on meeting the knowledge and skills defined by the competency framework. Recruiting students and counsellors to the training programme allowed a domestic abuse counselling service to open in October 2019 for everyone. By 2022, one-third of the clients seen were male and a quarter came from an ethnic minority background. The counsellors trained in this approach (now nearly 60 of them, over three years) have worked with hundreds of clients using the training and supervision provided to good effect. This book covers much of the teaching of that course, which allows us to share our understanding of the knowledge and skills that are required of domestic abuse counsellors.

So, we appear to have a successful model of practice, based on research. But is the model effective? Well, funding in counselling research is hard to come by and so the model has not been subject to clinical trials such as those reported in the literature. So, the short answer is no. However, we have collected data on mental health as part of our clinical process and can report that, on average, our clients present with moderately severe psychological distress, anxiety, and depression symptoms and, on average, end therapy with mild/moderate symptoms after, on average, 12 sessions (Roddy and Viliardos, 2022). We are, of course, aware that this data is affected by the people who present with a need to process memories of previous abuse but are not clinically anxious or depressed and therefore show little "improvement." We are also aware of supporting highly anxious people through court processes, where the success is being able to attend court and present their case, not reductions in anxiety scores. Finally, we screen clients for degree of complexity (three levels) and assign them to appropriately experienced therapists, which potentially affects our results. This is the problem with this type of research: there are so many variables it is very difficult to be able to run a trial that would be acceptable in terms of rigour and quality, without impacting on the client.

Although we have sessional data collection, hence the description of outcomes above, we cannot state whether this is better or worse than other therapies because we do not have a comparable data set with a similar service. What we can say is that our weekly client list has built up from zero in October 2019 to over 60 clients per week in May 2022, with a waiting list now in place. Many of the referrals are word of mouth. We know that some of our clients had tried many therapies before coming to us and then found something that worked. We believe we are providing a therapeutic service which has value.

Feedback from the domestic abuse service counsellors has indicated that the training has fundamentally changed their clinical practice for the better and many of the counsellors have gone on to gain employment in other services with complex clients. We have not noticed any differences in outcomes for clients, based on counsellor background or previous knowledge of domestic abuse. We recruit our therapists based on our competency model for personal characteristics (including a calm presence and positive outlook) and teach the skills and knowledge that are required. This seems to work well.

The purpose of this book is to provide information for counsellors, psychotherapists and other mental health practitioners who want to work with domestic abuse experiences but have not had a lot of training. Hence the book is aimed at informing those who are new to this area of work, rather than those who are already very experienced. Each of the chapters is written by the lecturer(s) teaching the topic to our clinic recruits. It is written as a teaching book, with learning objectives and activities. In many chapters, there are personal reflective exercises distributed through the text to help you to understand your own process, as well as the client's, which is a very important part of this therapeutic work. Some of the chapters are written with an emphasis on research, others with using the experience of the writer, in line with the teaching. Students have commented on how valuable different approaches to teaching have been in understanding the topics.

The book is laid out in a format that you can follow through from this chapter 1 to the end. It begins with the counselling model itself, what the different stages mean and what sort of clinical work might be required at each stage. This is followed up with chapters on understanding domestic abuse, the enhanced levels of therapeutic skills required, plus some issues of attachment and transference and ways that clients may protect themselves during the therapeutic process, core elements of the model. We then move into understanding and working with complex trauma, understanding the impact of previous childhood abuse on the adult client and compassionate mind training to help clients foster a positive self-view. We consider the different ways that abuse can be enacted based on the individual's life experience and, recognising that many people we see are going through legal processes, we have a chapter on the law and its potential impact. Finally, we look at creative ways of working with trauma, an important aspect of complex trauma work. These chapters are designed to support you with your client work. Chapter 14 concludes the taught sections with thoughts on self-care: what you might do to look after yourself amidst the traumatic material heard and ensure that you are ok to work with your clients.

The model can help you to track where your clients are in the therapeutic process and offers some ideas about issues that might arise at different stages and how you might approach these with clients. You will see that the chapters often refer to each other for additional information showing the interlinked nature of the skills and knowledge required in this work. It perhaps also begins to suggest why research trials highlighting different specific therapies are less likely to succeed, given the range of skills and knowledge required at each stage. The book contains a lot of information, with links to additional information, and may have value as a reference text after the initial reading.

Throughout the book, we use the term counsellor and therapist interchangeably and we also use the term abuser rather than perpetrator in many chapters, plus person or individual, rather than victim or survivor in most chapters. Some chapters do refer to perpetrators and victims: the choice of the author. We also use the non-gendered language of they, recognising that we could be working with anyone. Finally, it is worth saying that our client base is from those who have left the relationship, not those seeking support to leave, hence being able to set up the clinic at the university rather than within a domestic violence agency.

The purpose of writing the book was to facilitate an increased level of understanding amongst general mental health practitioners of what people who have experienced domestic abuse need from therapy. Having knowledgeable counsellors in this field across the United Kingdom, rather than in only a few funded areas, must surely be of benefit to our clients. However, please do remember that it is advisable to attend specialist training on the items covered in this book before you try them out on clients in your practice.

We hope that you enjoy the book.

References

Dutton, M. A. (1992). *Empowering and healing the battered woman: a model for assessment and intervention*. Springer Pub. Co.

Ferrari, G., Agnew-Davies, R., Bailey, J., Howard, L., Howarth, E., Peters, T. J., Lynnmarie, S., & Gene Solomon, F. (2016). Domestic violence and mental health: a cross-sectional survey of women seeking help from domestic violence support services. *Global Health Action*, *9*(1). 10.3402/gha.v9.29890

Golding, J. M. (1999). Intimate partner violence as a risk factor for mental disorders: A meta-analysis. *Journal of Family Violence*, *14*(2), 99–132. http://search.ebscohost.com/login.aspx?direct=true&db=sih&AN=18331395&site=ehost-live

Hameed M. O. D. L., Gilchrist, G., Tirado-Muñoz, J., Tan, A., Chondros, P., Feder, G., Tan, M., Hegarty, K. (2020). Psychological therapies for women who experience intimate partner violence. *Cochrane Database of Systematic Reviews*, *7*(7). Retrieved 24th October 2021, Jul 1; CD013017. doi: 10.1002/14651858.CD013017.pub2. PMID: 32608505; PMCID: PMC7390063.

Herman, J. L. (1992). *Trauma and recovery*. Pandora.

Hines, D. A., & Douglas, E. M. (2009). Women's use of intimate partner violence against men: prevalence, implications, and consequences. *Journal of Aggression, Maltreatment & Trauma*, *18*(6), 572–586. http://search.ebscohost.com/login.aspx?direct=true&db=cin20&AN=2010385644&site=ehost-live

Hines, D. A., & Douglas, E. M. (2011). Symptoms of posttraumatic stress disorder in men who sustain intimate partner violence: a study of helpseeking and community samples. *Psychology of Men & Masculinity*, *12*(2), 112–127. 10.1037/a0022983

Hines, D. A., & Douglas, E. M. (2015). Health problems of partner violence victims: comparing help-seeking men to a population-based sample. *American Journal of Preventive Medicine*, *48*(2), 136–144. 10.1016/j.amepre.2014.08.022

Humphreys, C., & Thiara, R. (2003). Mental health and domestic violence: 'I call it symptoms of abuse.' *British Journal of Social Work*, *33*(2), 209–226. 10.1093/bjsw/33.2.209

McManus, S., Walby, S., Barbosa, E. C., Appleby, L., Brugha, T., Bebbington, P. E., Cook, E. A., & Knipe, D. (2022). Intimate partner violence, suicidality, and self-harm: a probability sample survey of the general population in England. *The Lancet Psychiatry*, *9*(7), 574–583. 10.1016/s2215-0366(22)00151-1

ONS. (2021). Crime in England and Wales: year ending March 2021. Online: Office for National Statistics Retrieved from https://www.ons.gov.uk/peoplepopulationand-community/crimeandjustice/bulletins/crimeinenglandandwales/yearendingmarch2021

Ramsay, J., Rivas, C., & Feder, G. (2005). *Interventions to reduce violence and promote the physical and psychosocial well-being of women who experience partner violence: a systematic review of controlled evaluations*. D. o. Health. http://www.dh.gov.uk/prod_consum_dh/groups/dh_digitalassets/@dh/@en/documents/digitalasset/dh_4127426.pdf

Roddy, J. K. (2014). *A client informed view of domestic violence counselling* [PhD, University of Leeds]. Leeds.

Roddy, J. K., & Gabriel, L. (2019). A competency framework for domestic violence counselling. *British Journal of Guidance & Counselling*, *47*(6), 669–681. 10.1080/03069885.2019.1599322

Roddy, J. K., & Keech, C. (2019). Working with survivors of Domestic Abuse: addressing the needs of male and female counselling clients in the UK BACP Research Conference : Shaping counselling practice and policy: the next 25 years, Belfast.

Roddy, J. K., & Viliardos, L. A. (2022, 5th October). Improving mental health for domestic abuse survivors: A new model of counselling delivery effective interventions to prevent and reduce harm and abuse, Preston.

Sanderson, C. (2008). *Counselling survivors of domestic abuse*. Jessica Kingsley.

Walker, L. E. (1994). *Abused women and survivor therapy: a practical guide for the psychotherapist*. American Psychological Association.

Chapter 2

A Model of Therapeutic Practice

Jeannette Roddy

Learning Objectives

1 To understand a basic approach to domestic abuse (DA) counselling work
2 To recognise what clients may need as they begin counselling or psychotherapy
3 To prepare for the different ways that therapy can develop and why
4 To explore what you may find easy now, what may be more challenging and what you may still need to learn

Context

Working with survivors of DA has often been seen as challenging work. Clients have reported adverse experiences in counselling, feeling unheard and misunderstood (Farmer et al., 2013; Keech & Roddy, 2019; Roddy, 2014; Taskforce on the Health Aspects of Violence against Women and Children, 2010). There is anecdotal evidence that DA counselling student placements can lead to many "Did not attend" (DNA) sessions making it hard for students to gain placement hours. Professionals too have reported difficulty in giving the client what is needed, leading to early termination of therapy. Whilst there seems to be a willingness from all parties to give things a go, there are signs that it can be quite difficult "to find a way to work together".

The approach to practice described in this book provides a framework that organisations and therapists can use to help make the experience in therapy more helpful and constructive, leading to greater engagement and better outcomes for the client. Uniquely, this proposed approach is inclusive of individuals irrespective of their gender, sexuality, or race. The book works from the principle that human beings who wish to abuse another do so from their own motivation and world view, using the tools that are most effective based on their skill level and the perceived weakness of the victim. Hence the abuser may use gender, sexuality, class, social structure, parenting, family, religion, career, community, or anything else that they

DOI: 10.4324/9781003253266-2

perceive the victim may feel especially sensitive to, or ashamed of, to exert control. See chapters 3 and 11 for more information about how abusers may try to exert control.

Working from the client perspective of the abuse and the impact that this had on them means using a strongly person-centred approach, with aspects of cognitive behavioural therapy (CBT) and psychodynamic theory supporting the work. For example, psychoeducation can be used to help the client to understand, but with the agreement of the client rather than the insistence of the therapist. This allows facilitation of the client to understand what might have happened and respond to that knowledge in their own way. Whilst this approach draws on principles that are taught in most therapeutic training, and identifies others that are specialist in nature, it also provides insight into how these different elements can work together to meet the needs of this client group. This chapter draws on previously published work on the model and the competencies required for counselling work (Roddy, 2014, 2015; Roddy & Gabriel, 2019) which can provide much more detail than a short book chapter.

A Model of Practice

The proposed framework for counselling practice is shown in Figure 2.1. This shows three distinct stages of work with the client: stage 1 is where the client is making decisions to access and then engage with the counselling; stage 2 is where the client settles down into a much deeper exploration of their experiences, past and present; and stage 3 is where the client is making the decision to leave counselling as they feel able to move on with their lives. There are a few steps within each stage and the diagram arrows show that the steps taken are not always linear.

Although counsellors are only involved from step 3 in stage 1 where the counselling begins until step 7 in stage 3, the client sees their therapeutic journey beginning when they recognise the need for help and continuing beyond leaving therapy, as they embed what they have learned in their lives. Understanding the process that clients can go through prior to accessing counselling helps us to improve the systems and processes seen by the client prior to starting counselling to support them in their journey. Each of these stages and the steps identified are described below in more detail.

This chapter outlines the way a client might use counselling and also the skills, knowledge, and personal characteristics required of the therapist. Clear links are made to specific chapters to highlight when these may be most useful, depending on where the client is in their process. It is hoped that, in this way, the book may be used with clients at different stages in therapy to provide some new thoughts and guidance if therapy is becoming stuck.

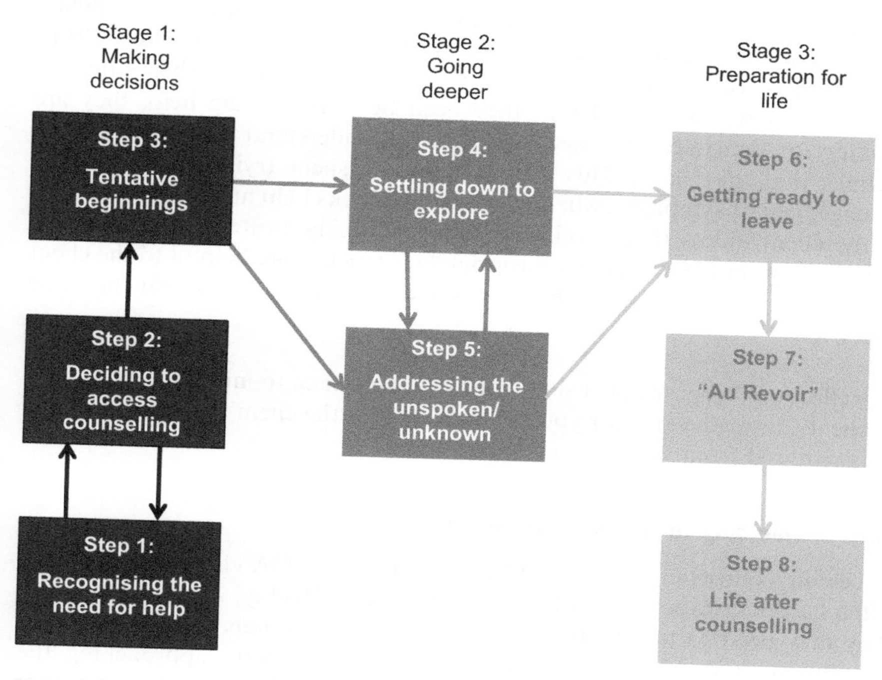

Figure 2.1 Client stages of therapy.

Stage 1: Making Decisions

As counsellors we often see counselling as starting when the client arrives for the initial session. However, there are three steps in stage 1, as seen in figure 1, which involve the client making decisions about how to, and whether to, access therapy (Steps 1 and 2) and then whether to continue counselling after the counselling has started (Step 3). If we understand the client's decision process for accessing counselling, we can help to facilitate an easier path into therapy. This stage highlights what clients may need to support their decisions and invites you to consider how well your service is currently meeting those needs.

Step 1: Recognising the Need for Help

The mental health consequences of experiencing DA have been well documented for the last 30-40 years, not just with adult DA but the experience of DA within childhood. Reports of high levels of anxiety, depression, trauma, and suicidal ideation are common (Ferrari et al., 2016; McManus et al., 2022). For some clients, recognising that they can no longer cope with their symptoms prompts them to seek help, for others it may be that their emotions are spilling out beyond their control at work or with their partners (Roddy, 2014). Clients have often tried everything they can to try to manage their situation and have finally concluded that they need help. In seeking help, they are looking for someone, or somewhere, that will understand the overwhelming feelings that they have. This means that time spent trying to discuss the management of symptoms when the client first seeks help may not feel helpful to the client unless they specifically ask for coping strategies. Hearing the client's story and responding appropriately is much more helpful to the client and their process. Look at chapters 4 and 5 to see how this can be done effectively.

> Reflection: When you consider your own approach to initial meetings with clients, how easy is it for you to simply follow the client's story? What else is required from you or your organisation?

Step 2: Deciding to Access Counselling

Accessing counselling can be a difficult decision for DA clients as they have often had poor experiences of counselling before (Roddy, 2014). As a result, they may need to talk to friends or trusted professionals to seek a recommendation or conduct their own research online before approaching the counselling service. Providing information that helps with making that decision, for example through a website or social media, is important and this can also be used by agencies who may suggest the service to clients.

> Reflection: How do your clients find out about your service? How useful is the information provided for making an informed decision about the counselling you offer?

Once the client has made contact, they are then gauging whether they feel the service will understand them and their specific situation. If the client is to be assessed for the service, the assessor needs to have a good understanding of DA and the way DA can affect someone (see chapter 3 for more information on this). Showing the client that they are understood at this stage builds hope that the counsellor may also understand and that the counselling may help. It is also useful to have an assessment process that allows the client to share their main areas of concern, without going into any depth, so that the client is less likely to be overwhelmed by the experience, and perhaps more likely to return.

Having a trained and qualified counsellor available to do this work can be helpful as they can manage the session carefully as well as assess the complexity of the client's current and past histories. In services where counsellors are allocated, counsellor experience should be carefully matched with the complexity of client experience. It is also important to manage client expectations, for example having an accurate idea of current waiting list times so that clients know how and when they might be called back as well as having a clear point of contact for any queries that might arise. Doing what we say we will do helps to build confidence and trust (important factors) in the organisation until therapy begins (see also chapter 3).

Ideally the first appointment will be arranged by the therapist by telephone to allow an initial connection to be made with the client. Not all clients will answer or allow telephone contact due to their previous experiences of telephone abuse and here, contact by email is better. It is important that any approach to the client is in a way that works for them.

Reflection: How are clients introduced to your organisation and how do they maintain contact if there is a waiting list? How well do staff in your organisation understand the complexities of DA? How are first appointments made? What impression is the client given?

Step 3: Tentative Beginnings

This is the beginning of sessions between the counsellor and the client. There are several areas to consider when starting therapy, identified in the following text.

Creating the Right Environment

The first session for a counsellor is simply establishing a relationship and finding something to talk about without necessarily pressing too hard. A comfortable, relaxed atmosphere of two equals, where everything is welcome, is a useful starting point. It can be helpful to start the session with some basic contracting, in particular confidentiality, establishing clear boundaries from the outset whilst also taking the focus away from the client if that is helpful.

Conversely, the first session can be quite an ordeal for the client. Facing the possibility that they are going to have to tell someone what happened to them can be frightening, shameful or anxiety provoking, or they simply may not know where to start. Clients may want to create different types of relationship with you with some clients wanting to share everything as fast as they can (which may mean over-disclosure and a careful checking in process at the end to manage any concerns which may have arisen) and others being quite guarded about what they say, talking mainly about what is happening now for them. In both situations, listening and showing you understand, and letting the client know that you welcome hearing more at the next session, can be enough. For more information on what might be required in working with clients at the beginning of therapy, please see chapters 4 and 5.

As the client discloses, being able to show you understand what was happening in the context of DA is important (see chapter 3 for background on this) as this is often not understood. Psychoeducation on DA theories can be an important part of the work if the client has not previously explored this. Helping the client to understand their own experience (such as why they are suddenly becoming very anxious) can be very helpful in establishing the potential usefulness of sessions. Adopting a stance of curiosity and interest, rather than any judgement, is also helpful as it facilitates the story. In listening to client stories, focus on the client's perception of the event rather than your own and respond objectively (see also chapter 11).

Clients are all different: some will bring one thing to explore in depth within a session, others will take several sessions of alluding to a particular incident before finally disclosing what happened. It is important to recognise the client's process, go at their pace and resist the temptation to push the client to disclose more than they are ready to do, as this can overwhelm the client. Working through things at the clients pace works best. For more information on pacing and session management, particularly with difficult disclosures, please see chapters 4 and 8. In either case, managing the end of the session to ensure the client is ready to reconnect with the outside world is important.

Finally, showing the client that you care about them is vital. This can be as simple as smiling as you meet them or wishing them well in any forthcoming events. When someone has been abused by the one person that they felt loved them, it can feel like no-one cares. Experiencing acceptance and warmth can be a welcome relief after their previous relationship experiences.

> Reflection: when you consider these elements of building a relationship with the client, which ones do you already do with your current clients? Which ones are left and how could you develop these? What could you do to integrate these into your current practice?

Dealing with Current Issues

Often people who have experienced DA will have many complex and difficult issues to deal with. Some may have court cases and child custody hearings, others might be struggling with access to their children post-separation, whilst others may be struggling to live on their own. Many will have some contact with their abuser and will continue to be abused in some way: verbally; by text or email; through social media; through professionals (by reporting or implying some issue that will warrant legal, social work, medical or police involvement: see chapters 3 and 12); through common friendship groups and so on.

Helping the client to understand the abuser's behaviours and motivations can be helpful in finding strategies to cope with the stress. For example, if the abuser uses the handover of children (as part of shared custody) as an opportunity to have a go at the client, it can be helpful to explore other ways of handing over the children, such as leaving them at a family member or close friend's house to be picked up there.

Equally, there may be a range of presenting emotions and behaviours which can be disruptive to their current life. See chapters 6, 7, 8, 10 and 13 for more information of the causes and what might be helpful to try in session. Working with a therapist who is actively engaged with their main concerns can feel like someone is on their side, sometimes a new experience. It may also prompt more disclosure as the client brings more into the session that they would like to understand.

Reflection: Think about the many ways that the abuser may use to try to control the client after separation. What simple ways could be used relieve the pressure on the client? Which agencies are you aware of locally to that you could refer the client to if they needed additional support (for example: court orders, legal aid, housing)?

Deciding to Continue

Remember that as you try to settle the client into counselling, the client is still trying to decide whether they want to stay or go. It is useful to bring out into the open any feeling that there may be a disconnect between you and the client to explore and resolve what might be going on (see also chapters 4 and 5). If the exploration of the client's experience has gone too deeply, too quickly, it is useful to discuss that with the client and try to establish how you might work together more effectively (see also chapter 8). Managing to talk through such relationship issues can create a stronger therapeutic relationship as the client can see that issues and any conflict can be resolved easily and non-defensively, and that their views are sought and valued.

The decision for the client to continue counselling can take up to 8 sessions. Hence a 6-session counselling model can be of limited value. Having the option to extend past 10 sessions can be very helpful as once the client feels comfortable, they often have a lot to say and a few additional sessions is just not enough.

Ultimately, it is for the client to decide. Creating a safe space and helping the client to disclose at their own pace, whilst helping them to put their experiences in context, are all helpful ways to encourage therapy to continue. Once the client decides to stay, there can be a shift in the sessions, with a clearer focus, fewer cancellations, and a sense of a deeper therapeutic relationship. At this point, the client is moving into stage 2 of the process.

Reflection: How might you know if the client was settling into therapy or considering whether to leave? What might be the best way to address this?

Stage 2: Going Deeper

In stage 2, the therapeutic relationship becomes much stronger and more secure as the client settles to look at the more difficult aspects of their life (step 4). Behaviours and responses to current events that were once helpful and soothing during the abuse may now be seen by the client as problematic (see chapters 6 and 7).

From a counsellor perspective, this is also when difficult, traumatic experiences from adulthood or childhood can be explored (step 5) (see chapter 8). Sometimes the experiences of childhood can set patterns for our responses to events in adulthood (see chapter 9) which are less effective as an adult. The two steps in this stage show that the client will not just focus on trauma but will also explore other issues in parallel with the trauma work, often swopping between the two as their life dictates the need to process other things in therapy. Sometimes clients have a very complicated past (see also chapter 9) which would need many more sessions to fully resolve.

This is a complex stage of the counselling as the client is balancing understanding and processing recent experiences and ongoing events, with deeper exploration of some of the factors in their past that may be impacting on their current life. Helping clients to see links between past and present provides a perspective that clients can find very useful.

Step 4: Settling Down to Explore

As the client starts to feel more secure in the therapeutic relationship, they share more about their experiences, often leading to their first ever disclosure about particularly difficult experiences to the counsellor. As the trust in the relationship builds, this also allows the client to consider alternative views about themselves and others through gentle therapeutic challenge. Elements of this step are highlighted below.

Feeling Safer

Building trust is a very important part of the work being done in counselling. In chapter 4, you can read about how trust is built and why a person-centred approach is particularly helpful in this. However, feeling safer within therapy can also lead to feeling safer outside the therapeutic space leading to more connections with friends and family being made as the client starts to believe in themselves again. This experience of greater sharing within therapy and externally is a good measure of how well the counselling is going.

> Reflection: How might you encourage a client to reconnect with friends and family without being directive?

Challenges to Client Perception of Themselves

As the therapeutic relationship grows and more experiences are explored, the client will begin to recognise that many aspects of the relationship which they held themselves accountable for were not necessarily their fault. As they begin to understand the dynamics of abuse, they can begin to recognise which aspects were entirely the responsibility of the abuser and when, perhaps, they made choices which they regretted but now recognise were the best choices available at that time. The counsellor's role here is to show that there is more than one way to look at a particular incident, especially considering roles, actions, choices, and responsibility. The information in chapter 3 will be helpful in facilitating this.

As the client begins to understand more about what happened, they often begin to recognise the way they are undermining and judging themselves, even when the abuser is no longer present. Here, the therapist must ensure that any interpretation of these thoughts is in line with the client's circumstances i.e. that the focus is on things that can be changed or affected. This requires some cultural skill on the part of the counsellor to explore what changes in thoughts or behaviours might mean for the client. This shift in perception of themselves also requires their trust in the therapist to challenge them appropriately. Without that trust, it could be construed as criticism, which feeds low esteem and self-confidence. Challenges need to be honest and heart-felt to be heard by the client. See chapters 3, 4, 5, and 11 for help with this.

Reflection: How do you feel about using challenge in counselling sessions? What do you understand as challenge? (Remember challenge could be as simple as providing two different perspectives on an event) When you think about challenging in this way, what do you see as the potential pitfalls?

Doing Things Differently

By spending time in therapy looking at how people interact and how that can affect them, the client can now start to apply this to situations in their life. These instances of the client recognising something different outside and bringing it back into therapy to discuss allows greater understanding of themselves. This can reduce levels of anxiety and anger, as the world is seen as less frustrating.

The client can also start to experiment outside of the sessions as they begin to challenge other aspects of their lives, for example, going along with others, rather than deciding what is right for them. Sometimes the confidence to voice something like "I don't like going to the market on Saturdays" can take a few weeks to talk through in therapy and yet once implemented in real life provides a great base to make and act upon other choices in their lives.

Reflection: How can you ensure that you provide positive encouragement for the client in making these changes, rather than implied criticism? How do you ensure that the client is making the changes for themselves, rather than for you?

Whilst these things may seem small, for people who have had many aspects of their lives controlled over an extended period of time, with consequences for dissent, working up the courage to make changes, to state their opinion, and to feel positive about themselves, helps them to regain control of their lives. Once one step has been taken successfully, many more often follow quickly. For more information on these aspects of the work, please see chapters 6, 7, and 10.

Reflection: Much of the work in this section is underpinned by a very good working knowledge of how abusers use their power and the impact that has on the individual. How much do you already know and what more do you need to find out? Remember, this isn't just about theory, but how it is enacted in practice.

Step 5: Addressing the Unspoken/Unknown

For some, but not all, clients who have experienced DA, memories of the abuse will leave them with difficult and challenging traumatic memories. There will also be a significant number of clients who will have previously had abusive childhood experiences which are also playing a part in their current difficulties. Often these memories have been suppressed for years, but as the work continues and different aspects of the current abuse are explored, these create links in the client's mind to other, similar events earlier on in their life. For those who experience these shifts whilst in counselling, it is important to work through what the client brings or feels. In this step, it is useful to understand more about the childhood experience of abuse, as well as how to work with abuse creatively and sensitively. Chapters 8, 9, 10, and 13 are particularly helpful for this part of the work, if required.

Identifying Past Experiences

Identification of past experiences comes from the client, not the therapist. Sometimes, as the experiences upper-most in the client's mind are addressed, the client starts to make links to previous experiences. These experiences may be things they are aware of, but not spoken of before, or they may be things on the edge of the client's awareness that have now been brought into focus as part of the therapy, perhaps by noticing body movements at particular times. It is important to stay at the pace of the client and not to move into directed exploration, as there is the chance that the client is not quite ready to see everything in full. This may require a number of sessions to fully process, as the client dips in and out to the extent that they can tolerate the emotions that emerge. Exercises to help with emotional regulation are helpful here (see chapters 8, 9, 10, and 13).

> Reflection: As a therapist, how do you develop the skill to go at the client's pace? How do you know when it is appropriate to let things go, and when to challenge the client to go just a little further?

Working through the Process

Working though traumatic experiences can be difficult for both the client and the therapist. Experiences that were too difficult to talk about at the time, or have sometimes been buried for some years, are rarely without emotional tension.

In these circumstances, it is important that the counsellor can normalise the experiences of the client within trauma theory (see chapters 8 and 9). The techniques and ideas described here can support the client to manage their emotions, which can allow closer examination of what the thoughts and feelings might be. Depending on the therapists training, they may use specific types of trauma-based interventions, or they may use imagery or other creative tools (see chapters 8 and 13 for some ideas on this). The therapist must be confident with, and trained in, whatever approach they decide to use with the client as they need to ensure that a safe space is maintained throughout any exploration.

> Reflection: What do you know about working with trauma already and what do you need to find out? Where could you find appropriate additional training?

In facilitating this process for the client, the counsellor must be fully engaged and connected with the client. This presents some risks to the therapist as they may be left with images, sensations and feelings related to the disclosure which will need to be processed. Repeated exposure to other people's trauma without necessary care could result in therapist burnout (see chapter 14). Self-care for therapists is particularly important when working with this client group.

> Reflection: What does self-care mean to you and how rigorously to you maintain work/life boundaries to ensure you have some recovery time? If this is not currently part of your working life, how could you change this?

Benefits of Resolving Past Experiences

Whilst the processing of trauma cannot be undertaken lightly the benefits to the client in processing the experiences are significant. Where before, the client may have been frightened by what was unseen or difficult to pull into conscious thought, there may now be a sense of a load lifted and more energy available for other things. Clarity on what happened can bring relief, even if it is not pleasant.

Seeing what had happened in the past can help the client to understand how they are in the world today as they try to protect themselves from this happening again. Yet, they are different people now, with different knowledge, experiences, tools, and better understanding of their strengths to help protect them. This change in self-perception can help with issues as diverse as relationships, work, and self-care. It also provides the client with a sense of control over their life, where the trauma had previously left them feeling out of control.

As the work continues, having the counsellor alongside, supportive, and caring at each step, provides a different role model to the one many clients have experienced before. There may not have been many people in their lives so interested in them for an extended period of time and the dynamic of feeling cared for helps them to grow in confidence and self-esteem (see chapter 4).

This is a complex stage of therapy and there can be times where the work seems to have stalled or becomes more difficult. There can be many reasons why this is the case, for example the client's response to traumatic memories (see chapter 8). Supervision for counsellors is vital here, for example to identify what may be going on the counselling room (see also chapter 5), as well as to support the counsellor (see also chapter 14). Finding ways through these difficulties together with the client can feel very rewarding to the counsellor and can be life changing for the client.

> Reflection: How comfortable are you with the possibility of processing such experiences with a client? How do you know that this type of work is right for you? What additional training might you need?

Stage 3: Preparing for Life after Counselling

As the client enters stage 3, there is a change in the sessions as the client starts to feel more in control of their life, more confident and has less to discuss in therapy. Although this stage can be quite short therapeutically, there are still important aspects of this process that require counselling support. Sensing that an ending may be approaching, the client starts to prepare to leave therapy and support themselves in the future (step 6). The therapist work in stage 3 is about supporting client independence whilst also re-assuring the client that they can access the counselling service again in the future, if needed (step 7). Research participants have reported using what they have learned in therapy to support themselves long after the counselling has finished (step 8).

Step 6: Getting Ready to Leave

The client will start to realise that they have covered most of what they wanted to cover (and perhaps more besides). This is the time where they begin to show much more interest in the outside world and session time may be spent more on what has changed, been achieved or on the different challenges that are appearing due to greater social activity. Gradually the client begins to recognise that they are supporting themselves much more now, that they feel more confident and positive about themselves and that it is time to move on and end therapy. Sometimes there is recognition that more could be done, but enough has been completed for now. When there are fixed numbers of sessions offered, this process tends to begin a few sessions before the end as the client prepares for the ending. Clients have reported how helpful it is when the counsellor confirms with them that they feel the client is ready for the ending.

> Reflection: How do you ensure that the client gets to process their feelings about leaving therapy without direction from the counsellor? How do you recognise that a client is starting to think about ending?

Step 7: Au Revoir

Recognising that they no longer need counselling and can support themselves is important; however, it is equally important that they know, should the need arise, that they can refer back into the service again to process anything that has come for them unexpectedly.

Whilst most clients will be fine, knowing that the support is there if needed, a small number of clients may re-access for specific issues, rather than to embark on a wider exploration of experiences. For a few clients, it may be appropriate to refer into another service to support some development needs, such as group work or work to address a particular area of difficulty. Having a list of referral options for such clients can also be helpful as part of the ending. For some clients, endings have previously been difficult, and ending counselling can seem particularly onerous. In these cases, it can be useful to arrange a special ending session, planned by the client. See also chapter 5 for a discussion on attachment styles.

Working with a client for an extended period of time (say 6 months or more) means that there is a close bond between therapist and client. Saying good-bye can be emotional and welcoming the next client in the following week can feel strange. However, it is as important for us to let the client go, as it is for the client to decide to go (see chapter 5). Supervision (both individual and group) can be very helpful in supporting this process (see chapter 14). Looking back at the work completed can also help with the letting go process.

Reflection: How do you deal with endings in your life? What would help you to manage such client endings well?

Step 8: Life after Counselling

Although therapy ends when the client leaves, the client often retains very fond memories of the counselling and draws upon their learning long into the future, as they navigate the new elements of their lives. Whilst they often recognise the progress they have made, some feel that there is more to do, particularly those clients with very complex past lives. There is a future focus now, planning what they might like to do, rather than existing day to day. Whilst the counsellors do not get to see the continued effect of the therapy, the clients continue to feel its effect and many remember their counsellor and the sessions.

Summary

This model depends upon the client making the decision to access counselling and therefore wanting, to some extent, to explore what is happening for them with a therapist. Building a therapeutic relationship based on trust, hope and understanding is a key foundation to future exploration. Therapists must be comfortable to work with anything the client brings and must have appropriate support measures in place for themselves. Ensuring a clear and appropriate ending is very helpful for both client and counsellor and both can find reflecting on the work done afterwards helpful.

Of course, not all therapy is as straight forward as is presented here. Stages presented may overlap and there may be some backwards as well as forwards movement. This approach can help to identify where the client is in the model and where there may be difficulties. If there are specific issues at particular stages of the therapy, the chapters suggested may provide some possible options or areas for further exploration.

Key Learning Points

In this chapter an approach to working with DA clients is presented. The key elements are:

1. Finding a way to engage with and help the client with whatever they bring is important in building the foundations for future work.
2. Understanding DA, how it affects the individual and the ways that abuse can be perpetrated is essential for this work.
3. Using high-level empathic skills plus psychoeducation on DA helps the client to fully understand their situation.
4. Being genuine and consistent session to session helps the client to feel safe within the session.

5 Working within your competence level helps you to feel confident in what you are doing, which in turn helps the client to feel safe.
6 Recognising that, whatever has happened in the abusive relationship, the client will have been trying their best to manage a difficult and challenging relationship can help counsellors to provide positive support and feedback.
7 Always work from the client perspective, bringing challenge where needed.
8 Review your client work regularly through supervision to facilitate better understanding of client work and self-care.

References

Farmer, K., Morgan, A., Bohne, S., Silva, M. J., Calvaresi, G., Dilba, J., Naloop, R., Ruke, I., & Venelinova, R. (2013). *Report 1 Comparative Analysis of Perceptions of Domestic Violence Counselling: Counsellors and Clients* (EU Comparative: Counselling Survivors of Domestic Violence, Issue. The Haven. http://www.dvcounselling.eu/images/report%201%20counselling%20survivors.pdf

Ferrari, G., Agnew-Davies, R., Bailey, J., Howard, L., Howarth, E., Peters, T. J., Lynnmarie, S., & Gene Solomon, F. (2016). Domestic violence and mental health: a cross-sectional survey of women seeking help from domestic violence support services. *Global Health Action*, *9*(1). 10.3402/gha.v9.29890

Keech, C., & Roddy, J. K. (2019). *Male survivors' experiences of psychological support following domestic violence: client insights from NHS and Third Sector provision.* BACP Research Conference 2019: Shaping counselling practice and policy: the next 25 years, Belfast.

McManus, S., Walby, S., Barbosa, E. C., Appleby, L., Brugha, T., Bebbington, P. E., Cook, E. A., & Knipe, D. (2022). Intimate partner violence, suicidality, and self-harm: a probability sample survey of the general population in England. *The Lancet Psychiatry*, *9*(7), 574–583. 10.1016/s2215-0366(22)00151-1

Roddy, J. K. (2014). *A client informed view of domestic violence counselling* [PhD, University of Leeds]. Leeds.

Roddy, J. K. (2015). *Counselling and psychotherapy after domestic violence: A client view of what helps recovery*. Palgrave Macmillan.

Roddy, J. K., & Gabriel, L. (2019). A competency framework for domestic violence counselling. *British Journal of Guidance & Counselling*, *47*(6), 669–681. 10.1080/03069885.2019.1599322

Taskforce on the Health Aspects of Violence against Women and Children (2010). *Responding to violence against women and children – the role of the NHS: The report of the taskforce on the health aspects of violence against women and children*. London: Department of Health. Retrieved from http://www.dh.gov.uk/prod_consum_dh/groups/dh_digitalassets/@dh/@en/@ps/documents/digitalasset/dh_113824.pdf

Chapter 3

Understanding Domestic Abuse

Jeannette Roddy and Rod Dubrow-Marshall

Learning Objectives

1 To understand current definitions of domestic abuse
2 To understand the different theories of domestic abuse and their limitations
3 To identify how abuse can be perpetrated in a range of social contexts
4 To recognise the effect of experiencing abuse on mental health
5 To recognise the many losses associated with experiencing abuse and the necessary grieving process for the client
6 To reflect on why single focus therapeutic treatments can appear to be ineffective

Context

In 2021, a legal definition in the United Kingdom for domestic abuse was introduced through the Domestic Abuse Act 2021. Although this was clearly developed from an earlier description (Home Office, 2012), it represented a change from the term domestic violence to domestic abuse. This definition acknowledged that abuse can be enacted in many ways, not just through physical force, to ensure the power and control of one individual over another.

The definition of domestic abuse in the United Kingdom includes physical or sexual abuse; violent or threatening behaviour; controlling or coercive behaviour; economic abuse; psychological, emotional, or other abuse; and it can be a single event or pattern of behaviour over time. Abuse is defined as being between two parties over the age of 16 who are connected to each other (at some point in their lives, not necessarily living together now, and including sibling and parent/child relationships) and is inclusive of all people, irrespective of gender, ethnicity, sexuality, or class. Although these forms of abuse are contained in a legal definition in the United Kingdom, they are not unique to the United Kingdom and can be seen in relationships across the world.

Whilst we focus on domestic abuse here, it can be useful to reflect on other more obvious relationships where power and control can be harmful, to

DOI: 10.4324/9781003253266-3

understand how this might work. For example, there can be workplaces where power dynamics associated with hierarchy, budget, and resources can play out, affecting an individual's job security, career, livelihood, and/or personal relationship. The threat of unemployment, a bad reference, or the misleading reporting of conversations can lead to emotional and psychological difficulties for the person affected, particularly when it is hard to show or prove what is real or true within the situation. The individual can become fixed on trying to resolve the difficulties that they perceive and to please the other. They may have previously enjoyed working there and therefore feel it must be them that is at fault. Other workers may tell them that this is just what it is like here and that they have to adapt to survive, leading to feelings of powerlessness or lack of resilience. It may be that even if they recognise the unfairness of the situation, they may not have options for leaving their employment at that time and do not want to risk reporting what is happening for fear of losing their job.

Reflection: Have you seen examples of power and control enacted in your life previously? How did you feel about it? Was there any motivation for the behaviour that you could see? What happened within the relationship involved as a result? What were the options for the person being abused (if any)?

In abuse situations, the method of control selected is the one thought to be most effective. In the example above, the abuser will work out whether the individual is particularly sensitive about team working, finance, career, flexible working, and so on, and will require the individual to deliver certain things to gain their support. Whilst this can be seen as a motivation tool in the short term, when the requirements are continually changed or added to and this extends over a long period of time without any resolution, this could be seen as abuse. As the individual fails to achieve anything, their self-confidence and self-esteem diminishes and their ability to look for other employment (or to be successful in gaining other employment) diminishes and they can become trapped in the job.

The same principles apply within a domestic abuse context. In a healthy relationship, the bond between the two provides support for both individuals to grow and flourish. In an abusive relationship, the relationship is designed to support the needs of one individual over the other. Here, the mechanisms of control will include withholding money or affection, restricting access to outside influences such as friends or family, insisting on specific behaviours or standards (such as the precise location of objects in the home), demeaning the person through language and intimidation, physical assault, spreading lies, and so on. Just as the employee can be trapped in a job, so the person in a domestically abusive relationship can be trapped as they may have no access to finance, may be told by others that all relationships have difficulties that must be worked through, or may fear losing their children if they leave (Beaulaurier et al., 2008; Hines et al., 2007). It is likely that the abuser will clearly deny any responsibility for the abuse, blaming the other. As self-esteem and self-confidence reduce, so it becomes harder to facilitate the changes that are required to live independently again.

Changes to the relationship and the shift to the focus on the abuser tend to happen over time, with the level of abuse gradually increasing without this necessarily being obvious. The Cycle of Abuse (Walker, 1979) is a well-known model of abusive behaviour taught throughout the world. It describes how a happy relationship begins to feel fraught, like walking on eggshells. As the tension builds stress and anxiety levels grow, until there is a significant event, physical, verbal, or emotional. This is followed by a period of calm (sometimes fleeting) before tension builds again. This cycle can happen many, many times. It is only when people step back and look at the changes in their relationship that they realise how bad it has become. It can be hard to believe that they stayed in the relationship and tolerated the abuse for as long as they did. This can lead to feelings of shame and guilt at what has happened, losing self-confidence and self-esteem, and doubting their ability to protect themselves. It is only by understanding the mechanisms of abuse used by the abuser, and its psychological impact, that the person can see why they stayed, how they did protect themselves (and any children) from the abuser when they could, and how they can protect themselves in future, if necessary.

For a therapist, understanding the types of domestic abuse that can be perpetrated and the way the abuse can be perpetrated is a vital aspect of the work (Dutton, 2006; Nicolson, 2010). This helps the therapist to link and explain theory to the client, helping the client to understand more clearly what had really happened (rather than the view put forward by the abuser). In exploring the client experience the counsellor can support and provide realistic challenge to the client perspective, often shaped by the abuser. Understanding the many aspects of how abuse can occur helps the therapist to bring to the client's attention the context of other stories and experiences shared in therapy which may have been minimised by the abuser. Developing a good understanding of domestic abuse not only supports the client with their recovery from previous experiences but also helps them to recognise and take appropriate action should they experience any future abusive relationships.

> Reflection: How well do you feel you currently understand domestic abuse and how it is perpetrated? What could you do to understand more? What is your plan for doing so?

Research with people who have experienced domestic abuse has consistently noted that a good working knowledge of how domestic abuse can be perpetrated is essential to the work (Roddy & Keech, 2019; Sanderson, 2008; Seeley & Plunkett, 2002). This element has also been identified within the

NICE guidance for supporting people who have experienced domestic abuse (National Institute for Health and Clinical Excellence, 2014). Whilst this need for knowledge is not new to specialist organisations working within this area, it is less widely acknowledged in a therapeutic context. The issue is to what extent this knowledge is required, with some organisations considering a short (two-hour) introductory course about domestic abuse to be sufficient. The premise of this book is that knowledge of domestic abuse is essential, but a course which only covers the mechanisms of domestic abuse is not enough. In a counselling context, the psychological impact of this on the client must also be recognised and appropriate skills and strategies employed.

This chapter will outline some of the theories on domestic abuse that can be helpful in client work and provide references for you to read as you want to expand your knowledge. The other chapters will support you to develop the skills and knowledge required to facilitate the client sharing and processing of their experience as well as their understanding.

Theories of Domestic Abuse

One of the complications of working in the field of domestic abuse in the United Kingdom is that there are several different philosophical bases that professionals can work from. The predominant voice in the media and much of the domestic abuse training available in the United Kingdom suggests simply that men perpetrate abuse on women (Donovan, 2014). This theory highlights the power differential between men and women based on gender inequality and, as much of the serious physical and sexual violence reported is enacted by men, data tends to focus on the serious consequences of rape or serious physical injuries. The nature of domestic violence has been identified through four categories of violent behaviour, described as intimate terrorism, violent resistance, mutual violent control, and common couple violence (Johnson & Ferraro, 2000). There are a number of commentators who can provide more details on this topic if you are interested in exploring this further (Nicolson, 2010; Whalen, 1996). This approach suggested that only the most serious forms of violence needed to be addressed. The proposed focus on severe violence rather than emotional or psychological abuse by front-line agencies has previously driven government policy in this area in the United Kingdom and around the world. Additional legislation to protect women, together with additional funding for a variety of initiatives to support women in leaving abusive relationships (such as Independent Domestic Violence Advisors (IDVAs) in the United Kingdom) and to support the medical needs of healing physical injuries, has dominated government spend in this area for the last 40–50 years. Whilst this has increased the legal options for victims against their abusers, an unforeseen consequence in the United Kingdom, and perhaps also elsewhere, has been a reduction in the funding available for specialist counselling and psychotherapy services to support survivors with mental health issues which continue after the relationship is over.

At the same time as Johnson was developing theories of violence against women, Murray Straus was looking at violence within families using family systems theory (Straus, 1979, 2008). He concluded that there were similar levels of abusive behaviour in men and women within the family environment, using the Conflict Tactics Scale (CTS) as a measure of abusive relationships (Straus, 1979; Straus et al., 1996). The CTS included elements of physical assault, injury, sexual coercion, psychological aggression, and negotiation (a positive way of handling conflict). Both Johnson and Strauss have argued in the literature over the years about which method of describing the abuse is better although there is no resolution to this. In fact, it can be argued that both are correct, as there are instances of extreme violence as described by Johnson and there are also reports of abuse as described by Strauss. The types of abuse described by survivors tends to reflect the context of the relationship and the individuals involved. Hence both authors theories have validity.

The final theory that it is useful to consider is that of psychological drivers for abuse. Here theorists have looked at why abuse might be perpetrated, rather than researching the type and prevalence of abuse (Dutton, 2006, 2007). These theories were brought together by Donald Dutton, showing clearly for the first time the potential for women as well as men to be abusers (Dutton, 2006). Dutton tried to stay away from the political arguments used by other domestic violence researchers and tried to be as objective as possible. He suggested that the perpetrator may well have issues which prompted a need for control or a response to a lack of control. This could be a result of, for example: attachment difficulties which may result in the partner being overly sensitive to relational difficulties; or the impact of previous trauma which could lead the individual to need control of a situation; or a personality disorder which could, for example, lead to a lack of emotional control which could cause tension in the relationship; or the intergenerational transmission of violence, which may mean that the individual is unaware that their behaviour is abusive as the environment they were brought up in displayed much worse behaviours. These theories suggest that abuse is, to some extent, environmental and that it can occur for many reasons. This is not to excuse such behaviour, simply to note that individuals will respond to their perceived relationship difficulty in different ways. This also starts to show how complex working with abuse can be, when the theories utilised can vary from situation to situation and requires some understanding of the client situation to determine which theory may apply in each case.

Reflection: How flexible can you be in amending your understanding of the client frame of reference based on new information? What would help you to have the confidence to do so? What can you do to support any professional growth that is needed?

From a counselling perspective, there is much in Straus' work to consider, particularly in the light of the new and expanded definition of domestic abuse today, to include emotional and psychological abuse and specifically coercive control. Over the last decade or so there has been a developing evidence base to suggest that emotional and psychological abuse can have serious mental health consequences too (Blasco-Ros et al., 2010; Potter et al., 2021), although there can be more serious outcomes when these are combined with other forms of abuse, for example sexual or physical abuse. Blasco-Ros et al. (2010) suggested that survivors can take longer to get over the impact of psychological and emotional abuse alone than when this is combined with physical or sexual abuse. This may be because emotional abuse was not always as easy to see or name when compared with physical evidence and therefore treatment was limited, or it may have been the use of medication in treatment rather than the potentially more helpful discussion of their experiences with trained mental health professionals. Either way, there is evidence to support earlier reports that emotional and psychological abuse can leave emotional scars long after the physical injuries have healed (Walker, 1979).

Within the framework we present here, we prefer to use a non-gendered model of domestic abuse such as they, rather she or he. This allows people to see the abuse as potentially happening from either partner, irrespective of gender or sexuality. There are resources using non-gendered abuse terms available for download (Wells, 2022) and these are recommended for use with clients.

Reflection: How do you feel about using a non-gendered approach? Where do your belief systems about domestic abuse come from? How will these beliefs both help and hinder you when working with clients?

Abuser Actions and Behaviours

Much of the literature available on perpetrators within domestic abuse looks at how men control women. One of the most used models of perpetrator behaviour is the Duluth Model (Domestic Abuse Intervention Programs, 2012), initially developed in the United States in the 1980s. A gender-neutral Power and Control Wheel can be used with people who have experienced domestic abuse to help them to recognise the abusive behaviours (National Sexual Violence Research Centre, 2023). Each spoke of the wheel describes a category of abuse together with examples of behaviours that might be seen. When a client can identify partner behaviours in several spokes, this would suggest that the relationship may have been domestically abusive. A helpful addition to the wheels developed by Duluth was an equality wheel which shows what a "healthy" relationship would look like and which can also be developed in a gender neutral context (University of Nevada, 2016). The cultural representation of this is American, nevertheless it provides ample challenge for someone from the United Kingdom to evaluate the health of their current relationship.

One of the main reasons that people stay in abusive relationships is that they do not recognise their experience as abuse. The level of abuse has probably crept up over time, without noticing, and they see the abuse as a factor in a difficult relationship rather than a potentially serious situation. It can be helpful to consider that there is no perfect relationship, just as there is no wholly imperfect relationship. Even within highly abusive relationships there are moments of connection and joy, it is just that they are few and far between. Thinking about relationships as moving on a continuum between the "worst ever" and the "best ever" experience can allow individuals to determine where they are on the line at any given time. All relationships have times where there is stress and other times where things are flowing and easy. The important factor is how often the relationship is at the "worst ever" end of the continuum. When doing this work, it is also helpful for counsellors in this field to consider their own relationships and behaviours in the context of this information, accepting that none of us are perfect and we can all learn from others.

Whilst we are suggesting that abuse can be perpetrated irrespective of gender, we do also understand that the type of abuse is likely to be selected based on the context of the relationship. For example, women are, in general, more likely to favour emotional and psychological abuse as a means of control as they tend to be physically smaller. On the other hand, men can favour more physical methods of control by using their strength and size. Needless to say, women can use violence in relationships and men can use emotional and psychological strategies too. When looking at abuse in relationships it is important to remember that anything is possible and, if you have no previous experience or knowledge of domestic abuse, the stories you hear may well be things you could never have imagined. Witnessing these accounts can have a cost and it is worth reading chapter 14 to determine ways of protecting yourself from the impact of hearing such stories.

> Reflection: How do you feel about listening to stories of abuse that may lead you to question your own views of humanity? How would you manage containing what you have heard when you may not be able to off-load immediately (e.g. home working)? What might your coping mechanisms be? How would you ensure that the client is not deterred from telling you more?

Abusers use many ways to control their partner. Some research conducted with men in the United Kingdom convicted of domestic violence against women suggested that there were specific types of abuse favoured by men (Craven & Fleming, 2008). However, these types of abuse also mapped well onto the experiences of men who were abused by women (Roddy, 2014). The categorisations used below are based on Craven and Fleming's (2008) work but have gender neutral descriptions. The types of abuser behaviours are as follows:

1 The Sexual Controller: Control can be exerted in two different ways here, either through rape of the other by forcing sexual intercourse, or by withholding sex until the other has complied with a command or instruction. Please note this is not about the individual's right to refuse to have sex if they do not wish to participate, this is about using sex as a means of controlling the other, not protecting themselves.
2 The King/Queen of the Castle: This is the domination of one partner in the home by making the other believe that their role is to do everything possible to meet their needs, even at the expense of their own well-being. When the individual fails to meet their expectations, as they often do (as the perpetrator makes it increasingly difficult to be successful or simply changes the requirements without telling the other this has happened) there will be punishment (such as psychological abuse by withdrawing communication for a period of days or weeks through to actual or attempted murder). This creates a climate of fear of getting things wrong, leading to high levels of anxiety.
3 The Bad Father/Mother: Children are, regrettably, often used as means of control over the parent who cares for and loves them. The abuser will spend time continually undermining the caregiver to suggest that they are a poor parent and, that if the person were ever to leave, they would lose custody due to their lack of parenting skills. Whenever the individual considers leaving, the abuser may become more vocal about their poor parenting to friends, family, and on social media. This sowing of doubt externally can make the individual more insecure and frightened, which makes it harder to leave and harder to resist specific commands given by the king/queen of the castle. Low levels of self-esteem and high levels of anxiety can result after a period of time.
4 The Liar: As above, abusers can lie not only about parenting but also about what has happened in the home and how it happened. This has two effects: firstly, to begin to make the individual doubt their own memory which undermines their self-confidence; and secondly to persuade the individual that all the difficulties and events in the relationship are the responsibility of the individual and not the abuser. The abuser is only responding to the individual and is not accountable for their actions. Often an important part of therapy is to unpick these events and start to understand what did happen, as well to start to build confidence in the individual that they can rely on themselves to remember things accurately. Undermining memory can result in the individual experiencing depression, lack of self-confidence and self-esteem, anxiety, and a lack of trust in themselves and others.

5 The Bully: Here the abuser uses their presence in the home to intimidate the other through shouting, glaring, and sulking. By creating an unpleasant atmosphere in the home, they can get their own way. The partner tries their best to meet the abuser's needs so that they can stop worrying about any further consequences of their apparent bad mood, but one issue is simply replaced by anoth. This has been described as "living on eggshells" and over time results in another high levels of anxiety from the individual.
6 The Jailor: Abusers are often aware that people outside the family would look at their actions and behaviour and know that things were not right within the relationship. A common response to this is for the abuser to gradually cut ties with the individual's friends and family. This may be by telling lies, for example, suggesting that they are the cause of relationship difficulties, or simply finding reasons for the individual not to go out socially or to work. As the individual becomes isolated, they become more dependent on the abuser and hear only their voice, making it harder to challenge what is being said. Lack of social contact and increasing levels of psychological and emotional abuse lead to depression and anxiety, as well as reduced self-esteem and self-efficacy.
7 The Headworker: Here, the abuser criticises and puts the individual down at every possible opportunity. This is a shared space with the bad father/mother, the liar, and the jailor. Often the abuser will tell the individual that only they would want them and tolerate them because they are so bad. The impact of being continually criticised is to erode the individual's self-esteem and self-confidence, making it harder to leave, and often leading to depression.
8 The Persuader: This type of abuse is threatening harm, to the partner, to the children, to pets, or to themselves. Harm in this case could be serious physical assault, murder, or suicide and the partner is often forced to make decisions to protect one of more people but at the expense of their own well-being. Often this will feel like the individual had no other choice, especially if the jailor and the headworker have already been working on reducing self-esteem and self-efficacy.

As you can see from the above, abusers may not use only one technique for overpowering and controlling their partner. They will use a combination of behaviours designed to be most effective against their partner. For example, if the partner is very fond of the children, the perpetrator may find ways to disrupt the relationship with the children; if the partner is close to their family, finding ways to discredit and diminish their family to create tension and arguments; if they are doing well in their career, the perpetrator may disrupt their workplace, make them take time off or telephone regularly through the day to disrupt their work. These actions would be presented as looking after or looking out for the partner, not a means to undermine and control them.

Reflection: Have you ever had experience of, or seen in another relationship, evidence of any of the behaviours above? Think about what that was like, either to experience personally or to see that happen to someone else? What would you do as a friend or family member? What would be different about being a counsellor?

Psychological and Emotional Abuse and the Impact on Self

Psychological and emotional abuse have been variously defined over many years and are often seen as relatively inter-changeable concepts (Marshall, 1996). Follingstad and DeHart (2000) define psychological abuse, from survey research with psychologists, as "threats to physical health, control over basic physical freedoms, and general destabilization" (p. 906).

The term "gaslighting" (Stern, 2007) has also become a popular way to describe the ways in which perpetrators induce victims to think they are imagining the abuse they are suffering and/or are otherwise losing their minds. This is also akin to the "mystifying of experience" noted by Laing (1967) in defining the family context and dynamics responsible for psychosis.

The overall psychological effects of psychological abuse have been well documented and can be summarised in broad terms as a form of complex post-traumatic stress disorder (PTSD) (Herman, 2015). It is also notable that these effects transcend the context for the psychological abuse whether it be in families, trafficking gangs, or extremist groups (Dubrow-Marshall & Dubrow-Marshall, 2015). In both psychology and law, the term "coercive control" can be seen as a unifying concept which explains the abuse and coercive influence in domestic abuse and in other coercive contexts.

Reflection: Intimate partner violence has sometimes been referred to as domestic terrorism. In what ways is being abused by an abusive partner like being abused in a group such as a gang or extremist group?

Legal definitions in England and Wales in Section 76 of the Serious Crime Act (2015) and Domestic Abuse Act (2021) regarding psychological, emotional, and physical abuse have enshrined in law principles from psychological theory and practice that have been developed over decades including Schechter's (1987) classic definition of coercive control as "a pattern of coercive control which one person exercises over another. Abusers use physical and sexual violence, threats, emotional insults, and economic deprivation as a way to dominate their partners ... " (in Kuennen, 2007, p. 8-9).

Controlling behaviour is defined in Section 76 of the Serious Crime Act (2015) as

> a range of acts designed to make a person subordinate and/or dependent by isolating them from sources of support, exploiting their resources and

capacities for personal gain, depriving them of the means needed for independence, resistance and escape and regulating their everyday behaviour.

Coercive behaviour is defined in the same section of the Serious Crime Act as "a continuing act or a pattern of acts of assault, threats, humiliation and intimidation or other abuse that is used to harm, punish, or frighten their victim."

A repeating pattern of coercive and controlling behaviour over time is identified as the common process of abuse, as opposed to isolated incidents (Stark, 2007). The structure of the victim's life, day after day, is enmeshed in this nexus of control. This is also a fundamental attack on their self-identity and traps them in a mystifying web of discourses and double binds (Bateson, 1972) which can be both blaming but also rewarding in a cycle (Walker, 1979). The degradation of the victim's identity is also akin to Lifton's (1961) pattern of thought reform whereby "milieu control," "confession," and "doctrine over person" lead to a "dispensing of existence" in psychological terms.

Reflection: To what extent is "coercive control" or "controlling and coercive behaviour" useful as unifying concepts to explain the pattern of psychological and physical abuse within intimate partner violence? How does this help in working with clients?

Existential Concerns and Multiple Losses

Survivors of domestic abuse and coercive control have often lived through the prolonged subjugation of their pre-existing self-identity while in the abusive relationship. It is common for much of the pre-relationship identity to survive this ordeal but while the person is being coercively controlled these other aspects of their identity are relatively inaccessible and may not be accessible at all (Dubrow-Marshall, 2010). As with Lifton's (1961) depiction of thought reform, this concept of a "totalistic identity" indicates that the usual, healthy cognitive functioning which allows for multiple aspects of self-identity to be psychologically salient on a minute-by-minute basis (Turner, 1987), is prevented from operating (Dubrow-Marshall, 2010).

The psychological journey to this point usually appears to involve a profound identification with the abuser which initially is based on positive attributes and qualities (Walker, 1979). This is akin to how cults "love bomb" their victims when recruiting them (Singer, 2003) and ensure an initial positive identification with the group. Once the abuser has enticed their victim to identify with them and their relationship, they go on to entrap them in what is described by Courtois (2008) and Herman (2015) as a form of trauma bond or trauma coerced attachment (Doychak & Raghavan, 2018).

The previously described pattern of psychological and physical violence (Stark, 2009), often over many months and years, involves a recurrent series of attacks, threats, and humiliation. These create a form of complex trauma, often with significantly heightened anxiety and dissociation, and a deep trauma bond whereby the victim is psychologically imprisoned and unable to escape from the mind of the abuser (Cantor & Price, 2007).

During the depths of this trauma bond, the victim will act according to patterns of referent informational influence (Turner, 1987) whereby their strong identification with the abuser will lead them to behave in ways which reinforce that dominant or totalistic part of their identity. This explains why current victims of domestic abuse may sometimes present as willingly acting on the wishes of their abusive partner. At that time such actions will actually bolster their self-identity which is totally bound up with that of their partner. The lack of positive behavioural reinforcement by the abuser, for whom the subservient actions of the victim are never enough to satisfy their narcissistic needs, can contribute to a form of cognitive dissonance amongst victims. Try hard as they might, their best is never good enough and this ultimately starts to corrode the totalistic identity allowing for chinks of doubt and light, as when ice cracks form on a frozen pond.

Some people will recount their journey up to realising the trauma bond in which they are enmeshed. This journey is typically not linear, and individuals are often not equipped with the psychological vocabulary with which they can fully interpret and understand what is happening to them at the time. At the heart of trauma-coerced attachment is a form of double bind wherein the victim feels unable to do right for doing wrong but simultaneously is unable to perceive how they could do anything else other than to try harder to satisfy their abuser and meet their needs. This double bind mystifies the experience of the person and creates an enveloping form of dissociation such that they are often unable to rationally decide what to do, except to ensure their survival.

The psychological blows and losses that can be suffered by people who have experienced domestic abuse and coercive control are therefore often profound and long lasting. However, the depth of psychological loss is different for each person, and it is vital to acknowledge those individual features which will allow for unique paths to recovery. The actions when eventually leaving the abusive relationship can be a key indicator of the extent to which the pre-existing aspect of the individual's identity remains intact or requires reconstruction. Bit by bit over time there has been a "drastic reinterpretation" of their history (Singer, 2003) and this history will require agentic re-reinterpretation by the person.

Leaving the totalising influence in one's life, whether an abusive partner, group or workplace, can involve a huge existential loss. Survivors have spoken movingly about how the thought of leaving their partner would be akin to losing a limb or breaking themselves apart. Such has the abuser's identity supplanted their own that people will often feel deeply that life without them has no meaning whatsoever. This process of existential domination, and the threat of loss beyond it, has been reported in survivors of genocides including the holocaust (Frankl, 2004) and survivors of trafficking gangs and extremist groups (Doychak & Raghavan, 2018).

The way in which individuals are dehumanised in abusive and coercive relationships is central to the existential loss that is left behind afterwards. In particularly abusive and damaging relationships, key aspects of self-identity from before the abuse can be preserved but are buried deep in the remains of the person's selfhood. Gentle exploration of times before the abuse, of activities that brought joy, and specific memories of pride or connection can be helpful here. This can be challenging for the individual. The temptation to give up, to allow the fragile remaining architecture to collapse in a cloud of dust, is a withering indication of learned helplessness and depression borne of the existential void into which the abuser has taken them. Given this potential level of destruction it is perhaps remarkable that so many people can rise again above the wreckage that has been wrought, and stand and walk tall again, free from the psychological bondage and shackles and free again to be themselves in a myriad of different ways.

Reflection: What particular challenges do you feel you might face working with a client who are no longer aware of themselves or their needs or desires? What might is you need to be aware of as you started the work?

Challenges and Pathways to Working Effectively with Clients

Working with clients who have experienced domestic abuse and coercive control presents particular challenges which relate to key questions of self-identity and self-efficacy. It is not just that survivors have been abused, physically and psychologically, denigrated and made to feel worthless, often over a lengthy period of time, if that were not enough to seek to recover from. In addition, there is the common and painful realisation that they identified fully and wholeheartedly with an abusive charlatan who took away not only their dignity but also their identity and humanity. Sometimes survivors will ask "how did I get this so wrong"? As with the gaslighting with which they have been acculturated, survivors will sometimes seek certainty by blaming themselves for their abuse. While taking responsibility for future safety is potentially agentic ("I will not make that mistake again"), a causal analysis which limits the extent of existential recovery through self-blame is also potentially damaging to longer-term recovery.

It is therefore important for survivors to (re)learn and remember step by step what took place and why and how this led them to the humiliation and existential destruction which they have suffered. Re-self-actualisation, bereft of self-blame, allows for the person to regain their sense of self such that the core conditions of person-centred humanistic therapy can be helpfully deployed. Without that core sense of self being re-established, there is not enough inner psychological "rope and pulley" for the survivor to use to chart their own recovery course. Initially, then, it is critical for survivors to learn, through a form of non-directive psychoeducation, about the nature of the abuse that they suffered and their responses to it, such that they can use that knowledge to reconstruct their self-identity piece by piece.

> Reflection: What sort of responses could you make to a client in this circumstance? What do you think might be helpful? What might be unhelpful is this situation?

In these regards, the *Power, Threat, Meaning (PTM) Framework* (Johnstone & Boyle, 2018), published by the British Psychological Society's Division of Clinical Psychology, is a non-diagnostic method by which survivors can come to a better understanding of "what happened to me" as opposed to "what is wrong with me?" Firstly, the PTM framework allows for the survivor to more fully understand the nature of the power that was operating in their abusive relationship and how undue influence and coercive control was deployed at different stages. As the power differentials deepened and the coercion worsened, the survivor can come to see how there were a series of threats to their health and well-being (some actually enacted), and sometimes to their children, all of which led them to react with a series of "threat responses." The way in which victims of domestic abuse can use protective behaviours as a means of surviving are explicated further in chapter 7. For now, the threat responses in the PTM framework can also be usefully noted as akin to classic diagnostic psychological symptomology. For example, anxiety, often seen as a personal characteristic, is better reframed as a rational response to significant threats to self and well-being. Dissociation, often seen as a feature of psychological ill health, is instead recast as a response to existential threats and gaslighting. Similarly, depression, whether reactive or with a longer aetiology, is now seen as a threat response to the double bind and totalism of the trauma bond which makes it appear that there is no way out.

In these ways, the PTM framework can be potentially used with survivors to help them regain an agentic understanding of how they were coercively controlled and how their reactions to that, while also sometimes forms of psychological distress, were and are actually forms of self-survival and resilience. Shorn of much of the diagnostic labelling of modern psychology, complex post-traumatic stress disorder can perhaps be relearned and understood as a series of threat responses from which the survivor can ultimately emerge. While the longer-term effects of such complex trauma are acknowledged (Herman, 2015), understanding the roots and structure of this empowers people to self-manage their own recovery.

Reflection: How would using something like the PTM framework fit within your practice? How could you integrate it, if you found the content useful for your practice?

Mental Health Consequences of Domestic Abuse and Current Treatment Limitations

The description of abuser behaviours above allowed some conclusions to be drawn about the mental health impact of living within an abusive relationship. Individuals could experience one or more of depression, anxiety, low self-esteem, low self-confidence, lack of trust in self or others, lack of self-efficacy, lack of identity, or ongoing fear of what might happen next. Some people may also experience high levels of anger either because they have been forced to contain their own natural anger responses as a protection and this has now built up and spilled over, or they have developed a pattern of self-harming as a means of releasing their emotions when it was not safe to do so with their partner (see also chapter 7).

In addition to this, where the level of abuse has been high and has continued for a lengthy period, the individual may also have experienced living on high alert for a long time, leading to a hyper-arousal trauma response, or feeling so overwhelmed by what was happening that they developed a coping strategy of dissociating from what was happening, a hypo-arousal trauma response. See Chapter 8 for more details on what to look out for and how to work with complex trauma, which forms when multiple serious physical and/or emotional incidents happen over a period of time. Experiencing multiple life-threatening events can also lead to suicidal ideation with one in four individuals likely to experience this (Calder et al., 2010). As a domestic abuse counsellor, it is important that you feel able to deal with the presentation of suicidal thoughts as it is very likely that this is something that will come up within the client base.

Finally, some people may find it difficult to identify who they are or what their needs might be, having spent time working to meet the needs of the abuser to keep themselves safe. Once removed from the abuse, it can be hard for individuals to work out what is next for them and what they might want to do with their lives leading to a sense of hopelessness.

Reflection: Not all clients will bring all of those issues, but some may. How well do you feel you would cope with clients who are experiencing high levels of distress? What do you think you would need to support you in the work? How do you think you could access this support?

These mental health issues are all highlighted in the literature on domestic violence and mental health which you can read about if you are interested. Please note that the level of mental health difficulty is often related to the context of the research i.e. data from a domestic violence refuge intake interview tends to show higher levels of distress than data from a walk-in A&E unit at a local hospital, as you might expect (Afifi et al., 2009; Araszkiewicz & Dabkowska, 2010; Bargai et al., 2007; Barrowclough et al., 2001; Blasco-Ros et al., 2010; Boyle & Todd, 2003; Ferrari et al., 2016; Golding, 1999; Hines & Douglas, 2011, 2015; Hines et al., 2007; Holly, 2013; Humphreys & Thiara, 2003; Trevillion et al., 2012). For a brief summary of the mental health issues see Roddy (2015) Chapter 1.

The effects on mental health can be significant. Yet, despite several trials using developed therapies being conducted to look at specific outcomes such as reductions in depression or in PTSD, much of the research has been determined as not of sufficiently high quality, leading to complications with achieving treatment recommendations. Instead, further calls for more research have been made (Hameed et al., 2020; Ramsay et al., 2005).

Part of the issue with working with this client group is that they need to work through the whole experience, rather than a part of it. For example, working on strategies to reduce anxiety and depression will only be effective if the issues relating to this are addressed i.e. the domestic abuse itself. Relational issues such as lack of trust and lack of sense of self, or complex trauma, may mean being referred to different therapists for each identified issue. This will make it hard to establish a relationship trusting enough to tell all. A relational trauma is helped by a relational approach. The client's loss of their relationship, their imagined future and their loss of belief in their own judgement, can be significant losses that require a period of mourning and grief (Herman, 1992) before the work to move on can take place.

Having one specific person who can deal with most of what is presented allows trust to build and the story to be told at an appropriate pace. A trauma informed therapy is helpful to manage trauma symptoms, but often it is the ideas and feelings that are left over rather than the symptoms that are of more difficulty. Hence a symptom reduction-based treatment can be less helpful than an exploration and processing of relevant experiences.

The therapy proposed in this book allows flexibility in what is required by the client in a counselling situation. It highlights a range of issues that may need to be addressed, together with some hints and tips about how to do so. This recognises that one size does not fit all and that, perhaps unsurprisingly, therapy must be adjusted to fit the needs of the individual.

Summary

This chapter highlights different theories as to why domestic abuse occurs and suggests that there is merit in each of these. The impact of predominantly following one theory of male on female violence means a focus of available resources for domestic abuse in protection and recovery from physical harm, rather than mental harm. Yet psychological and emotional abuse can leave debilitating mental health consequences as abusers target their partner's weaknesses to undermine their sense of self, to enable control of their lives. The loss of the relationship, their imagined future and, in particularly serious cases, their identity, can be difficult to acknowledge. Grieving the loss can support transition into action. Understanding and using theories of domestic abuse to assist the client in understanding what happened during therapy can be very helpful in changing perspective on their experiences.

Key Learning Points

1 There are many theories of domestic abuse which allow for abusers to be any member of the population. Social power can be a factor, but so can childhood experiences and the dynamics and stresses of family life.
2 There are a range of tactics that abusers can use which appear often when working with clients who have experienced domestic abuse. Understanding these can also help to identify areas with which a client may need most help and support.
3 Emotional and psychological abuse can be devastating to the identity of the abused person, requiring careful work to discover the person they are today.
4 The breakdown of a relationship can result in many losses for the individual, which require time to grieve and then move on with the next stage of their life. The psychological loss of the abuser alone can be significant.
5 The mental health consequences of domestic abuse are well documented but there are currently no research informed practice models for treatment. Recommended treatments are for aspects of the experience, not the experience as a whole which many clients would benefit from.

References

Afifi, T. O., MacMillan, H., Cox, B. J., Asmundson, G. J. G., Stein, M. B., & Sareen, J. (2009). Mental health correlates of intimate partner violence in marital relationships in a nationally representative sample of males and females. *Journal of Interpersonal Violence*, *24*(8), 1398–1417. 10.1177/0886260508322192

Araszkiewicz, A., & Dabkowska, M. (2010). Women's mental health: P02-372 – Social and demographic factors and severity of symptoms of posttraumatic stress disorder in victims of intimate partner violence [Abstract]. *European Psychiatry*, *25*(Supplement 1), 1388. 10.1016/s0924-9338(10)71374-2

Bargai, N., Ben-Shakhar, G., & Shalev, A. Y. (2007). Posttraumatic stress disorder and depression in battered women: the mediating role of learned helplessness. *Journal of Family Violence*, *22*(5), 267–275.

Barrowclough, C., King, P., Colville, J., Russell, E., Burns, A., & Tarrier, N. (2001). A randomized trial of the effectiveness of cognitive-behavioral therapy and supportive counseling for anxiety symptoms in older adults. *Journal of Consulting and Clinical Psychology, 69*(5), 756–762. 10.1037/0022-006x.69.5.756

Bateson, G. (1972). Steps to an ecology of mind: Collected essays in anthropology, psychiatry, evolution, and epistemology. Intertext.

Beaulaurier, R. L., Seff, L. R., & Newman, F. L. (2008). Barriers to help-seeking for older women who experience intimate partner violence: a descriptive model. *Journal of Women & Aging, 20*(3–4), 231–248.

Blasco-Ros, C., Sánchez-Lorente, S., & Martinez, M. (2010). Recovery from depressive symptoms, state anxiety and post-traumatic stress disorder in women exposed to physical and psychological, but not to psychological intimate partner violence alone: a longitudinal study. *BMC Psychiatry, 10*, 98. 10.1186/1471-244x-10-98

Boyle, A., & Todd, C. (2003). Incidence and prevalence of domestic violence in a UK emergency department. *Emergency Medicine Journal, 20*(5), 438–442.

Calder, J., McVean, A., & Yang, W. (2010). History of abuse and current suicidal ideation: results from a population based survey. *Journal of Family Violence, 25*(2), 205–214. 10.1007/s10896-009-9284-x

Cantor, C., & Price, J. (2007). Traumatic entrapment, appeasement and complex post-traumatic stress disorder: evolutionary perspectives of hostage reactions, domestic abuse and the Stockholm syndrome. *The Australian and New Zealand Journal of Psychiatry, 41*, 377–384.

Courtois, C. A. (2008). Complex trauma, complex reactions: assessment and treatment. *Psychological Trauma: Theory, Research, Practice and Policy, 8*, 86–100.

Craven, P., & Fleming, J. (2008). *Living with the dominator: a book about the freedom programme*. Gardners Books.

Domestic Abuse Act 2021 (2021). Retrieved from https://www.legislation.gov.uk/ukpga/2021/17

Domestic Abuse Intervention Programs (2012). *Home of the Duluth Model: Social Change to End Violence against Women*. Domestic Abuse Intervention Programs. Retrieved 7th September from http://www.theduluthmodel.org/about/index.html

Donovan, C. (2014). *Living in a homo/bi/transphobic society: implications for DVA in LGB and/or T relationships*. The Coral Project: exploring Abusive Behaviours in LGB and/or T Relationships, Sunderland.

Doychak, K., & Raghavan, C. (2018). 'No voice or vote': trauma-coerced attachment in victims of sex trafficking. *Journal of Human Trafficking*. 10.1080/23322705.2018.1518625

Dubrow-Marshall, R. P. (2010). The influence continuum – the good, the dubious and the harmful – evidence and implications for policy and practice in the 21st century. *International Journal of Cultic Studies, 1*(1), 1–13.

Dubrow-Marshall, R., & Dubrow-Marshall, L. (2015). Cults and mental health (chapter 153), in Friedman, H. (Ed.). *Encyclopedia of Mental Health*, Second edition. Oxford: Academic Press (Elsevier), pp. 393–401. doi: 10.1016/b978-0-12-397045-9.00153-1.

Dutton, D. G. (2006). *Rethinking domestic violence*. UBC Press.

Dutton, D. G. (2007). *The abusive personality: violence and control in intimate relationships*. Guilford Press.

Ferrari, G., Agnew-Davies, R., Bailey, J., Howard, L., Howarth, E., Peters, T. J., Lynnmarie, S., & Gene Solomon, F. (2016). Domestic violence and mental health: a cross-sectional survey of women seeking help from domestic violence support services. *Global Health Action*, *9*(1). 10.3402/gha.v9.29890

Frankl, V. (2004). *Mana's search for meaning*. Rider.

Follingstad, D., & DeHart, D. (2000). Defining psychological abuse of husbands toward wives: contexts, behaviors, and typologies. *Journal of Interpersonal Violence*, *15*, 891–920.

Golding, J. M. (1999). Intimate partner violence as a risk factor for mental disorders: a meta-analysis. *Journal of Family Violence*, *14*(2), 99–132.

Hameed, M. O. D. L., Gilchrist, G., Tirado-Muñoz, J., Tan, A., Chondros, P., Feder, G., Tan, M., Hegarty, K. (2020). Psychological therapies for women who experience intimate partner violence. *Cochrane Database of Systematic Reviews*, *2020*(7). Retrieved 24 October 2021. Doi: 10.1002/14651858.CD013017. https://doi.org/10.1002/14651858.CD013017.pub2

Herman, J. L. (1992). *Trauma and recovery*. Pandora.

Herman, J. (2015). *Trauma and recovery* (2nd Edition). Pandora.

Hines, D., Brown, J., & Dunning, E. (2007). Characteristics of callers to the domestic abuse helpline for men [corrected] [published erratum appears in *Journal of Family Violence* Nov;22(8): 773]. *Journal of Family Violence*, *22*(2), 63–72.

Hines, D. A., & Douglas, E. M. (2011). Symptoms of posttraumatic stress disorder in men who sustain intimate partner violence: a study of helpseeking and community samples. *Psychology of Men & Masculinity*, *12*(2), 112–127. 10.1037/a0022983

Hines, D. A., & Douglas, E. M. (2015). Health problems of partner violence victims: comparing help-seeking men to a population-based sample. *American Journal of Preventive Medicine*, *48*(2), 136–144. 10.1016/j.amepre.2014.08.022

Holly, J. A. (2013, 14th January). *Complicated matters: addressing domestic and sexual violence, mental ill-health and problematic substance abuse.* Domestic Violence and Mental Health: Empowering Women and Professionals, University of Turin.

Home Office (2012). *New definition of domestic violence*. Retrieved 27th November 2012 from http://www.homeoffice.gov.uk/media-centre/news/domestic-violence-definition

Humphreys, C., & Thiara, R. (2003). Mental health and domestic violence: 'I call it symptoms of abuse'. *British Journal of Social Work*, *33*(2), 209–226. 10.1093/bjsw/33.2.209

Johnstone, L., Boyle, M., Cromby, J., Dillon, J., Harper, D., Kinderman, P., Longden, E., Pilgrim, D., & Read, J. (2018). The Power Threat Meaning Framework: Towards the identification of patterns in emotional distress, unusual experiences and troubled or troubling behaviour, as an alternative to functional psychiatric diagnosis. *British Psychological Society*.

Johnson, M. P., & Ferraro, K. J. (2000). Research on domestic violence in the 1990s: Making distinctions. *Journal of Marriage & Family*, *62*(4), 948–963.

Kuennen, T. L. (2007). Analyzing the impact of coercion on domestic violence victims: How much is too much. *Berkeley J. Gender L. & Just.*, *22*, 2–30.

Kuennen, T. L. (2007). Analyzing the Impact of coercion on domestic violence victims: how much is too much. *Berkeley J. Gender L. & Just.*, *22*, 2–30.

Laing, R. D. (1967). *The politics of experience and the bird of paradise*. Penguin.

Marshall, L. (1996). Psychological abuse of women: six distinct clusters. *Journal of Family Violence, 11*(4), 379–409.

National Institute for Health and Clinical Excellence (2014). PH50 domestic violence and abuse – how services can respond effectively: supporting evidence [NICE Guidance]. Retrieved 28th February 2014 from http://guidance.nice.org.uk/PH50/SupportingEvidence

National Sexual Violence Research Centre (2019). Power and Control Wheel. National Sexual Violence Research Centre. Retrieved 3rd March 2023 from https://www.nsvrc.org/sites/default/files/2019-08/Gender%20Neutral%20Power%20Control%20Wheel.pdf

Nicolson, P. (2010). *Domestic violence and psychology: a critical perspective.* Routledge.

Potter, L. C., Morris, R., Hegarty, K., Garcia-Moreno, C., & Feder, G. (2021). Categories and health impacts of intimate partner violence in the World Health Organization multi-country study on women's health and domestic violence. *International Journal of Epidemiology*, 652–662. 10.1093/ije/dyaa220

Ramsay, J., Rivas, C., & Feder, G. (2005). *Interventions to reduce violence and promote the physical and psychosocial well-being of women who experience partner violence: a systematic review of controlled evaluations.* D. o. Health. http://www.dh.gov.uk/prod_consum_dh/groups/dh_digitalassets/@dh/@en/documents/digitalasset/dh_4127426.pdf

Roddy, J. K. (2014). *A client informed view of domestic violence counselling* [PhD, University of Leeds]. Leeds.

Roddy, J. K. (2015). Counselling and Psychotherapy After Domestic Violence: A client view of what helps recovery. Palgrave Macmillan.

Roddy, J. K., & Keech, C. (2019). *Working with survivors of domestic abuse: addressing the needs of male and female counselling clients in the UK.* BACP Research Conference: Shaping counselling practice and policy: the next 25 years, Belfast.

Sanderson, C. (2008). *Counselling survivors of domestic abuse.* Jessica Kingsley.

Seeley, J., & Plunkett, C. (2002). *Women and domestic violence: standards for counselling practice.* T. S. A. C. Service.

Singer, M. (2003). *Cults in our midst: the continuing fight against their hidden menace.* Jossey-Bass.

Stark, E. (2009). *Coercive control: how men entrap women in personal life.* OUP.

Stern, R. (2007). *The gaslight effect: how to spot and survive the hidden manipulations other people use to control your life.* Morgan Road Books.

Straus, M. A. (1979). Measuring intrafamily conflict and violence: the conflict tactics (CT) scales. *Journal of Marriage & Family, 41*(1), 75–88.

Straus, M. A. (2008). Dominance and symmetry in partner violence by male and female university students in 32 nations. *Children and Youth Services Review, 30*(3), 252–275. 10.1016/j.childyouth.2007.10.004

Straus, M. A., Hamby, S. L., Boney-McCoy, S., & Sugarman, D. B. (1996). The revised Conflict Tactics Scales (CTS2): development and preliminary psychometric data. *Journal of Family Issues, 17*(3), 283–316. 10.1177/019251396017003001

Trevillion, K., Oram, S., Feder, G., & Howard, L. M. (2012). Experiences of domestic violence and mental disorders: a systematic review and meta-analysis. *PloS One, 7*(12), e51740–e51740. 10.1371/journal.pone.0051740

Turner, J. (1987) *Rediscovering the social group: a self-categorisation theory.* Blackwells.

University of Nevada (2016). Gender Neutral Equality Wheel. University of Nevada. Retrieved 3rd March 2023 from https://med.unr.edu/Documents/med/statewide/echo/clinics/public-health/2016/Gender%20Neutral%20Equality%20Wheel.pdf
Walker, L. E. (1979). *The battered woman*. Harper & Row.
Wells, R. S. (2022). *The Duluth Model, why it's time to remove it from domestic abuse training*. Domestic Abuse Business Services Ltd. Retrieved 10th January from https://www.d-a-b-s.co.uk/post/power-control
Whalen, M. (1996). *Counseling to end violence against women: a subversive model*. SAGE Publications.

Chapter 4

Enhancing Therapeutic Skills

Jeannette Roddy, Leigh Gardner, and Linda Dubrow-Marshall

Learning Objectives

1 To understand the importance of advanced counselling skills in creating trust and working with clients who have experienced domestic abuse
2 To recognise how and when advanced skills can be used
3 To assess current competency levels for advanced skills and create a plan to address any gaps or upskilling required
4 To recognise the context of client material brought to session and how to respond, particularly in the context of ethics and safeguarding

Context

Domestic abuse is complex. The relationship that began in love and commitment begins to unravel and becomes uncertain and difficult or harsh. As discussed in chapter 3, the behaviour of a domestically abusive partner can lead to isolation and shame, a heightened sensitivity to meeting the needs of their partner, and a lack of self-belief, self-esteem, and trust in others. Silence can become a frightening experience, as it has previously resulted in more abuse from their partner, and needs to be considered therapeutically. The relational aspect of counselling is key to recovery, as the individual must build at least one safe, secure relationship which is helpful to them, to begin to trust in others again. Yet there may be uncertainty from the client about engaging with the counsellor. Building the therapeutic relationship requires high levels of counselling skills, building on the counsellor's own significant personal development, to ensure a trustworthy, consistent, and understanding presence as the client recounts their story.

In this chapter, we discuss different ways to develop the therapeutic relationship and what additional levels of skill may be required.

Building Trust

Building trust with the client is an essential part of the early sessions in domestic abuse work. Clients who have experienced domestic abuse can often

DOI: 10.4324/9781003253266-4

find it difficult to trust anyone completely. In part, this is due to the emotional or psychological abuse they have experienced, as it may have become difficult to believe what was being said and/or to decide who can or cannot be trusted. This lack of relational certainty can then undermine other relationships outside of the abusive relationship, even those with individuals or organisations who are trying to help.

The therapeutic relationship offers an opportunity for clients to test out trust in a safe space, which can then have very positive outcomes for the client outside of the counselling room. This was put very well by one previous research participant:

> Lucy (pseudonym): "The sense to be able to trust somebody again, because in trusting the counsellor and informing that relationship where everything that was said there was just between the pair of us, I actually began to trust other people more."
>
> (Roddy, 2015, p. 82)

However, it is important to recognise that building trust can begin before entering the counselling room. In many therapeutic contexts today, a person within the organisation is the first point of contact for the individual. This initial contact is frequently followed by an assessment session with a second person before an offer of counselling by a therapist, yet another person to meet. This means that the client may have already met two or three different people in the organisation before they begin therapy. Hence, when we talk about building trust, we must build trust in the organisation as well as in the therapist. See stage 2 in the process model in chapter 2 to understand more about this part of the work.

Developing organisational trust to the extent that someone may be prepared to take a risk (Mayer et al., 1995), such as a client who is uncertain about what to disclose, requires the following elements:

1 Ability – the client must believe that the organisation is competent enough to deliver the service they require. This is not just about the website or the client contract, but a sense of whether each of the individuals they meet understands their situation and needs.
2 Benevolence – there is a feeling that the organisation wants to and is motivated to help the client and is not seeing the client only because they have been paid or mandated to do so.
3 Integrity – the client understands the principles of the organisation and sees that there is a match between words and action over time. For example, communication is clear, consistent and any issues are properly and reasonably addressed. In this way the reputation of the service in the community and of the therapist that they see, can both assist trust in the therapeutic process even before therapy has started.

Reflection: When you think about the client journey into your organisation, what could you do to ensure that a potential client will see these characteristics at each stage of their journey? What might be useful to consider or change in the way that you assess clients to make it easier for them to engage?

As counsellors, it is easy to see that these defined ideas for organisations to build trust (ability, benevolence, and integrity) map nicely onto the three core elements of good therapeutic practice: empathy, positive regard, and congruence.

We must understand our clients to build their trust in us, as therapists. This client group may have difficulty voicing the depth of their experience or understanding what might have happened. A therapist who can tentatively offer some insight into what might have happened to the client can help trust to build. This provision of a different context for the client, that of surviving and/or having normal responses to experiencing abuse (see also chapter 8), can feel supportive and caring to the client, and hugely beneficial (Roddy, 2014). Whilst we can help the client to see what they have achieved in the face of enormous difficulty, we can also witness and help the client to process the feelings that they have about their experiences. Focusing too soon on client strengths may negate the client's experience of abuse, leading to early termination of therapy. Focusing too much on the terror of the situation may be overwhelming for the client (see also chapter 8), also leading to early termination. The therapist skill is to balance these two aspects of the work, through acknowledging the extent of the abuse as well as the client's strengths and resilience, providing positive regard for them and valuing and caring for them, as well as holding hope for the future. Balance and honesty in holding each of these positions are key aspects of the work, providing a relationship which can be trusted and is not overwhelming.

Seeing this positive therapeutic stance may be challenging for clients who have been living with an abuser who undermined and put them down. Sharing a space with someone who wants the best for them and sees the potential for positive change can be both welcome and a little scary, as they may wonder about the therapist's motivations. People living with abuse can become very good at reading people, at looking for signs that all is not well, or that something else is happening under the surface. Clients often test a therapist's reaction by offering something relatively small about their experiences first and then checking the therapist's response to this before offering anything bigger. Here, congruence is important, so that the client can see that they have been understood and received by the counsellor. In the past, picking up dissent from the abuser and shifting their position to align with the abuser helps to keep them safe. If they sense dissent from the counsellor, then this shift may happen in the therapy room and trust is lost.

From a counselling perspective, it is therefore important that you bring your open and honest, whole self into the counselling session. If you are saying one thing and thinking another, it is likely that the client will pick this up and change their story to suit what they feel you want to hear, to ensure that they maintain the relationship. If this continues, it will be difficult for the client to bring what they need to bring and it is likely that therapy will stop. Hence, congruence with the client is at least as important as empathy. If this is something you find particularly difficult, then working with this client group may not be for you. The section on congruence below will help you to determine your own levels of congruence and how comfortable you may feel with clients.

> Reflection: When you think about how you practice empathy, positive regard, and congruence, how would you currently rate your skills? Which one of these do you feel would need most development prior to working with this client group?

There are, of course, some difficult aspects of working with this client group whilst building and maintaining trust. For example, should you self-disclose your own experiences of abuse or not? The short answer is only when it is in service of the client, that is, it can be very helpful to client to hear what you have to say, but anything said should be brief and focused on helping the client, not providing an opportunity to discuss your experience. Another example is what to do if there is, as sometimes happens, evidence of harm to self or harm to others (including children). This is a very important ethical issue, which we will discuss in chapters 6, 7 and 12 and requires a consistent and open discussion with the client about the organisation's protocols in the event of such disclosures. The key here is that when the disclosure is passed on, it is done with and alongside the client transparently, and not excluding the client.

In building trust, high levels of empathy, congruence and positive regard are important elements of therapeutic practice. Each of the elements are discussed in more detail below.

Advanced Empathy

> We think we listen but very rarely do we listen with real understanding, true empathy. Yet listening of this very special kind, is one of the most potent forces for change that I know.
>
> (Rogers, 1995 p. 134)

Advanced skills are an essential part of training for working with this client group to facilitate clients to form a deeper and longer lasting, life changing relationship with themselves and subsequently, others. These skills are extremely challenging for some and need to be modelled as part of the therapeutic relationship to establish trust and to allow depth to grow in the therapeutic relationship. This developing depth and trust helps the client to move through the model of practice from stage 1 to stage 2 (see chapter 2).

Elliott et al. (2018) note the many and varied definitions of empathy and, when discussing Rogers' "seeing through the client's eyes, to adopt his frame of reference" (Rogers 1980, p. 85), describe this aspect as "higher-order process." This matches well with Kohut's "a higher form of empathy" (Lohut 1959 in Natiello, 2001, p. 10) which talks of taking the empathy from beyond the "formulaic empathic responses" (McLeod, 1999, p. 386) into something different, "the process of weaving together the fragments and threads of the client's experiences over a period of time" (Lohut in Natiello, 2001, p. 10). This way of listening and being allows the therapist to hear "the music behind the words" (Tolan & Wilkins, 2011 p. 105). It is through this deep understanding and willingness to be alongside, that the client will start to feel heard in a different and more compassionate way, will start to feel that they can open up more to the therapist, and also feel that the therapist will be able to tolerate anything that they are going to tell them, without judging or responding from their own frame of reference. This kind of "hearing," being truly seen in all aspects of themselves when they have previously spent time trying to hide from the abuser and others, can be overpowering for a client. Hence the therapist must determine the extent of using this skill, whilst establishing a trusted relationship (see above).

Knowing as the therapist when to offer deeper empathy is a necessary part of working with domestic abuse – it is essential that we work within the client's window of tolerance and work at the client's pace (see chapters 2 and 8) to continue to build a healthy and trusting relationship. Deep empathy is touching on an edge of awareness (Gendlin, 1984) and an inexperienced therapist may want to join the dots. Yet this work needs to be done by the client, at their own pace, to make meaningful understanding it must come from them, rather than the counsellor. Working with domestic abuse clients can be slow, gentle work, what can be described as putting out the breadcrumbs for the client to pick up when they are ready. This may include general psychoeducation around domestic abuse or stories of how domestic abuse can be, to facilitate the client understanding more about their own process, without being told.

Part of providing empathy is being with the client and both client and therapist taking in the nonverbal clues such as body language, eye contact (empathy can be shared with no words but through eye contact). Using the telephone for counselling may mean no face to face contact or screen to aid in visual clues, but the therapist can listen for breathing, changes to breathing, catches of the breath, cracks in the voice; there is an incredible intimacy to working on the telephone that can lend itself well to deep empathy creating therapeutic depth as both client and therapist are focused on the client's disclosure. Of course, any over sharing as noted by the disinhibition factor (Suler, 2004) needs to be noted and discussed with the client prior to the end of the session.

> Reflection: What is your experience of providing advanced empathy? What do you find easier and what more challenging? What would be the signs from the client that they have had "too much" empathy? How could you deal with this with the client in the moment?

Deep empathy may also include working with similes and metaphors, e.g. "it sounds like you are on a roller coaster with moments of exhilaration then moments of sheer terror and just wanting it to stop." Often clients will offer their own metaphors, e.g. "I am stuck in room with no windows and I can't get out and there is no air coming in." When a client offers images in this way, it is important to pick them up and work with them to explore their meaning and really show empathy. A therapist may be tempted to change the metaphor to something that they were imagining, but the client is giving a wonderful insight into their world through metaphor, so use it and work with it. This develops the sense of the client feeling understood, to impart what Bozarth calls "idiosyncratic" empathy (Bozarth, 1984, p. 74 in McLeod 1999, p. 386). For more information on how to work with metaphor, see chapter 8.

Congruence

When Carl Rogers (1957) developed person-centred therapy, he conceived of clients as being in a state of incongruence based on their earlier experiences where they were not free to express themselves fully and instead learned to behave in ways that were rewarded rather than being loyal to their own beliefs and feelings. This incongruence was perceived as leading to the distress that the clients felt as it produced anxiety and avoidance of uncomfortable feelings. Rogers postulated that it was very important therefore for the therapist to be congruent within themselves and with their clients so that they established a safe place for the clients to become attuned to their true selves. Through the role-modelling of the therapist's inner congruence in session, and the interpersonal experience of congruence that is felt by the client within the therapeutic relationship, the client would be able to recover. Kolden et al. (2018, p. 425) describe congruence as meaning that "both therapists and patients are accessible, approachable, and sincere rather than obscured behind stereotypical roles or hidden behind protective facades." Congruence, which is often also described as genuineness, works alongside the other core conditions of empathy and unconditional positive regard to set the stage for clients to recover and to be able to express themselves congruently to their inner states, thereby reducing their symptoms of distress.

Whatever the client's childhood experiences may have been, it can be assumed that in having been in an intimate relationship where they experienced domestic abuse that they certainly will have learned to be incongruent as a means of survival. A barrier to accessing help by victims of domestic abuse is listed in the Statutory Guidance for the Domestic Abuse Act (Home Office, 2021, updated 2022, p. 58) as "Shame and stigma – including fear of not being believed, feeling shame around disclosing abuse." This would certainly be an inhibiting factor in congruent expression in the psychotherapy room. The Statutory Guidance furthermore makes the point that "the abuse may make the victim feel isolated, worthless, to feel they are to blame for the abuse and/or be convinced they cannot look after themselves" (p. 57). It would be only natural for the client to want to avoid a genuine expression of such painful feelings.

It follows that the challenge for the domestic abuse counsellor is to demonstrate through words and non-verbal expressiveness that they believe the accounts of abuse by the client and that they see the actions of the perpetrator, not the victim, leading to the abuse. Furthermore, they genuinely believe in the client's ability to recover from abuse and go on to have a better life, both through the support of therapy as well as other resources. In clinical practice, countertransference may make it difficult for the therapist to always genuinely believe this when there may be so many serious obstacles to the client's recovery even after the person has left the relationship (see chapter 5 for more on countertransference). This might include continued threats by the perpetrator to life and safety, and post-separation legal abuse including motions to obtain custody of the children. If the therapist becomes traumatised by disclosed or subsequent events, their genuine response to working with other victims might include feelings of fear and powerlessness, in tandem with how victims feel (see also chapter 14).

Kolden et al. (2018, p. 425) state that: "The therapy process promotes congruence, that is, the development of the capacity to approach, recognise, and reflect upon problematic mind states with openness and authenticity rather than fear and avoidance." This is an aspirational goal and for it to occur, both the therapist and client would move away from fear and avoidance, even though these may be powerful feelings to acknowledge when the danger that clients are experiencing is present. It is important for therapists to openly acknowledge their own painful feelings in relation to domestic abuse so that they can be more genuine when working with clients, and supervision is the perfect place to work on this. Personal therapy may also be indicated, especially for therapists who have personally experienced or witnessed domestic abuse. Peer supervision can also be invaluable in helping counsellors working with domestic abuse survivors as painful feelings can be validated by others who are feeling similarly and furthermore hope can be instilled by sharing accounts of clients who are successfully recovering from abuse. See also chapter 14 for more on self-care.

Reflection: How do you manage congruence when you are feeling revolted by the story of violence that the client has presented? How would you respond to a client when their timeline of events does not seem to add up?

Unconditional Positive Regard

The third "necessary and sufficient condition for therapeutic change" postulated by Rogers (1957) is unconditional positive regard, another aspirational goal within the therapeutic relationship. This core condition in client-centred therapy has been widely valued by other psychotherapeutic approaches who share the assumptions that positive regard, caring, respect for the client, accepting them and trying to understand them no matter what they may reveal about themselves, are key elements of the psychotherapeutic relationship.

In a meta-analysis of the relationship between positive regard and therapeutic outcome, Farber et al. (2018) reported a positive correlation between these two variables and suggested the need for further research to determine the role of non-verbal communication in expressing positive regard. Norcross and Lambert (2018) reviewed psychotherapy outcome research and characterised positive regard and empathy as effective, together with collaboration, therapeutic alliance, and goal consensus.

Goal consensus can present challenges within client-centred counselling generally as well as specifically with survivors of domestic abuse. Client-centred counselling allows the client to direct the content of the session, in contrast with more directive approaches used in cognitive-behavioural and solution-focused therapy approaches. An example of when goal-setting and unconditional positive regard can clash is when the client in a violent relationship presents that they believe that their partner wants to change and that they wish to remain in the relationship whereas the therapist recognises signs that the perpetrator is unlikely to change and interprets the situation as representing that the couple are in the "honeymoon stage" which precedes the eruption of violence (Walker, 1979). A reflective model of how to consider this tension in the therapeutic relationship may come from approaches in client-centred therapy offered by occupational therapists and dilemmas they experience when clients set goals that involve physical activity that is unsafe for them. Kessler et al. (2019) noted that therapists would "override" goals set by clients that were unsafe and suggested that they reflect on the power imbalances of the relationship and propose ways to deal with their concerns while continuing to support the client's goals. They cautioned:

> While therapists were able to listen for and adopt many client-suggested goals, this study highlights the ongoing need for therapists to be keenly attuned to the balance of power during goal setting conversations as well as to their underlying, perhaps professionally engrained, values and beliefs

> around risk and attainability of goals. Conscious effort may be needed to actively listen, clarify meaning attached to goals and respect client choice. (p. 324)

A further complicating factor in working with survivors of domestic abuse is the competing obligation of the psychotherapist to assess risk and safeguarding issues on a regular basis, and to uphold a commitment to the ethical value of "protecting the safety of clients" (BACP, 2018). A principle of good practice from the BACP Ethical Framework (2018) is: "We will give careful consideration to how we manage situations when protecting clients or others from serious harm or when compliance with the law may require overriding a client's explicit wishes or breaching their confidentiality" (p. 14). These tensions between supporting client goals that the therapist has safeguarding concerns about and wanting the best for the client (which the therapist believes is a different course of action) can challenge the therapeutic alliance and therapist aspirations to feel unconditional positive regard towards the client. Feelings of frustration and anger towards the client for making what is perceived as "poor" decisions can pull apart empathy for the client's point of view and make it difficult to truly listen to the client's perceptions.

Keeping in mind that clients benefit from unconditional positive regard which facilitates more in-depth therapeutic work, if the counsellor begins to feel disapproval towards the client, they should consider the client's point of view more carefully and remember that the person is coming to therapy to try to improve their situation. It is also worth considering what the therapist respects, admires or likes about the client, to counter-act these mainly negative feelings. Such feelings should be discussed in supervision to determine whether they are experiencing "compassion fatigue" which is interfering with their work (see also chapter 14). If they are feeling dissociated and distant from the client, they may want to seek personal therapy to determine if client stories are affecting them or bringing up past experiences.

> Reflection: Have you experienced dislike towards clients when they expressed positive feelings towards their abusive partner? Have you been angry at clients for making poor decisions or returning to an abusive partner after having left? How did you restore your feelings of unconditional positive regard?

Working with Silence

Silence in therapy can be an important processing place. In a busy world, where we are connected to phones, computers, the internet/social media, we are not often able to sit and really experience silence. We are conditioned as children to "take turns" to speak and not to interrupt and, when in conversation, there is a tendency to follow on quite quickly to keep the dialogue moving. Hence, silence may be a concept that neither client nor trainee therapist may be overly comfortable with, yet is something that can develop as part of a growing relationship. In silence there is opportunity for something to happen … There can be something highly spiritual about silence – many religious orders use the Great Silence, as a time to pray, contemplate and meditate to gain insight and awareness both within and universally without:

> As with prayer, there are many different levels of silence. At one end of the spectrum it can be felt as isolation and, at the other, silence offers the deepest connection to life and an opening to a unifying movement towards the greatest truths.
>
> (McNeilage, 2015)

Silence though, can also be a charged and threatening place- used for holding power over someone – probably most connected to being a child and told to "be quiet" and, in terms of abuse, a huge connection to being forced into silence and secrecy. How then as therapists do we use silence in the counselling room in a beneficial way? Classic client centred therapists are most likely to maintain that silence needs to be broken by a client, the space is theirs, they need to lead. However, when working with vulnerable clients, especially DA, this may not always be useful and could feel intimidating and scary – as if they are doing something wrong or someone hasn't quite explained the rules to them. There are many types of silence – a comfortable one, an uncomfortable one – a battle of who breaks the silence first perhaps? And each person in the relationship may be, and probably is, experiencing it differently. There may be an expectation that it will be the client that breaks the silence, yet the client has not been trained in what the silence may be there for or that it is part of the process. This may show a misbalance of power (Proctor, 2017), where the therapist may be "expecting" the client to speak. This is not to dismiss silence in any way – it is an important part of learning, growing, and changing in therapy but the point here is that it has to be beneficial to the client. It has to be an "active" part of the dialogical encounter: "Humans do not only substantially rely on dialogue they are dialogue. Therapy does not only substantially rely on dialogue, therapy is dialogue" (Schmid, 2006, p. 251) and "True dialogue is not transmission of information; it is participation in the being of the other which is only possible if it includes metacommunication" (Rennie, 1998; Schmid, 2006, p. 246).

This metacommunication or "talking about communication" is an essential part of looking at being in relationship and working in relationship during therapy. This allows clarity, congruence, and complete non-judgement in noting what is happening in the encounter between therapist and client, bringing into awareness some essential learning: "we have to realise that there is dialogue regardless of whether we are aware of it or not" (Schmid, 2006, p. 250).

Silence is therefore about being and not doing but this "being" is in the presence of another. It is important that psychological contact is kept throughout any silences in order to maintain the therapeutic relationship and the six necessary and sufficient conditions (Rogers, 1957, 1995). It may be that silences are much fewer earlier on in the therapy to allow the client to settle and the relationship to develop. Establishing ways of working with a client is very important for the use of silence in therapy – clients may need to know that there could be silences and to have explained how these could be useful – thus sharing therapist power in sharing knowledge. A part of contracting may be explaining this way of working, especially if contracting to work over the phone or internet where it may be useful to work out between client and therapist what may be needed if there is a silence, for example, a reassurance that both parties are still there and that the connection is not lost or a check-in to see where the client is in their process.

Reflection: What is your own relationship with silence? How long could you hold a silence with a client comfortably? How do you know that the silence is also comfortable for the client? How do you know that you still have psychological contact with the client during silence?

This collaborative way of working is encouraged through the use of empathy, unconditional positive regard and congruence at deep levels, thus enabling relational depth (Mearns & Cooper, 2020) and providing what Winnicott called "a holding environment" (Winnicott, 2018).

Working with Hope

Many studies of counselling have seen hope pushed into the category of "placebo" rather than an "active" ingredient (Wampold & Imel, 2015) and the debate around the nature of hope and methodological integrity of measuring the effect within psychotherapy continues. In this model of practice, we consider that the common factors of therapy are the important underpinning aspects of the work and that hope, which is highlighted in this work, plays an important part (Frank & Frank, 1991; Lambert, 1992).

The concept of hope has divided opinion for centuries, with Ancient Greeks considering it unhelpful to hope for things as there was no way of knowing whether what was hoped for would be delivered (Menninger, 1959). On the other hand, world religions have encouraged hope that the next life will be better than the current one. Within domestic abuse relationships, there are some signs that hope is a very strong element of staying in the relationship, that in some way, if the right combination of behaviours or actions can be determined, that the relationship will revert to the positive experience of early courtship. Of course, this is not part of the abuser's plan as perpetrating abuse ensures their needs are met. This state of believing that the relationship can be improved has been described as wishful thinking, but perhaps the term "unrealistic hope" (O'Hara, 2011) is a better term, as if the hope experienced is heartfelt rather than fanciful. When individuals finally recognise that the relationship will not improve and that all their efforts have been in vain, this can lead to a feeling of hopelessness (Roddy, 2012) which can be linked with higher levels of suicidal ideation (Beck et al., 1974). This also appears to be a point where the individual finally begins to reach out for help as they no longer believe they have the resources required to solve their problems. The situation they find themselves in seems very appropriately described by a Bennett and Bennett (1984) quotation cited in Frank and Frank (1991, p. 562): "In the acceptance of helplessness and hopelessness lies the hope of giving up impossible tasks and taking credit for what we endure. Paradoxically, the abandonment of hope often brings new freedom."

The movement from unrealistic hope through hopelessness to realistic hope has been previously documented (O'Hara, 2011). The journey that we take with a client of abuse through hopelessness, and existential crises (Beck et al., 1974) can be challenging for therapists. However, we can hold onto the possibility of a new and different life for the client. We may not know what that life will be as we start the work, but we can hold hope for the future of the client, when the client has lost hope themselves.

There have been various authors who have examined what can create hope within a therapeutic relationship and these papers will provide you with many ideas of what you might do in practice (Larsen & Stege, 2010a, 2010b, 2012; O'Hara, 2013; O'Hara & O'Hara, 2012). Examples of ways to prompt hope in clients include: witnessing the stories of abuse openly and with care and compassion; highlighting client resources (what they can do rather than what they cannot); separating the client from the problem (understanding the impact of the abuse on an individual irrespective of who they are); or using metaphor and creative work to create a different perspective or new insight (see chapters 8 and 13). If you are interested in more details around working with hope, please do access these papers as they provide a valuable resource for therapists.

In summary, it is important for counsellors to have hope *for* the client, *in* the client, *in* the counselling process and *in* life in general. Maintaining an optimistic view of the world, despite the presentation of abuse, is a gift for the therapist as well as for the client (see also chapters 10 and 14).

> Reflection: What is your own relationship with hope as a person, as a therapist, and from your experience of therapy? How might these views impact on your counselling practice?

Understanding Abuse Narratives

Whilst we have talked about hope as a means of maintaining therapeutic presence when the client is sharing deeply distressing memories or feelings, it seems appropriate to share some of the ways that clients will tell, or not tell but imply, what has happened. The title of this section, understanding abuse narratives, is not about the stories that the clients tell, it is about understanding the way that stories are told and why that might be the case.

Often the extent of the abuse or any injuries sustained will be minimised. There are many reasons for this, such as:

1 The abuser will have explained in detail why the client was at fault or responsible for what happened: the story has become one of guilt and shame that they could have behaved in such a way making it hard to disclose the whole story (see also chapter 6).
2 The abuser may have claimed that the abuse was "nothing" with the threat that there could be a lot worse to come: the client is now unsure that they can trust themselves to judge the seriousness of incidents and are reluctant to share for fear of misrepresenting the facts and being "caught out" by the counsellor.
3 The client may still feel traumatised by the events and may not be able to go anywhere near the story as they may feel too distressed to do so (see also chapter 8).
4 There may be cultural issues associated with the abuse, for example religious beliefs or sexuality, which may bring conflict and confusion within the client not only about their experience but in their sense of themselves and their life (see also chapter 11).
5 There may be historical issues, for example, if they grew up in a domestically violent family and/or have had friends who have been in particularly violent relationships not identified as domestic abuse (see also chapter 3), they may consider that what has happened to them is not as bad as for others and hence minimise based on their own judgement and experience (intergenerational transmission of abuse).

When listening to the client, it is important to look out for signs that there is more to the story than is being told. A very matter of fact presentation of the story, despite some gruesome aspects, may suggest either that they have already repeated the story many times to other professional services or that they have disengaged with the material and are not prepared to feel the enormity of what happened. A gentle enquiry about some aspect of the story will usually provide evidence of the client situation and what might be behind the reticence.

It is important when listening to stories of the client's life today and in the past to be able to hear the dismissing of things, the passing over things quickly, and the elements that are missing, such as the emotional content. It is not just what is being said, but what is not being said. Using highly attuned empathic skills, together with your own understanding of what you have heard/noticed, allows you to speak for the client in situations where they want to tell you something but cannot find the words.

> Reflection: How comfortable do you feel in "guessing" what might be going on for the client and sharing your thoughts about this with them? What might be difficult about doing this? How can you share this with the client without "telling" them what happened?

Summary

Working with clients who have experienced domestic abuse is complex, not just due to the issues that can potentially be brought, but also due to the relational complexity that working with a survivor of abuse brings. A simple summary is to suggest that a relational abuse requires a relational approach for healing. In this chapter, we have explored the need for trust and outlined some ways to develop trust with the client. Within this, key elements of person-centred work presented as vital to working with the client, specifically high levels of empathy, beyond those normally required for standard counselling training, high levels of congruence, beyond those generally required for client work, and positive regard for the client and the ability to accept and respond appropriately to whatever the client might bring.

These core counselling skills are also used to bring gentle challenge to perceptions about the abuse and help with client understanding about what might have happened. Silence and hope within therapy can provide both positive and difficult experiences with clients and learning how to use them in the context of the client is useful for this work. Understanding why stories may have been presented in particular ways can help with exploration, particularly in noticing any missing gaps and supporting the client to tell the whole story.

Issues which come up for therapists as a result of hearing client stories or remembering their past history as a result of client work need to be dealt with in supervision and/or personal therapy.

Key Learning Points

1. Building trust in the therapeutic relationship is the foundation upon which counselling is built. This may need particular attention and skill with this client group due to their past experiences.
2. Advanced empathy, where the counsellor can understand and share what is going on for the client without specific narrative, is extremely helpful in working with and facilitating the client.
3. Therapists need to be very comfortable with themselves, their skills and their process to ensure that they present a competent, confident and consistent presence in the counselling room.

4 At times, the client may opt for courses of action that the therapist may judge unhelpful, yet they must also continue to offer positive regard to the client as such issues are worked through.
5 Silence in therapy can be difficult for some clients, particularly if the abuser was silent before an attack. It is important to have strategies to both manage and explain silences for the benefit of the client.
6 Hope within therapy can have positive effects on both the client and counsellor during the work and can usefully be brought into the therapy room as appropriate.
7 Learning how to hear stories of abuse and quickly understand the hidden and underlying meanings of what has been told can help to facilitate a more helpful telling of the abuse narrative.

References

Beck, A. T., Weissman, A., Lester, D., & Trexler, L. (1974). The measurement of pessimism: the hopelessness scale. *Journal of Consulting and Clinical Psychology*, *42*(6), 861–865. 10.1037/h0037562

British Association for Counselling and Psychotherapy (BACP) (2018). *Ethical framework for the counselling professions*. BACP.

Elliott, R., Bohart, A. C., Watson, J. C., & Murphy, D. (2018). Therapist empathy and client outcome: an updated meta-analysis. *Psychotherapy*, *55*(4), 399–410.

Farber, B., Suzuki, J., & Lynch, D. (2018). Positive regard and psychotherapeutic outcome: a meta-analytic review. *Psychotherapy*, *55*(4), 411–423.

Frank, J. D., & Frank, J. B. (1991). *Persuasion and healing: a comparative study of psychotherapy* (3rd ed.). Johns Hopkins University Press.

Gendlin, E. T. (1984). The client's client: the edge of awareness. In R. L. Levant & J. M. Shlien (Eds.), *Client-centered therapy and the person-centered approach. New directions in theory, research and practice*, pp. 76–107. Praeger. From http://previous.focusing.org/gendlin/docs/gol_2149.html

Home Office (2021, updated 2022). Domestic abuse act statutory guidance. Domestic Abuse Act statutory guidance – GOV.UK (www.gov.uk)

Kessler, D., Walker, I., Sauve-Schenk, K., & Egan, M. (2019). Goal setting dynamics that facilitate or impede a client-centred approach. *Scandinavian Journal of Occupational Therapy*, *26*(5), 315–324. 10.1080/11038128.2018.1465119

Kolden, G., Wang, C., Ausin, S., Fraser, S., Chang, Y., & Klein, M. (2018). Congruence/genuineness: a meta-analysis. *Psychotherapy*, *55*(4), 424–433. 10.1037/pst0000162

Lambert, M. J. (1992). Psychotherapy outcome research: implications for integrative and eclectical therapists. In J. C. Norcross & M. R. Goldfried (Eds.), *Handbook of psychotherapy integration*, pp. 94–129. Basic Books.

Larsen, D. J., & Stege, R. (2010a). Hope-focused practices during early psychotherapy sessions: part I: implicit approaches. *Journal of Psychotherapy Integration*, *20*(3), 271–292. 10.1037/a0020820

Larsen, D. J. & Stege, R. (2010b). Hope-focused practices during early psychotherapy sessions: part II: explicit approaches. *Journal of Psychotherapy Integration, 20*(3), 293–311. 10.1037/a0020821

Larsen, D. J., & Stege, R. (2012). Client accounts of hope in early counseling sessions: a qualitative study. *Journal of Counseling & Development, 90*(1), 45–54.

McLeod., J. (1999). *Practitioner research in counselling*. London: Sage Publications Ltd.

Mayer, R. C., Davis, J. H., & Schoorman, F. D. (1995). An integrative model of organizational trust. *Academy of Management Review, 20*(3), 709–734. 10.5465/amr.1995.9508080335

McNeilage. A. (2015). *The heart of silence*. https://www.bacp.co.uk/bacp-journals/thresholds/winter-2015/the-heart-of-silence/ accessed 20/12/21.

Mearns, D., & Cooper, M. (2020). *Working at relational depth in counselling and psychotherapy*. SAGE Publications.

Menninger, K. (1959). The academic lecture: hope. *The American Journal of Psychiatry, 116*, 481–491.

Natiello, P. (2001). *The person-centred approach: a passionate presence*. PCCS Books.

Norcross, J., & Lambert, M. (2018). Psychotherapy relationships that work III. *Psychotherapy, 55*(4), 303–315.

O'Hara, D. J. (2011). Psychotherapy and the dialectics of hope and despair. *Counselling Psychology Quarterly, 24*(4), 323–329. 10.1080/09515070.2011.623542

O'Hara, D. J. (2013). *Hope in counselling and psychotherapy*. SAGE Publications.

O'Hara, D. J., & O'Hara, E. F. (2012). Towards a grounded theory of therapist hope. *Counselling Psychology Review, 27*(4), 42–55.

Proctor, G. (2017). *The dynamics of power in counselling and psychotherapy: ethics, politics and practice*. PCCS Books.

Rennie, D. L. (1998). *Person centred counselling: an experiential approach*. SAGE Publications.

Roddy, J. (2012). *Hope, belief and compassion: values for the therapist, researcher and client*. 2012 Value and Virtue in Practice-based Research Conference, York St. John University.

Roddy, J. K. (2014). *A client informed view of domestic violence counselling* [PhD, University of Leeds]. Leeds.

Roddy, J. K. (2015). Counselling and psychotherapy after domestic violence: A client view of what helps recovery. Palgrave Macmillan.

Rogers, C. R. (1957). The necessary and sufficient conditions of therapeutic personality change. *Journal of Consulting Psychology, 21*(2), 95–103. 10.1037/h0045357

Rogers, C. (1995). *A way of being*. Miffin Harcourt.

Rogers, C. (1980). *A way of being*. Boston: Houghton Mifflin.

Schmid, P. F. (2006). The challenge of the other: towards dialogical person-centered psychotherapy and counselling. *Person Centered & Experiential Psychotherapies, 5*(4), 240–254. 10.1080/14779757.2006.9688416

Suler (2004). The online disinhibition effect. *Cyberpsychology & behavior: the impact of the Internet, multimedia and virtual reality on behavior and society, 7*(3), 321–326. 10.1089/1094931041291295

Tolan, J., & Wilkins, P. (2011). *Client issues in counselling and psychotherapy*. SAGE Publications.

Walker, L. (1979). *The battered woman*. Harper Collins.

Wampold, B. E., & Imel, Z. E. (2015). *The great psychotherapy debate* (2nd ed.). Routledge.

Winnicott, D. W. (2018). *Holding and interpretation, fragment of an analysis*. Routledge.

Chapter 5

Understanding Attachment and Transference

Jeannette Roddy and Sarah Eccleston

Learning Objectives

1 Understand how the effects of domestic abuse can affect the way the client may respond
2 Identify appropriate strategies to be able to work effectively with clients
3 Recognise the importance of clear boundaries when working with clients
4 Be aware of the potential problems with transference and countertransference
5 Understand why a consistent and honest relationship is important in this work

Context

The relational nature of domestic abuse means that relationships can become problematic for the survivor, not only in the context of the abusive partner, but also in the context of past, current, and future relationships with friends, family, and employers. Understanding the impact of domestic abuse on the individual in the context of attachment theory can be very helpful in building strong therapeutic relationships.

The therapeutic relationship can also be tested through transference (from client to counsellor) and countertransference (from counsellor to client) occurring during therapy. This chapter highlights how to recognise when transference issues may be affecting the relationship and need to be worked through in supervision. Attachment theory also helps to explain why maintaining appropriate boundaries in the therapeutic space is important.

Background to Attachment Theory and Its Role in Relationships

Attachment theory is still a relatively new addition (<100 years) to psychological thinking. Whilst we have always known the value of relationships as

DOI: 10.4324/9781003253266-5

human beings, we have only recently looked at the effect of relationships from a very early age on the outcomes of our lives.

Important studies that have shaped our views today came from studies of animals and birds. For example, Lorenz's (1935) study of ducks and geese helped to shape maternity practice in promoting human bonding between mother and child straight after birth. Harlow and Zimmermann (1958) experimented with a baby monkey showing that being close to a warm and comforting object was preferable to being with a hard and cold object, even when that object was the only source of food and water.

Some of the most well-known names in psychology were involved in early research on attachment theory. John Bowlby, Mary Ainsworth, Melanie Klein, and John and Joyce Robertson were all conducting research from the 1940s to try to understand the effect of life experiences and caregiver relationships on children. They noted that not having a caregiver who was consistent and available affected children in different ways. Some children tried to stay as close as they could to the caregiver when the caregiver was available becoming *anxious* when separated; other children would ignore *(avoid)* and keep a distance from the caregiver, taking care of themselves (Ainsworth et al., 1978). Those children who were happy to see the parent and happy to play separately knowing the parent would still be available had a *secure* relationship. These early terms, secure, avoidant, and anxious attachment styles were initially defined with Mary Main identifying a fourth category of disorganised/disorientated attachment, where the child displays an inconsistency in their attachment to others (Main & Solomon, 1986), sometimes being anxious and sometimes avoidant, without any particular pattern observed. These four attachment styles form the basis of what we understand today.

A similar set of definitions relating to adult attachment were published by Bartholomew and Horowitz in 1991. These were: *secure* (confident in their own ability to solve their problems and if they cannot, they feel they can rely on others); *preoccupied* (fear of rejection and focused on maintaining relationships, lacking confidence to rely on themselves); *dismissing* (confident and defensive in their self-sufficiency and lacking desire for close relationships); and *fearful* (lacking confidence in themselves and others, fearful of intimacy and socially avoidant). You can see very clear links between the models for adults and children, although the terms are slightly different.

Importantly, the broad categorisation for attachment is secure or insecure, where insecure attachment includes all categories, excluding secure attachment. It is useful to be aware of these terms as they are sometimes used interchangeably in the literature. Hopefully, as you think about these different relational styles you will be able to think of friends and family members who fit into one or more of these categories to help you to recognise it elsewhere.

Reflection: Thinking about these different styles of attachment, where do you feel you are most of the time? If you were working with someone with a different attachment style, how might that feel for you?

One of the important aspects of attachment is that it can change over time, depending on a person's experiences. For example, someone who is securely attached can show signs of insecure attachment if their partnership is in difficulty. Equally, someone who is insecurely attached can start to show secure attachment if they form a loving and consistent relationship with their partner.

Often people in abusive relationships become insecurely attached, due to the uncertainty of their partner's behaviour. Understanding that having an abusive relationship does not preclude having a healthy relationship in future can provide hope to people who have been abused, as they can see the potential for positive change and new relationships in their lives.

The Effect of Domestic Abuse on Attachment Style within a Relationship

Intuitively, we know where we prefer to be and with whom. Generally, we choose people whom we like, respect and care for, and who reciprocate these feelings towards us. Most of us will also be aware of why we tolerate relationships which are harmful to us, what our coping strategies might be in that instance and a clear idea of why we stay (or we plan to leave). So why then, do people stay in abusive relationships?

If we go back to chapter 2 and remember that often in domestically abusive relationships the initial period of courtship was very romantic, kind, caring, and respectful. In other words, the sort of relationships we would ordinarily choose over others. As time goes on, the atmosphere begins to change and the abuser holds their partner responsible for the change: if only they could do more of this or less of that, be more understanding, be more/less demanding (depending on the abuser's attachment style). In other words, the "perfect relationship" could return if only their needs were being attended to. This type of approach is designed to focus the victim on meeting the needs of the abuser at the expense of themselves i.e. the sort of behaviour associated with *preoccupied* attachment. Even if the person had started the relationship as securely attached, the desire to do their best for their partner may mean a change in behaviour and attitude, as they become fearful of losing their partner due their inability to be "good enough."

As time goes on, the person can become less sure of themselves, due to the many problems being brought by the abuser, but they also begin to wonder about the abuser themselves and whether their partner really does have their best interests at heart. As they lose confidence in the abusive partner and no longer have confidence in themselves, they may move into *fearful* attachment.

If the person has been isolated as part of the abuse, making approaches to friends and family for help is far from easy as often relationships have been disrupted by the abuser. Reconnecting with people once known is increasingly difficult to do as trust in them and others around has been severely eroded. It is sometimes at this point that people opt to seek therapy, knowing that there is something that is not quite right, that they used to be different in their relationships with others and that something needs to change. Talking over their difficulties can be more important at this point than medication, which can dull the pain of the situation and potentially reduce help-seeking activities.

Many domestic abuse services focus primarily on increasing the individual's self-confidence and self-esteem. As they begin to see how much more they can do and how the abuser had changed and shifted their view of things into something both wrong and harmful, they start to feel more in control of their own lives and can trust themselves to make good and appropriate decisions in their lives. This can result in a move into *dismissing* attachment, where they keep themselves safe by relying on their own resources and becoming quite independent.

Ideally, the next step of the process, that of re-integrating into society and starting to trust others and create meaningful and supportive friendships can also be facilitated. This helps the individual to move into a more securely attached place, being able to trust and rely on others as well as themselves (see also chapter 8 for the final stage in the trauma model of reconnecting). However, as there are often quite small amounts of funding available, the focus tends to be on facilitating independence. You can see how the attachment style moves from section in Figure 5.1, which is based on Bartholomew and Horowitz' (1991) model of adult attachment.

Whilst this pattern of attachment change and development can be seen often, there are possible differences to this pattern if the individual starts the relationship as someone who is generally *dismissing* rather than *securely*

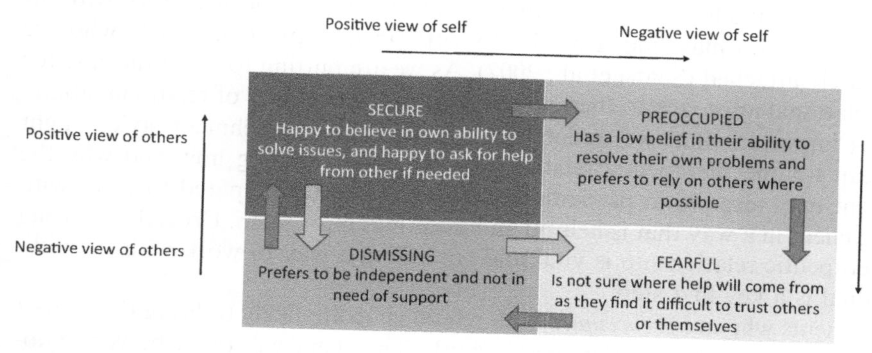

Figure 5.1 How domestic abuse might affect attachment styles.

attached. In this case, the abuser is still looking for more attention, but the individual is likely to try harder to stay away from the abuser to minimise the disruption to their life. The abuser is then more likely to pursue the person and the situation may escalate or else the person will leave.

Escalation by the abuser may also have the effect of undermining the person's confidence in their ability to read situations and look after themselves, which can start to show up as *fearful* attachment. Friends and family, if still around, can be very helpful here in noticing the decline in the individual as their confidence seems to seep away. For those isolated, the situation can deteriorate until the individual feels they cannot cope anymore, and they seek support, as above.

> Reflection: Think about your own attachment style. What are the benefits to client work of this and what are the limitations? What behaviours or attitudes would it be helpful for you to look out for when working with clients, for both you and the client?

Studies on attachment in people who have been in domestically abusive relationships have shown that individuals can show any of the attachment styles mentioned above after abuse (Gormley, 2005; Henderson et al., 1997; Henderson et al., 2005; Hick, 2008; Walker, 2009). It is possible that psychological abuse may engender a more dismissing style of relationship whereas physical abuse, with an existential threat, may prompt a more preoccupied style responding to the need for self-preservation and dependency on the abuser. However, all types of attachments style are possible, although the number of people still showing secure attachment at the end of an abusive relationship is suggested to be small.

Working with Insecure Attachment in Counselling

Given that many people leaving an abusive relationship may have become insecurely attached, it is likely that therapists in this field will work with individuals who may find it harder to settle in therapy than people who are securely attached (Saatsi et al., 2007). As we are putting forward the case for a relational approach to therapy to counteract the effects of relational abuse, it is important that we understand what insecure attachment styles might mean for the therapeutic relationship. By understanding how and why the client may respond in particular ways, we are better prepared to work with the client in a way that is helpful and meaningful for them. Crucially a strong therapeutic relationship is vital and so finding a way to work with the individual is a key first step.

Clients who are *preoccupied* with relationship are likely to bring that aspect of themselves into any therapeutic work. The client will often be very emotional and may have problems ending sessions as they want to prolong contact for as long as possible. They may seek reassurance from the therapist about what they are doing or are thinking about doing. Sometimes, if things go wrong, they may text, call or message the therapist between sessions as they seek to use the therapist as a means of managing their emotions, finding it hard to manage on their own. It is not simply that they lack emotional regulation skills, but their previous experiences may have taught them to express extreme emotion as a means to gain attention from their caregiver (Holmes & Slade, 2018). Not having that attention can result in collapse, dependency, chronic depression or anxiety, for fear that the relationship may end as they are unable to do anything to put it right (Holmes & Slade, 2018).

A strong therapeutic relationship that can withstand the gaps between therapy is a key element of this work. Having very clear boundaries, such as keeping sessions to time and ensuring between session contact is within clearly defined limits is helpful, as the therapist models consistent and caring behaviours which the client can begin to rely on and trust.

A therapist using an open and honest approach (congruence) to address any distress or unexpected response seen or sensed during a session helps to minimise the risk of the client leaving the session with a misunderstanding or misinterpretation about something that they perceived happened during a session. Being able to explore those thoughts with an honest response from the therapist of their experience of what happened, allows the client to be part of resolving potential conflict in a relationship constructively.

For clients who present with very high levels of emotional distress, working with emotional regulation techniques such as breathing (see chapter 8) or mindfulness and self-compassion (see chapter 10) can also be useful. Helping the client to understand that they can manage their emotions themselves allows more independence in their lives: "rescuing" the client from emotions particularly once the therapeutic relationship is established, can re-enforce their view that they need someone else to help them to self-regulate and slow down therapeutic progress.

Showing that you care about the client deeply, whilst keeping boundaries and facilitating their self-soothing process, is very helpful, to avoid boundaries being seen as a form of rejection (see the section on boundaries below). It is interesting to note that there is research to suggest that *preoccupied* clients are the most difficult clients to work with therapeutically (Saatsi et al., 2007) perhaps due to the issues of building a strong, yet independent therapeutic relationship. Nevertheless, it can be done, although it can take a lot of care and attention, as well as supervisory support.

Clients who are *dismissively* attached present very differently. Here, the individual will have suppressed emotions from their caregiver as they recognise that their emotion is not welcome. Interestingly, where a person has detached from the caregiver, it is possible that they have a much stronger sense of self, which they needed to be able to choose and withstand separation. However, their reliance on themselves may not have served that well in the abusive relationship as it may have made the relational dynamics worse (see the section on effects of attachment above). Dismissive clients may be reluctant to engage with a therapist at depth, initially. They are used to working things out on their own and may challenge the therapists' competence or question their approach, requiring a non-defensive response from the therapist. Clients may not necessarily value or be in touch with their feelings. Working with such a client requires a focus on the individual's thoughts and perceptions first, as they process what has happened in a way that they can relate to, with a move to looking at their feelings and their relationships with others once the therapeutic relationship is established. This allows them to be seen and accepted for who they are, before the gentle challenge of acknowledging the pain and grief of trauma and loss (Muller, 2009).

> Reflection: Working with people who are insecurely attached can sometimes be frustrating as it can seem the relationship is going well one week and badly another. How might you deal with this inconsistency in the way the client responds to you in session?

Establishing a Safe Space: Boundaries, Contracting, Congruence

Contracting is the beginning of our journey with clients, and we need to set out our clear expectations of what will happen in the sessions. The current BACP Ethical Framework (2018) reminds us that we need to communicate with our clients in ways that are suitable for the context in which the client finds themselves. It is important to consider how leaving a violent relationship may mean a client has different needs to other clients. In some instances, our clients can lead quite chaotic lives, and in particular those clients who find themselves in sole charge of children following a relationship breakdown may feel overwhelmed.

The frequent cancellation of sessions can be an issue for single parents or for those parents who have left the family home and have appointments with housing, social workers and perhaps professionals involved in the legal side of any ongoing court proceedings. Boundaries for dealing with the cancellation and/or rescheduling of appointments need to be clear and need to be enforced if the working relationship is to be effective. Breaks in counselling can be very disruptive and impair the development of the therapeutic relationship and we need to be clear with our clients that continuity is a key factor in whether therapy is successful or otherwise.

As a therapist, you might find your personal feelings about cancellations is at variance with your place of work and you may need to negotiate to find the right balance. I have known of instances when the organisation has accepted repeated missed appointments, often by phone at the last moment. What does it mean when a client cancels at the last moment like that? Sometimes the reasons are genuine but often it signifies that a client forgot, and this can again be indicative of a disorganised pattern of cognitive processing and/or lifestyle. I think the fact that they took the time to phone, all be it too late to fill the slot, suggests that they want the therapeutic relationship to continue. They want you to know that they would like to attend and that they value what you are doing but today is not the day! A good practice is to sit with clients at the end of the session and encourage them to put the appointment and an alarm call for the day before in their phone. Reiterate, that the consequences of non-attendance are that other clients cannot fill the slot and most importantly that they are not engaging in the therapeutic process in a meaningful way. If a client repeatedly misses a session or is late, this is a good time for you to recontract and this may lead you to an understanding of the sporadic nature of their attendance. It can be that we need to terminate the therapy. Just because a client may seem to us to be in need, it does not necessarily mean that they feel the same way. Some clients are just not ready to talk about their lives at this point. Revisiting significant events can prompt very emotional responses and they may feel that returning to those events is impeding them in their efforts to "pull their lives together." It is important that their autonomy in this decision-making process is respected, even though we may feel that therapy would be hugely beneficial.

At the other extreme of the spectrum are those clients that seem to have become over dependant on us. Indicators of this include a reluctance to leave the therapeutic space and contacting us outside of the agreed sessions. People leaving relationships can be lonely and feel the need to connect with someone who seems to understand and value them and so they begin to see the relationship between you both as a friendship. We want our clients to know that we care but we also need to keep in mind that our relationship with them is finite. Holding boundaries about contact and time are important aspects of this.

The exploration of risk is an integral part of the contracting process (Reeves, 2015) and we need to be especially aware with clients who have experienced partner abuse. Their own concept of what constitutes a risk may be significantly different to other clients. They may have minimised their own safety and that of their dependants as part of the pattern of violence and/or control. An exploration of what would constitute risk is an important part of the contracting process and this initial clarity ensures that clear boundaries are maintained from the outset. There may, for example, be occasions when a client will tell you that an abusive partner has visited, and an argument has taken place. You may need to ask if any dependent children witnessed this as the damage this may do is not always understood by the client. They may put the emotional needs of the abusive partner above their own and so not always be considering how that partner adversely affects other family members. When we counsel clients with dependent children, we need to be very clear about how we will assess risk and the limits of confidentiality that we can offer.

The need for confidentiality is often foremost in their minds. They may have a history of having been closely monitored and interrogated about ways in which they have breached the boundaries placed on them by the abuser. Endless questioning and accusations of secretiveness and lying are often a key feature in abusive relationships, particularly those in which sexual jealously has been a feature. Many clients are very worried that their abuser may be able to access their notes or that you would give them information without their permission. It can be hard for them to believe that you will not be coerced or bullied in the way that they may have been. Reassurances about confidentiality may be important throughout the length of the work that you do together and to create the necessary trust needed to form a working alliance. Statements made by the client may be prefaced by them asking "You won't tell anybody will you?" and it is worth reiterating at this point the confidentiality agreement that exists between you. What they are really asking is, are you someone that will not be coerced or bullied into betraying them. This behaviour is also indicative of how the client is now remapping their own boundaries, considering who they can and should trust and may be experiencing for the first time, a person who values their privacy and autonomy.

Reflection: What is your experience of maintaining boundaries in counselling? What do you find easy and what is more challenging for you? How would you deal with some of the scenarios outlined above in a way that is comfortable for you?

What Is Transference and Countertransference and How to Spot and Work with It

With insecure attachment, it is important that we understand our own attachment patterns and our own issues. In doing so, we can understand better what is going on in the room with the client when there is a disconnect between the two and whether it is us (countertransference) or the client (transference) who is not seeing the other fully.

Transference and countertransference are terms that are used throughout psychotherapy and a definition at this point is useful. First described as a concept by Breuer and Freud (1893–1895), transference is an interaction between both the therapist and the client and is contributed to by both parties. Strong feelings, often rooted in childhood experience are projected towards the therapist who is now substituted in the client's subconscious for a mother, father, sibling or significant authority figure. Although the client is not aware that a shift has taken place, they are responding to subconscious internal models. Countertransference is a similar process taking place in the therapist.

The childhood experiences of clients can become very present in the room both through the displaying of attachment style and the subconscious enactment of transference. An initial sign that transference is taking place is a sense that the client's responses are not in proportion to the stimulus that the therapist is providing. The client may seem very threatened by the therapist and adopt an almost childlike "victim" position. This may be rooted in early experience of parental aggression and/or control experienced by the client and so, when we offer care and attention, the client responds to us as they have their parent in the past. If this is the nature of the transference taking place, then it severely hinders the client's ability to progress to a more autonomous state. They see the therapist as "in control," like a parent, and this can severely rupture the therapeutic relationship. We may see the client relinquishing control of their therapy and begin to ask, "What should I do?" and to attempt to push us into making decisions for them. This carries the possibility that the therapist may then take on that parental role and start to offer solutions as a counter transference starts to take place. As an older woman, I have seen this dynamic occur when I have worked with younger clients. If this transference and counter transference goes unchecked, then we risk becoming "advice givers." When one considers that the very nature of partner violence requires the victim to relinquish control, we can see that this situation is in no way advantageous to the client as it returns them to a state of helplessness when we are actively trying to foster independent thinking.

Transference may take the form of anger towards the therapist as the internal models of the client start to impose on the therapist the attributes of those that have tried to control the client in the past. I have worked with clients who seem quite irrationally angry towards me and I have then had to question whether this is something that I am creating or if this is transference taking place. My experience has been that they see me as the "professional" in the room and that much of their experience of professionals has involved having their autonomy removed from them and so they may begin to distance themselves from the therapist and their lack of trust can be displayed as anger and hostility. Their internal models may also view our professional boundary keeping as an attempt to manipulate or control them and so they start to transfer onto us their unconscious feelings of resentment and fear, playing into the belief that people are not what they seem and should not be trusted.

Another interesting aspect of transference can become apparent when the client works with a younger therapist. The client may need to be deeply held and understood and so they may be looking for the "parent" in the therapist. I have seen instances of student therapists who have been unable to form a working alliance with clients who believe that their experience can be neither held nor understood by someone who seems not to have had the necessary life experience to hold their pain. They equate youth with inexperience and so the transference may manifest itself in dismissive or in some cases, quite hostile behaviour.

Countertransference can occur when we work with clients who have suffered violence from an intimate partner. They can often engender in us a "rescuing" tendency that we might not experience in other situations. This can be particularly relevant if you yourself have been or are still engaged in a violent or coercive relationship. You may find that you are over identifying with the client and their situation, and this can be highlighted by you having a sense that you understand how they are feeling or reacting, that seems to exceed what we would normally expect from our own empathetic responses. You may see similarities between your situation and your client's, and this can lead you to make assumptions and, in some instances, to become irritated when your client does not make the connections or come to the realisations that you have. An awareness of this heightening of feeling is important and should be taken to supervision. It can seriously impair the quality of the therapeutic relationship and needs to be addressed as soon as you become aware of it.

> Reflection: Have you had any instances in your client work where you have become aware that you no longer know what is happening in the room? If so, how did you manage to re-establish psychological contact with the client? If this happened now, what strategies do you feel could be used?

Summary

Attachment is an important area to explore when working with people who have experienced domestic abuse. Identifying what clients need from a therapist to counterbalance their previous relationships can be a very helpful factor in the work completed. Whilst we often focus on the client in terms of attachment, we also need to be aware of our processes and what we are bringing into the therapy room that could disrupt the client, ourselves and the therapeutic relationship. Being aware of some of the presentations in counselling of insecure attachment allows us to understand the client process and the enforcement of boundaries can be seen as client facilitating rather than client limiting.

Key Learning Points

1. Thinking about the relational dynamics of domestic abuse helps us to understand how a client may have changed in the way they relate to people.
2. Therapy provides opportunities to try out new or previously known ways of relating as the person starts to move towards having trusting relationships with themselves and others again.
3. Insecure attachment can be difficult to deal with and finding strategies to work with complex clients is helpful. Working with a supervisor who understands these complexities is also helpful.

4 Be aware of any changes to your usual therapeutic practice as this may provide some insight into the relational process developing between you and the client.
5 If there are any relational ruptures in your client work, try to address them in the moment, before they become rooted as another example of the client's normal experience.
6 Be clear about the boundaries in your work, either organisational or personal, and consider how these can be managed with this client group.

References

Ainsworth, M. D., Blehar, M. C., Waters, E., & Wall, S. (1978). *Patterns of attachment: asessed in the strange situation and at home*. Hillsdale, NJ: Lawrence Erlbaum.

Bartholomew, K., & Horowitz, L. M. (1991). Attachment styles among young adults: a test of a four-category model. *Journal of Personality & Social Psychology, 61*, 226–244.

Gormley, B. (2005). An adult attachment theoretical perspective of gender symmetry in intimate partner violence. *Sex Roles, 52*(11/12), 785–795. 10.1007/s11199-005-4199-3

Harlow, H. F., & Zimmermann, R. R. (1958). The development of affectional responses in infant monkeys. *Proceedings of the American Philosophical Society, 102*(5) (October 20, 1958), 501–509. Philadelphia: American Philosophical Society.

Henderson, A. J. Z., Bartholomew, K., & Dutton, D. G. (1997). He loves me; he loves me not: attachment and separation resolution of abused women. *Journal of Family Violence, 12*(2), 169–191.

Henderson, A. J. Z., Bartholomew, K., Trinke, S. J., & Kwong, M. J. (2005). When loving means hurting: an exploration of attachment and intimate abuse in a community sample. *Journal of Family Violence, 20*(4), 219–230.

Hick, K. (2008). *Moving beyond power and control: a qualitative analysis of adult attachment and intimate partner violence.* Alliant International University. psyh. San Francisco.

Holmes, J., & Slade, A. (2018). *Attachment in therapeutic practice*. SAGE Publications.

Lorenz, K. (1935). Der Kumpan in der Umwelt des Vogels; der Artgenosse als Auslosendes Moment sozialer Verhaltunsweisen. *Journal of Ornithology, 83*, 137–213; 289–413. (English translation: Companionship in bird life; fellow members of the species as releasers of social behavior. In: *Instinctive Behavior* (Ed. by C. H. Schiller).) New York: International University Press.

Main, M., & Solomon, J. (1986). Discovery of an insecure-disorganized/disoriented attachment pattern. In T. B. Brazelton & M. W. Yogman (Eds.), *Affective development in infancy*. Westport, CT US: Ablex Publishing.

Muller, R. T. (2009). Trauma and dismissing (avoidant) attachment: intervention strategies in individual psychotherapy. *Psychotherapy: Theory, Research, Practice, Training, 46*(1), 68–81. 10.1037/a0015135

Reeves, A. (2015). Risk assessment: talking and ticking boxes. *Working with risk in couselling and psychotherapy*. SAGE Publications.

Saatsi, S., Hardy, G. E., & Cahill, J. (2007). Predictors of outcome and completion status in cognitive therapy for depression. *Psychotherapy Research, 17*(2), 185–195. 10.1080/10503300600779420

Walker, L. E. A. (2009). *The battered woman syndrome* (3rd ed.). Springer Publishing Co.

Chapter 6

Working with Protective Emotions

Linda Dubrow-Marshall and Laura Viliardos

This chapter will examine common emotions which are experienced by survivors of domestic abuse which may appear to be "negative," but which can be better understood as "protective emotions." Whilst in an abusive relationship, a range of overwhelming emotions may be experienced by the victim including abject fear. "Protective emotions" can shield the person from feeling terrified of the other person and completely powerless by putting the blame on themselves or placing emphasis on self-deficiencies which could potentially be rectified and restore some feeling of self-control.

The sections covered in this chapter are as follows:

1. Understanding the concept of protective emotions
2. Shame
3. Guilt
4. Self-criticism
5. Anxiety
6. Suicidal ideation
7. Exercises to enhance therapeutic practice

Understanding the Concept of Protective Emotions

It can be assumed that victims of domestic abuse are beset with tumultuous emotions due to the unpredictability of their partner's emotions and behaviours and the intensity of the experience of physical and emotional abuse. Walker's (1979) seminal work on the cycle of domestic violence outlined the stages of tension building leading up to a violent incident followed by the expression of remorse and reconciliation and the establishment of a period of relative calm or honeymoon phase, a pattern which repeats itself continually and which creates a barrage of overwhelming feelings that feel intolerable. This can then lead to a layer of feelings that builds on top of the overwhelming feelings that can be called "protective emotions."

This chapter focuses on a counselling approach to the common emotional reactions to being in a violent relationship of shame, guilt, self-criticism, anxiety,

DOI: 10.4324/9781003253266-6

and suicidal ideation from the lens of being "protective" against even more painful, raw, and unmanageable feelings, such as abject fear. Psychotherapists who lack an appreciation of the emotional experience of being in an abusive relationship may at first glance view these powerful emotions as "negative" and interpret them as being self-destructive and as an impediment to therapeutic change. They may even find it difficult to maintain the core conditions in their therapeutic work, especially empathy. For example, the practitioner may internalise the anger that should rightly be directed to the perpetrator, which the client is not expressing, to the point that they feel anger towards the client for demonstrating feelings of self-blame and self-criticism. It can become much easier to restore feelings of empathy and unconditional positive regard towards the client when the practitioner can appreciate that these painful feelings *protect* the client from feeling powerless to control the actions of their partner and at least give the illusion that their reactions might ensure their safety. Blaming themselves or placing emphasis on self-deficiencies that could potentially be rectified may restore some feeling of self-control. To put it simply, the painful feelings that the client experiences protect them from even more painful emotions.

With this understanding and the core conditions now securely in place, the safety and integrity of the psychotherapeutic space can be maintained, and the practitioner can contain the painful emotions and facilitate movement beyond the protective emotions to address the extremely difficult underlying issues. There are several psychotherapeutic strategies that could assist the practitioner, including guiding the exploration of the *purpose* that the protective emotions serve as it is only then that less painful and self-destructive solutions can be found to address the underlying difficulties. The therapist can do this by accepting the protective emotions as being valid in their own right, and helping clients to label these. Clients may observe that their emotions reflect the volatility of the perpetrator's emotions and behaviours, and the therapist can affirm the client's right to have, own and express their emotions, without having to hide them for fear of retaliation. The acceptance and unconditional positive regard expressed by the psychotherapist allows the client to be more in touch with their feelings and less dissociative within the safety of the therapy room. A growing awareness of how feelings change can help clients to feel less stuck and powerless. The practitioner can accompany the client's journey so that they can gently explore the feelings that are underneath the protective emotions.

Reflection: Can you identify a time in your own life when you were stuck in a painful emotional state and later discovered that you had underlying feelings that were even more unpleasant? If you cannot think of an example, consider times when you felt unsafe or how you felt at hearing of a significant death. What helped you to understand the purpose and meaning of your protective emotions?

Shame

It is argued that feelings of shame can be more prevalent in survivors of interpersonal trauma, such as domestic abuse, compared with non-interpersonal trauma (Amstadter & Vernon, 2008). Lewis (1971) described shame as an interpersonal emotion and argued that shame emerges when an individual is in a relationship in which they feel dependent and vulnerable to rejection. When an individual in this relationship fails to meet the standards of a superior and admired other, it can lead to profound feelings of rejection, humiliation, anger, and shame.

Platt and Freyd (2015) suggest that shame is a dominant influence in perpetuating an abusive relationship and they argue that it is a more powerful emotion than fear when it comes to maintaining these relationships. With the origins of the shame response being defensively rooted, which ensured connection to a tribe and enhanced survival, it is putative that shame will ignite when leaving (or contemplating leaving) an abusive relationship. Further, when a person has been consistently shamed, they can feel worthless and unlovable. Someone experiencing shame in an abusive relationship will likely seek out predictability or familiarity, despite the maltreatment, thus continuing the bond with the perpetrator. In domestic abuse cases shame can be actively fostered in the victim by the perpetrator, by behaving in a way that makes the victim feel ashamed. Additionally, a perpetrator of domestic abuse will rarely accept responsibility for their behaviour, leaving an explanatory gap for the victim to understand what has happened and take on the responsibility for the perpetrator's actions and the outcome. This can exacerbate feelings of self-blame which in turn can leave the victim feeling ashamed ("I am such a bad person as I made this happen").

Shame is an uncomfortable emotion which can lead to an urge to hide and withdraw; it is a common response following an abusive experience (Dutton, 1992; Sanderson, 2008; Wilson et al., 2006). An individual experiencing the painful emotion of shame can feel flawed, defective (Bradshaw, 1990), diminished, inadequate, and not good enough (Miller, 1985). Cognitively, the individual can ruminate on thoughts such as "something is wrong with me." As the individual tends to focus on the negative, often viewing themselves as insufficient, they can employ subjective reasoning and obsessive thinking (Harper & Hoopes, 1990). Shame centres around the feeling of being exposed and criticised, both internally and externally (Banmen, 1988). Consequently, enduring feelings of shame can lead to social withdrawal. Such feelings can become so embodied, that eventually an individual can experience the painful shame response without an activating event (Kaufman, 1989).

This could raise questions as to why shame is considered to be a *protective emotion*. Whilst shame is often thought to be a negative or unhelpful emotion, it serves an essential role in species survival. According to social preservation theory, the shame response, which appears around the second year of life

(Cozolino, 2010), is believed to ensure that an individual adheres to social and cultural norms and to prepare for the possibility of being attacked (Platt & Freyd, 2015). In terms of how shame manifests behaviourally, an individual in a state of shame will likely look downwards, lower their head and round their shoulders; a posture associated with social exclusion and loss (Cozolino, 2010). Despite shame being an important protective emotion, experiencing a prolonged and reoccurring shame state can cause physiological dysregulation, and can negatively impact affect regulation, the development of networks of the social brain and attachment (Schore, 1994).

Although disclosure and help-seeking are influential in ending ongoing abuse and increasing emotional wellbeing, shame and embarrassment often act as a barrier to disclosing abuse experiences and seeking help (Rose et al., 2011). As well as reducing the likelihood of abuse survivors seeking support, shame can also result in clients withholding material they could present in counselling. In research on the client's perspectives of counselling for domestic abuse survivors (Roddy, 2015), one participant described issues that she perceived held her back from disclosing her experiences sooner, as she was aware that at times she responded to or pre-empted the abuse, or went along with her partner's behaviour, in the heat of the moment. Acknowledging that this was not what she considered to be her normal standards of behaviour, she reported feelings of shame. Here, the participant described two distinct characteristics of shame: shame related to the abuse that happened behind closed doors; and shame related to her own behaviour as a consequence of the abuse. Due to the profound feelings of shame, the participant explained that she needed to feel that the counsellor would be able to understand her situation and, crucially, she wanted the counsellor to help her understand what had happened and why she reacted the way she did. Building trust with the counsellor was vital for her to be able go further and share aspects that she found difficult to endure due to her feelings of complicity in the abuse (see also chapter 4).

Experiences that lead to shame are often kept secret or they can be repressed. Despite being outside of conscious awareness, the individual could experience it as depression, uneasiness, anxiety, and guilt (Loughead, 1992). Kaufman (1989) argued that shame seldom remains a wholly conscious process, as repression is the main defence mechanism to protect against the painful emotion. Further, when an individual is repeatedly shamed, they will have a tendency to hide or supress the thoughts, feelings, and behaviours which caused them to feel bad or unworthy (Kaufman, 1989).

Reflection: In childhood, we experience feelings that cause us to feel shame. Because we are children, we just feel the shame and have a difficult time in challenging whatever caused the shame. Do you remember any time in your childhood, possibly at school, when you felt shame? How did you deal with it? What would have been helpful for you at the time, looking back?

When working with domestic abuse survivors, many clients will express feelings of shame for not having left an abusive relationship sooner; or perhaps for making excuses to themselves and others for covering up the abuse they were experiencing; or for not recognising that children have been psychologically or physically harmed by the domestic abuse (Stanley et al., 2012); or for the social isolation they now experience from friends and family.

Herman (1997, p. 200) argued that breaking the silence about their experiences is important for all survivors in relinquishing their own "burden of shame, guilt and responsibility and plac[ing] this burden on the perpetrator, where it properly belongs." If the therapist is congruent, empathetic, and accepting and proceeds gently and patiently, there is the potential to help the client to heal their shame within the relational depth of the therapeutic relationship. DeYoung (2015) advocates that a relationship of mutual connectedness can become a safe enough environment for a client to discuss their feelings of shame. The therapist can help to educate the client about the development, function, and characteristics of shame. Further, DeYoung (2015) also suggests that some clients find it helpful to allow their shamed and shaming "parts of self" speak to the therapist and to one another.

A client who is a domestic abuse survivor may have experienced situations which they find deeply shaming and they may find it difficult to articulate, fearing judgement from others. When a client is struggling to communicate shameful experiences, they will benefit from a counsellor who understands these complex responses to abuse and also empathises with the client's experience on a deep level. Non-judgement has been found to be an essential aspect of the counselling process with domestic abuse survivors in developing a therapeutic alliance and reducing feelings of shame (Roddy, 2015). Furthermore, clients benefit from the counsellor explaining how domestic abuse plays out, the impact of domestic abuse on the individual and the therapist normalising the individuals' behaviour and reactions in the context of the domestic abuse situation. For a counsellor inexperienced in working with domestic abuse survivors, listening to traumatic stories can be uncomfortable and distressing which can make it difficult for the therapist to connect psychologically with the client (Dutton, 1992; Sanderson, 2008). If the client perceives the therapist as unable to cope with the material they are sharing, the counsellor can further increase feelings of shame and cause the client to limit their disclosures in the future. It is imperative for a counsellor to be able to empathise with stories of abuse and understand the client's experience, rather than responding sympathetically. Sympathetic responses can cause the client to feel pitied, which in turn heightens feelings of shame (Roddy, 2015).

Shame has the potential to be more painful and harmful than guilt, for example, because shame is a generalised feeling about oneself. Nevertheless, guilt is an important protective emotion to understand in the context of domestic abuse and it will be discussed next.

Guilt

It is important to differentiate shame from guilt, which is a more complex, language-based response related to psychosocial context (Cozolino, 2010) and occurs due to a perceived transgression or the individual behaving in a way that they feel is wrong. Although there is some similarity in their meaning, guilt occurs following actions that are perceived as wrong (Wilson et al., 2006) and can be attributed to a particular context or event. Shame on the other hand is an emotion that is internalised and represents a belief about the self. To illustrate, someone experiencing the emotion of guilt might believe "I did something bad," whereas someone experiencing the emotion of shame might believe "I am bad" (Cozolino, 2010, p. 194). As with shame, guilt serves as a protective emotion and can motivate people to behave better in the future.

Shame and guilt can be major factors in how an individual responds to the abuse they have experienced and can determine whether the individual seeks the support needed to overcome the abuse or leave an abusive relationship (Williams, 2021). Despite perpetrators being ultimately responsible for domestic abuse, many victims will blame themselves (Street et al., 2005). An individual overwhelmed with feelings of guilt might be reluctant to leave due to feelings of responsibility for specific behaviours they displayed due to the abuse. They might be hesitant in reaching out for help and support if they feel that the abuse was their fault and that they will be blamed, not believed, or judged by others.

Research suggests that guilt and shame can increase the likelihood of developing PTSD symptoms after traumatic events (Andrews et al., 2000; Kessler & Bieschke, 1999). Furthermore, Street et al. (2005) found that individuals with histories of traumatic events in childhood were more likely to report trauma-related guilt after experiencing domestic abuse. It could therefore be helpful for practitioners to have an awareness of adverse childhood experience (see chapter 9). Street et al. (2005) advocate that practitioners should pay particular attention to the trauma related guilt and potential avoidant coping strategies displayed by the victims.

In families where there is domestic abuse, guilt can be masterfully manipulated by the perpetrator by, for example, making their victims feel guilty if they try to leave. Perpetrators can also instil guilt in the victim by blaming them for making their anger and abusive behaviours. Domestic abuse survivors commonly report feeling guilty that they remained in an abusive relationship for a prolonged period or that they returned to an abusive partner after leaving. Domestic abuse can erode a survivor's sense of competency, initiative, and autonomy which can lead to guilt and an overwhelming sense of failure (Sanderson, 2008). Female survivors are socially conditioned to take responsibility for the success of a relationship and their partner's emotional wellbeing. Therefore, when a relationship fails, self-blame, guilt, and shame can manifest (Sanderson, 2008).

For individuals experiencing guilt for remaining in an abusive relationship, knowledge that children are direct victims could further reinforce the emotion of guilt. Indeed, Callaghan et al. (2018) emphasise that children are significantly affected by domestic violence and coercive control, and they should therefore be recognised as direct victims, as opposed to "witnesses." As a counsellor working with domestic abuse survivors, it is important to help the client identify and label the emotions of shame and guilt and to support them in accepting these emotions. Validating and normalising the protective emotions often experienced by survivors can help them to realise the impermanence of the emotions and perhaps also that there was little to be ashamed or guilty of, given the circumstances and/or the actions taken by the perpetrator.

An exercise: guilt

- Think of an example where a victim of domestic abuse might feel guilty.
- Think of an example where a perpetrator of domestic abuse might feel guilty.
- Consider how in both cases the guilt might protect the person from feeling more painful feelings such as: I am worthy of abuse; I am a monster.

Self-Criticism

Self-criticism is when an individual has a tendency to engage in negative self-evaluation that can result in feelings of failure, worthlessness, and guilt when expectations are not met (Naragon-Gainey & Watson, 2012). An individual will generally experience self-criticism as negative internal thoughts directed at the self or about their behaviours or attributes. An individual having awareness of their perceived flaws can arguably be a positive way to increase self-awareness and achieve personal growth by enabling the process of learning from mistakes and overcoming weakness or bad habits. However, high levels of self-criticism can have a negative impact on self-esteem and self-belief, sometimes also resulting in avoidance when it comes to taking risks and asserting opinions. Self-blame can cause feelings of responsibility and guilt for not being able to control the abusive situation. In turn, self-blame and guilt can result in increasingly more submissive and compliant behaviour to appease the abuser (Sanderson, 2008). Hence, abusive partners will tend to focus on any perceived flaws and magnify those to help maintain control of the other, which in turn leads to much higher internalised self-criticism.

Thompson and Zuroff (2004) developed "The Levels of Self-Criticism Scale" which measures the two types of self-criticism: comparative and internalised. Comparative self-criticism is when an individual holds a negative view of the self when compared to others and finds themselves inferior or lacking. People who experience self-criticism in this form commonly base their self-esteem on the perceptions of others. They may also view others as superior, hostile, or critical. The prevailing feeling of inferiority can lead to an inability to cope with life and thus result in avoidant behaviours when it comes to dealing with problems (Thompson & Zuroff, 2004).

At the other end of the spectrum is internalised self-criticism. This self-generated criticism causes a chronic sense of falling short of one's own ideals or standards. An individual experiencing internalised self-criticism might make repeated attempts to achieve impossibly high goals and success can be viewed as failure.

Self-criticism is universally experienced. Many people are often their own worst critics and able to be much more sympathetic or empathic towards others going through similar situations. However, this is often greatly intensified for people who experience domestic abuse. As discussed in this chapter, survivors often attribute blame and responsibility for domestic abuse towards themselves. This can lead to self-criticism, which intensifies internalised feelings of anger, contempt, and hostility (Crapolicchio et al., 2021). As well as being associated with shame and self-criticism, self-blame can lead to psychological issues such as depression and social anxiety. Further, it can result in feelings of anger, revenge, holding a grudge and avoidance (Gilbert & Irons, 2005).

Self-Criticism: An Exercise

- Think of an example of how a victim of domestic abuse might criticise themselves.
- Think of an example of how a perpetrator of domestic abuse might criticise themselves.
- What are your feelings of countertransference towards these scenarios?
- When you think of your own process of self-criticism, is it mainly comparative or internalised?
- What do you find helpful in your own process in reducing the amount of self-criticism you experience?
- What might be the benefits and difficulties of using your own experiences as a template for your client work?

Research has demonstrated the relevance of self-criticism and dependency to vulnerability for depression. Self-criticism may cause the individual to ruminate over their experience of violence and abuse and their perceived "responsibility" for the abusive relationship. A major consequence of self-blame, guilt and self-criticism is a lack of self-compassion and self-acceptance (Sanderson, 2008). Reduced self-acceptance can be a significant barrier to disclosure and hinder a survivor from sharing their personal story of domestic abuse. This could increase the likelihood of psychological issues such as Post Traumatic Stress Disorder (Crapolicchio et al., 2021).

Techniques for therapists working with self-criticism:

- Helping clients to talk about and admit their feelings of self-criticism.
- Exploring whether self-criticism is wrapped around guilt and shame.
- Using a strengths-based approach, where we focus on what the client does well rather than on what needs to be improved.
- Being aware that there may be even more painful feelings underneath these feelings.

Compassion based approaches can help to reduce shame and self-criticism (see chapter 10). This process can be assisted by clients learning to challenge self-criticism and their own "internal bully" in a non-judgemental way. A therapist can help to assist a client to practice self-kindness and compassion, whilst exploring the potential barriers to self-compassion. Mindfulness interventions can also be an effective approach in reducing self-criticism. As mindfulness serves to facilitate non-judgemental awareness of the client's thoughts and feelings it is known to improve self-esteem and challenge negative thoughts. Clients could also be signposted to self-compassion self-help resources online. For instance, Dr Kristin Neff has developed an exercise "changing your critical self-talk" to be practiced over the course of several weeks: https://self-compassion.org/exercise-5-changing-critical-self-talk/

Anxiety

Anxiety and fear are related, but where fear can be attached to a particular stimulus, anxiety is more free-floating and chronic. Anxiety can be a normal and valuable feeling which allows us to take precautions where there are risks and we can take preventive actions, but an anxiety disorder creates a sense of danger where none is apparent and interferes with the quality of daily living. Anxiety becomes a protective emotion when a generalised feeling of distress leads to avoidance behaviours which may be counterproductive. The anxiety may serve a protective function in shielding the person from the underlying fear associated with being with an abusive partner. If the relationship has been abusive and life-threatening, the individual may continue to hold onto the anxiety which has become habitual, automatic, and a way of coping, and may also reflect the risks of post-separation violence or abuse.

There are many types of anxiety disorders and people can become fixated on specific issues, including health anxiety and social anxiety. The Beck Anxiety Inventory (Beck and Steer, 1991) assesses symptoms that are associated with a generalised anxiety disorder including physical sensations such as numbness, feeling hot and sweating, heart pounding, indigestion, dizziness, and feeling shaky; and more psychological symptoms such as being unable to relax, feeling that the worst possible thing will happen, terror, nervousness, and fear of losing control. Anxiety can sometimes lead to a panic attack where people may feel like they are about to pass out, die, go crazy, or lose control in another way. In some cases, it will lead to a panic disorder and agoraphobia where avoidance behaviours predominate and limit the person's ability to fully engage in ordinary life.

When a victim/survivor of domestic violence presents with symptoms of anxiety which have reached pathological levels, that is, they are interfering with the person's quality of life and ability to function, anxiety is usually viewed as a symptom of post-traumatic stress disorder (PTSD), rather than an anxiety disorder in its own right (although PTSD was considered an anxiety disorder in earlier versions of the *Diagnostic Statistical Manual of Mental Disorders*). By viewing anxiety as a symptom of post-traumatic stress, the purpose that the anxiety serves can become clearer as the diagnosis acknowledges that there has been exposure to a stressor where there is the threat of death, injury, or violation. While the aetiology of the anxiety is clear, the problem is that the anxiety interferes with life and persists even when the perpetrator is not present – it becomes an overarching frame through which the world is viewed. Perpetrators further reinforce a world view in which the outside world is unsafe and other people are not to be trusted to induce and reinforce dependence where the victim will be unable to leave (Fontes, 2015).

Sanders et al. (2003) advocate for a cognitive behavioural therapy model to understand anxiety with a recognition of the biological, mood, behavioural, cognitive, and environmental factors. Bourne (1990) recommends a three-pronged approach to recovery from anxiety: reducing physiological reactivity; eliminating avoidance behaviours and changing interpretations which are sustaining the anxiety. Applying these traditional approaches to the treatment of anxiety focuses attention on the symptoms, whereas a more person-centred approach accepts the person where they are and fully appreciates the obstacles to establishing a trusting relationship when a person has been betrayed in an intimate relationship (Roddy, 2015). Schiraldi (2000) refers to the need in the treatment of PTSD to help people to make sense of the "bewildering symptoms" of anxiety and dissociation and adds the layer of "spiritual fatigue" as a feature of anxiety which needs to be addressed in therapy. Within this are existential therapy issues of despair, hopelessness, and discouragement.

In working with survivors of domestic violence, it is paramount to make sure firstly that the person is safe (Herman, 1992). Here the therapist can help the client to assess the actual level of danger and what aspects of anxiety are appropriate responses to the situation. However, as perpetrators minimise the abuse, so do victims (Sarkis, 2019), so this can be a challenging task and one which needs to be addressed with sensitivity to client autonomy and ability to make their own decisions. Such decisions may be anxiety producing for the psychotherapist and should be brought to supervision. Client-centred approaches will support client empowerment but at their own pace so that therapist affirmations, reflections, summaries, and challenges help the client to let go of the protective emotion of anxiety and face the real dangers and accompanying fears as well as other painful emotions that may be underlying the protective layer of anxiety.

Reflection: Have you ever been so anxious that you didn't notice something important that happened during the day? Were you so worried that you did not pay attention to your body, mind, and spirit or something happening with your family or colleagues?

Suicidal Ideation

Suicidal ideation can be one of the most challenging set of thoughts and accompanying feelings for a psychotherapist to consider as a "protective emotion" when it is brought up by a client. This is to be expected as it will put the therapist on alert to considering safeguarding issues initially, but at a personal level there may be feelings of fear and dread. It is important therefore to assess whether it is suicidal ideation alone or whether there is a risk that it will lead to a suicide attempt.

The British Association for Counselling and Psychotherapy (BACP, 2021) offers some guidance for working with suicidal risk that begins with setting the contract with a new client around confidentiality. The BACP Ethical Framework for the Counselling Professions (BACP, 2018, p. 24) outlines the need to inform clients:

> about any reasonably foreseeable limitations of privacy or confidentiality in advance of our work together, for example, communications to ensure or enhance the quality of work in supervision or training, to protect a client or others from serious harm including safeguarding commitments, and when legally required or authorised to disclose.

The Ethical Framework also points out (BACP, 2018, p. 14): "In exceptional circumstances, the need to safeguard our clients or others from serious harm may require us to override our commitment to making our client's wishes and confidentiality our primary concern" which highlights the tension between the ethical principle of autonomy – "respect for the client's right to be self-governing" (BACP, 2018, p. 9) and beneficence – "a commitment to promoting the client's wellbeing" (BACP, 2018, p. 9).

The assessment of risk can be addressed by the therapist with their supervisor to make sure that they are not missing any imminent risk to life, which can include risk of murder by the intimate partner. Monckton-Smith (2022) has researched homicide within intimate relationships and outlined eight stages leading up to murder, and counsellors working with clients who have experienced domestic violence would be well advised to familiarise themselves with this.

Assuming that there is not an *imminent* threat to life through homicide or suicide (e.g. there is no suicide plan or provision for how suicide might occur such as by stockpiling pills), the practitioner can support an exploration of suicidal ideation as a protective emotion. Suicidal ideation can protect the survivor of domestic abuse by giving a sense of agency that if things become completely intolerable, they can take control and end the abuse. If they have left their partner, suicidal ideation can protect the person from staring into the existential void and feeling the depth of their loss as they may be physically apart but maintaining a trauma-coerced attachment to their partner (Doychak & Raghavan, 2020). After an experience of being subjugated to the coercive and controlling behaviours of the perpetrator, the person may feel at a complete loss about how to make decisions or to understand what their preferences and desires are. Consequently, profound feelings of grief and despair may emerge, and the therapist can be expected to feel challenged to listen to these feelings with empathy and unconditional positive regard.

It is of vital importance to make the therapeutic relationship one in which it is safe for the client to speak about their innermost thoughts and feelings that they may not be able to express to anyone else, especially if their intimate partner is someone who would put their lives at risk rather than save them. This can only be achieved if the therapist moves beyond the role of "safeguarding officer" to someone who can provide a non-judgemental space where feelings can be heard with empathy and understanding. Reeves (2022) has eloquently described this role:

> Our task, I would argue, is not simply to ask about suicide in order to determine a mitigation plan, or to assess for the presence of risk factors. Rather, our task is to open the door labelled "risk" and walk through, as we explore with our clients their experience of engaging with their feelings of suicide, what it means and what sense the client is able to make of it. Our task is to go there, to be brave and to really hear what others are often unable to tolerate.

Summary

Protective emotions, caused by the experiences of abuse, are very common amongst survivors of domestic abuse. Understanding why such behaviours might have occurred and being open to the exploration of these with the client in an empathic, supportive, and congruent way can support a deep and helpful therapeutic relationship. Topics such as shame, guilt, and suicidal ideation are topics that most people would find difficult to discuss. The additional difficulties of lacking trust and having experienced behaviours from the abuser to instil these responses mean that therapists need to go gently and carefully with clients to ensure that they are comfortable disclosing and saying what they need to say. As these emotions served the client well in surviving, it is likely that they will require some time to fully resolve, even when the relationship has been over for a while.

Key Points to Take Away

1 Protective emotions have value to victims of abuse by helping them to reduce the conflict in the relationship by taking responsibility for whatever had gone wrong.
2 Shame is an emotion where the individual feels that any difficulty is a result on their being, whereas guilt is linked to a specific event where the person felt that they had not lived up to their own standards of behaviour.
3 Self-criticism helps to alleviate any sense of responsibility for the abuser and can become a way of being for people who have experienced abuse, yet causes significant mental health issues as a result. Introducing self-compassion can be very helpful in working with this.
4 Anxiety can result fear in which cannot be projected onto the abuser and is therefore internalised. CBT approaches can be helpful for this issue.
5 Suicidal ideation is common in this client group. After ensuring the client is safe, it is very helpful to be able to explore what that means for them in a caring and open way.
6 Understanding the nature of protective emotions can help therapists to provide more empathy and positive regard in the face of challenging emotions.

References

Amstadter, A. B., & Vernon, L. L. (2008). Emotional reactions during and after trauma: a comparison of trauma types. *Journal of Aggression, Maltreatment & Trauma, 16*, 391–408.

Andrews, B., Brewin, C. R., Rose, S., & Kirk, M. (2000). Predicting PTSD symptoms in victims of violent crime: the role of shame, anger, and childhood abuse. *Journal of Abnormal Psychology, 109*, 69–73.

Banmen, J. (1988). Guilt and shame: Theories and therapeutic possibilities. *International Journal for the Advancement of Counselling, 11*, 79–91

Beck, A., & Steer, R. (1991). Relationship between the Beck Anxiety Inventory and the Hamilton Anxiety Rating Scale with anxious outpatients. *Journal of Anxiety Disorders, 5*, 213–223.

Bourne, E. (1990). *The anxiety and phobia workbook*. New Harbinger.

Bradshaw, J. (1990). *Homecoming*. Bantam.

British Association for Counselling and Psychotherapy (BACP) (2018). *Ethical framework for the counselling professions*. BACP.

British Association for Counselling and Psychotherapy (BACP) (2021). *Good practice in action 042 fact sheet: working with suicidal clients in the counselling professions*. BACP.

Callaghan, J. E. M., Alexander, J. H., Sixsmith, J., & Fellin, L. C. (2018). Beyond "witnessing": children's experiences of coercive control in domestic violence and abuse. *Journal of Interpersonal Violence*, *33*(10), 1551–1581. 10.1177/0886260515618946

Cozolino, L. (2010). *The neuroscience of psychotherapy: healing the social brain* (2nd ed.). Norton.

Crapolicchio, E., Vezzali, L., & Regalia, C. (2021). "I forgive myself": the association between self-criticism, self-acceptance, and PTSD in women victims of IPV, and the buffering role of self-efficacy. *Journal of Community Psychology*, *49*(2), 252–265. 10.1002/jcop.22454

DeYoung (2015). *Understanding and treating chronic shame a relational/neuro-biological approach*. Routledge.

Doychak, K., & Raghavan, C. (2020). "No voice or vote": trauma-coerced attachment in victims of sex trafficking. *Journal of Human Trafficking*, *6*(3), 339–357. 10.1080/23322705.2018.151862

Dutton, M. (1992). *Empowering and healing the battered woman: a model for assessment and intervention*. Springer Pub. Co.

Fontes, L. (2015). *Invisible chains: overcoming coercive control in your intimate relationship*. The Guilford Press.

Gilbert, P., & Irons, C. (2005). Focused therapies and compassionate mind training for shame and self-attacking. In P. Gilbert (Ed.), *Compassion: conceptualisations, research and use in psychotherapy*, pp. 263–325. Routledge.

Harper, J. W., & Hoopes, M. L. (1990). *Uncovering shame: an approach integrating individual and the family systems*. Norton.

Herman, J. (1992). *Trauma and recovery*. Basic Books.

Herman, J. L. (1997). *Trauma and recovery*. Pandora.

Kaufman, G. (1989). *The psychology of shame theory and treatment of shame-based syndromes*. Springer.

Kessler, B. L., & Bieschke, K. J. (1999). A retrospective analysis of shame, dissociation, and adult victimization in survivors of childhood sexual abuse. *Journal of Counseling Psychology*, *46*, 335–341.

Lewis, H. B. (1971). *Shame and guilt in neurosis*. International Universities Press.

Loughead, T. A. (1992). Freudian repression revisited: the power and pain of shame. *International Journal for the Advancement of Counselling*, *15*(3), 127–136. 10.1007/BF00116484

Miller, S. (1985). *The shame experience*. Lawrence Erlbaum.

Monckton-Smith, J. (2022). *In control: dangerous relationships and how they end in murder*. Bloomsbury Publishing.

Naragon-Gainey, K., & Watson, D. (2012). Personality structure. In V. S. Ramachandran (Eds.), *Encyclopedia of human behavior*. San Diego: Elsevier Science & Technology.

Platt, M. G., & Freyd, J. J. (2015). Betray my trust, shame on me. *Psychological Trauma: Theory, Research, Practice, and Policy*, *7*(4), 398–404. 10.1037/tra0000022

Reeves, A. (2022). Suicide risk: explore or evade? *Healthcare Counselling and Psychotherapy Journal*. https://www.bacp.co.uk/bacp-journals/healthcare-counselling-and-psychotherapy-journal/july-2022/suicide-risk/

Roddy (2015). *Counselling and psychotherapy after domestic violence: a client view of what helps recovery*. Palgrave Macmillan.

Rose, T. K., Woodall, A., Morgan, C., Feder, G., & Howard, L. (2011). Barriers and facilitators of disclosures of domestic violence by mental health service users: qualitative study. *British Journal of Psychiatry, 198*(3), 189–194.
Sanders, D., Wills, F., & Hallam, R. (2003). *Counselling for anxiety problems*. SAGE Publications.
Sanderson, C. (2008). *Counselling survivors of domestic abuse*. Jessica Kingsley.
Sarkis, S. (2019). *Gaslighting: how to recognise manipulative and emotionally abusive people … and break free*. Orion Spring.
Schiraldi, G. (2000). *The post-traumatic stress disorder sourcebook: a guide to healing, recovery and growth*. Lowell House.
Schore, A. N. (1994). *Affect regulation and the origin of the self: the neurobiology of emotional development*. Erlbaum.
Stanley, N., Miller, P., & Richardson Foster, H. (2012). Engaging with children's and parents' perspectives on domestic violence. *Child & Family Social Work, 17*(2), 192–201. 10.1111/j.1365-2206.2012.00832.x
Street, A. E., Gibson, L. E., & Holohan, D. R. (2005). Impact of childhood traumatic events, trauma-related guilt, and avoidant coping strategies on PTSD symptoms in female survivors of domestic violence. *Journal of Traumatic Stress, 18*(3), 245–252.
Thompson, R., & Zuroff, D. C. (2004). The levels of self-criticism scale: comparative self-criticism and internalized self-criticism. *Personality and Individual Differences, 36*, 419–430.
Walker, L. (1979). *The battered woman*. Harper Collins.
Wilson, J. P., Droždek, B., & Turkovic, S. (2006). Posttraumatic shame and guilt. *Trauma, Violence & Abuse, 7*(2), 122–141. 10.1177/1524838005285914
Williams, T. D. (2021). The relationship among guilt and shame, and religion for women victims of domestic violence. [Doctoral dissertation, Liberty University].

Chapter 7

Working with Protective Behaviours

Linda Dubrow-Marshall and Rod Dubrow-Marshall

Learning Objectives

1 To understand the concept of protective behaviours
2 To understand the ambivalence experienced by people in abusive relationships which can prevent action
3 To understand self-harm, returning to an abuser and addictions as protective behaviours
4 To consider our own responses to these behaviours and identify constructive ways to work with clients

Understanding the Concept of Protective Behaviours

Domestic abuse survivors sometimes present in counselling with a series of self-destructive behaviours that at first glance might seem mentally unhealthy and may inhibit understanding, empathy and compassion from the psychotherapist. These behaviours can include a variety of self-harm behaviours, addictive behaviours, ambivalence, and the perplexing pattern of staying with and returning to the abuser. Psychotherapists can find these behaviours very frustrating especially if they have been working with the client for some time, seen good progress, only to see them slipping back into self-destructive behaviours. This can lead to intense counter-transference reactions that are best addressed in supervision. In this chapter, we will examine these behaviours from the perspective of "protective behaviours," similar to the concept of "protective emotions" where the behaviours serve the function of protecting the client from overwhelming pain and intolerable feelings. In this way, the protective behaviours provide the counsellor with a window into the intensity of the painful feelings and experiences of the client. A respectful perspective can facilitate both empathy towards the client and the establishment of a safe therapeutic relationship that can contain overwhelming emotions. The client can learn to let go of the protective behaviours and adopt more adaptive coping mechanisms that facilitate a deeper recovery from the trauma of having been abused.

DOI: 10.4324/9781003253266-7

Through the lens of protective behaviours, therapists facilitate a deep exploration of the more painful feelings behind the behaviours to uncover what lies beneath and to consider the purpose served by the behaviours. For example, protective behaviours may involve taking risks or making unsafe decisions so while not overtly protecting the person, they may keep the person from confronting the danger they are in by staying with an abusive partner. Protective behaviours may serve to numb painful feelings, distract from the danger, and help the person to dissociate from the pain.

The perspective of protective behaviours aligns with the British Psychological Society's Power Threat Meaning Framework (PTMF) (Johnstone and Boyle, 2018) which replaces the usual concept of "symptoms" which pathologises people with the concept of "threat responses" where the behaviours can be understood as what the person had to do to survive. The PTMF advocates that practitioners understand these behaviours from the perspective of functionality and meaning and as an understandable and not necessarily pathological response to the abuse, recognising that:

> These strategies arise out of core human needs to be protected, valued, find a place in the social group, and so on, and represent people's attempts, conscious and otherwise, to survive the negative impacts of power by using the resources available to them.
>
> (Johnstone and Boyle, 2018, p. 12)

The framework further suggested that people "can be recognised and validated as activating threat responses for protection and survival. The experiences that are described as 'symptoms' are therefore better understood as reactions to threat, or 'survival strategies'" (p. 192).

The practitioner can assess if the threat responses are adaptive and helpful to the client under the circumstances or whether they have lost their meaning and can be replaced with more adaptive behaviours. They can only do so by carefully considering the context for the behaviours and through providing a safe therapeutic environment in which the person feels free to break the secrecy and isolation of their abuse and to tell their story without being judged or devalued. This acknowledgement and empathetic acceptance of the client no matter how negative their behaviours may appear will offer a relationship that is the antithesis of the experience of a person who is actively being abused by a partner, where they will have been made to feel worthless and utterly dependent on the abusive, overly critical partner. The irony is that the perpetrator will make the person feel that they are nothing without them (and therefore dependent on them for their very survival) while simultaneously trapping the person in a dangerous relationship which can escalate to murder (Monckton-Smith, 2022).

Guidelines for a client-centred approach to helping survivors of domestic abuse include accepting the behaviours as valid in their own right, while helping clients to recognise which feelings are behind or underneath the behaviours. The therapist can help by not negatively judging the person who is displaying unsafe behaviours, instead offering unconditional positive regard to gently explore the meaning of the behaviours, ultimately helping the client to reconsider their choices and behaviours. Therapeutic tasks can include helping clients to notice their feelings and pause and reflect on them before acting, a strategy that is commonly used with impulsive and self-destructive behaviours.

In this chapter, we will examine some protective behaviours which are commonly exhibited by survivors of domestic abuse: ambivalence, self-harm, returning to the abuser, and addiction. Sometimes these protective behaviours appear together or lead into one another where they represent a negative interweaving of attempts to ward off the pain. For example, you can have a negative trio of protective behaviours where ambivalence leads to self-harm, which leads to returning to the abuser, and this cycle can repeat in any order as illustrated in Figure 7.1.

Addiction is a further challenge to recovery as it sometimes begins at the instigation of the perpetrator and may have created a physical dependency which requires treatment. Other times it is an understandable response to coping with a very painful and difficult situation from which escape seems impossible.

Figure 7.1 A trio of protective behaviours.

Reflection: Have you ever been ambivalent and stayed too long in a romantic relationship or a friendship when it has become painful to you? Can you identify how your difficulty in leaving may be understood from the viewpoint of a threat response/what you had to do to survive at the time?

Ambivalence

People who are in intimate relationships involving violence can be expected to express feelings that reflect ambivalence as well as exhibiting ambivalent behaviours, and therefore ambivalence can be viewed through the lenses of both protective emotions and behaviours. It can be bewildering and even frustrating for psychotherapists to observe ambivalence in their clients towards their abusers following a violent incident, but this becomes more understandable when seen as protecting the clients from overwhelming and intensely painful feelings that underlie the ambivalence. For example, a person may simultaneously feel very positive and negative feelings towards their partner which leads to ambivalent behaviours where they move both towards and away from their partner. These behaviours may protect the person from facing the terror of leaving a partner who has convinced them that they are completely incapable of survival without them and the despair of labelling their relationship as abusive. Survivors of domestic abuse, and current victims, regularly report feelings of ambivalence towards their partner who has also been their abuser (Courtois & Ford, 2015) and this chapter focuses on an understanding of the resultant behaviours.

Classical theories of learning (Olson & Hergenhahn, 2015) can explain the persistence of ambivalent behaviours. When people are positively reinforced for their behaviours on a consistent basis, they will learn to continue these behaviours. If they are consistently negatively reinforced for certain behaviours, they will learn to discontinue or "extinguish" these behaviours. However, "intermittent reinforcement" leads to the most resistance because the same behaviours are rewarded and subsequently punished. This makes it impossible for the person to predict the response of the abuser so they keep returning to the behaviours in the hope that this time it will lead to a positive response. This theory can help explain the persistence of Walker's (1979) cycle of violence (see chapter 3) where the person is always hoping and believing in the return of the attentive, romantic partner if they can just work out how. If the abusive partner is a substance abuser, their reactions may become even more unpredictable. It can become even harder for the victim to let go of behaviours which they think may placate or sooth their partner only to be devastated by the next episode of emotional and/or physical abuse.

Lewin's (1935) influential theories of conflict and conflict resolution identified three basic types of conflict: plus-plus (approach-approach), minus-minus (avoidance-avoidance), and plus-minus (approach-avoidance) which can further enrich the understanding of the role of intermittent reinforcement within intimate relationships. Victims of domestic abuse are torn between push-pull factors in their ambivalence about their relationship, and approach-avoidance conflicts may persist as the barriers to resolution remain high. Levinger (1957) extended Lewin's concept of conflict to interpersonal relationships and noted that interpersonal elements of the conflict must be considered in addition to intra-personal elements. This can deepen our understanding of tensions within the relationship, such as the consequences if one person does not comply with the wishes of the other, or conflict between each person's goals. It can be assumed that the exertion of power and dominance is a central goal for the perpetrator of domestic abuse and that this can be expressed both physically and psychologically, contributing centrally to the distress and painful feelings of the victim who becomes trapped within the approach-avoidance conflict.

Festinger's (1957) theory of cognitive dissonance helps to explain some of the ambivalent behaviours that are present within an abusive relationship as he postulated that conflicting beliefs or behaviours lead to an uncomfortable state which results in people changing their beliefs or behaviours in order to feel consistent and more comfortable. These behaviours can include a series of protective behaviours which can be seen to lead to a reduction in that dissonance. At its core the ambivalence reflects the psychological investment or contract (Rousseau et al., 2013) which the survivor has had with their partner. This has often been entered into with great hope and enthusiasm for the future. It is also enshrined in marriage or civil partnership contracts and financial contracts including for property and savings. However, the initial prospects which are often sold so persuasively by the abuser (Walker, 1979) are not realised and the recognition of betrayal this constitutes is sometimes both shaming and humiliating, as well as deeply depressing to the survivor.

The psychological profundity of this betrayal explains why the pattern of post-traumatic distress amongst survivors of domestic abuse is often characterised as complex (Herman, 2015). As well as recovering from high levels of fear and anxiety, wrought by a continued pattern of psychological and physical abuse and threats thereof, the breaking of the psychological contract or trauma bond (Courtois & Ford, 2015) can also leave survivors asking critical existential questions about who they are and their place in the world, in a context where some of their key previous certainties about life and love have been seemingly destroyed. All these mixed feelings lead to a liminal state in which ambivalent behaviours towards oneself, the erstwhile partner and abuser, towards friends, family, work colleagues and towards the world in general, often thrive. Such behaviours are also protective against the growing and visceral understanding of the betrayal and trauma which the survivor has suffered.

The challenge to the counsellor is to create a therapeutic relationship in which the client is able to trust the therapist to share their innermost feelings despite the betrayal trauma which they experienced at the hands of someone they believed loved them (see also chapters 2 and 4). Freyd (1996) has articulated the conundrum where the therapeutic relationship has the potential to help the client to recover but also has the potential for harm given that the conditions for trust have already been profoundly violated. Patience on the part of the therapist and openness towards clients' questions or expressions of anger and distrust can be helpful in this regard.

Humanistic and existential approaches to psychotherapy can be incorporated into other therapeutic approaches and emphasise the importance of exploring deeper issues of meaning and purpose. Hartman and Zimberoff (2004) conceptualise that ambivalence is a form of "existential resistance" where the potential for "existential embrace of life for being fully alive" is sabotaged, denied and thwarted (p. 3). They reinforce the idea of ambivalence as a protective behaviour by pointing out that it focuses attention away from the underlying anxiety such as "fear of annihilation or engulfment (loss of self)" (p. 3). This characterises the experience of victims of coercive control in an intimate relationship where power is abused, and the person is made to feel completely dependent on their partner.

An empathetic stance towards the expression of ambivalent feelings and behaviours and a curiosity to explore what these mean for the client will deepen the therapeutic relationship and facilitate recovery.

> It is important for psychotherapists to acknowledge the client's need to express the positive side of their relationships or what they may have learned or enjoyed during an otherwise traumatic experience, and to deal with personal anger and countertransference in supervision and consultation.
>
> (Dubrow-Marshall, 2013, p. 22)

Reflection: In what areas of their personal life do psychotherapists experience ambivalence and in what ways is the ambivalence protective? Does the ambivalence that the client exhibits become mirrored in the countertransference of the psychotherapist? How can the psychotherapist use their own ambivalence to enhance the therapeutic relationship?

Self-Harm

Living in a continuous state of protective ambivalent behaviours within an abusive relationship where it may feel like there is no way to escape the underlying pain can lead to a host of self-harm behaviours. Although self-cutting is often the first example that comes to mind when people think of self-harm, self-harm behaviours can be very varied and can infuse many aspects of being in an abusive relationship. In the United Kingdom, the National Health Service (NHS UK, n.d.) includes as examples of self-harm: cutting, picking skin, pulling hair, eating disorders, poisoning oneself, excessive work, and addictions (which will be discussed separately in the next section). Taking the perspective of self-harm as protective behaviours puts the emphasis on the meaning of the symptom, which means that treatment should include medical treatment where necessary for the harm that was done (e.g. dressing of wounds, treating burns; nutritional interventions) and psychological treatment should focus on uncovering the underlying meaning and functionality of the symptoms, which transcends the symptom itself, and exploring the role of the abusive relationship in the aetiology and development of the self-harm behaviours.

Self-harm behaviours can be challenging for practitioners to work with whether or not they occur within a violent relationship. For example, while some people hide their self-inflicted wounds where they cannot be seen while they are dressed, other clients may want to show their wounds to the counsellor, who may find this distressing or even disgusting, and therefore difficult to resist being judgemental and to maintain unconditional positive regard.

Mind (2020) reported some of the ways that people have described self-harm:

> a way to express something that is hard to put into words; turn invisible thoughts or feelings into something visible; change emotional pain into physical pain; reduce overwhelming emotional feelings or thoughts; have a sense of being in control; escape traumatic memories; have something in life that they can rely on; punish themselves for their feelings and experiences; stop feeling numb, disconnected or dissociated; create a reason to physically care for themselves; express suicidal feelings and thoughts without taking their own life. The NHS (n.d.) included the above reasons for self-harm and added that it can be a way of "relieving unbearable tension; a cry for help; a response to intrusive thought."

These lists can be helpful to clients in letting them know that they are not alone if they recognise their motives in the list. The lists can be helpful to therapists in suggesting possible meanings for clients' self-harm behaviours, but helping clients to uncover the *individual* meanings that the behaviours have for them is of utmost importance. The Power Threat Meaning Framework (Johnstone and Boyle, 2018) reminds us it is important to help the client to tell their story of what happened to them, how power has been abused, the threats that they have experienced, and how this has led to threat responses. Similarly, Mind (2020) advises people who are seeking help for self-harm that although the behaviours may provide a temporary short-term sense of release, it is necessary to address the "difficult feelings, painful memories or overwhelming situations and experiences" that are driving the behaviours. Such feelings might include anger, rage or shame or it may be a means of punishing or attacking either themselves or others for any perceived wrongdoing and a way to gain a sense of power and control, if only fleetingly (Pickard, 2015).

It is important to include self-harm in the assessment of domestic violence survivors as it has been noted by Boyle et al. (2006) that people going to emergency departments for self-harm in the United Kingdom were more likely to be victims of domestic violence, and they also advised assessing for suicidality. The National Institute for Health and Care Excellence (NICE) guidelines (2022, 1.61) advocate for an individualised approach to assessment of self-harm and warn: "Do not use risk assessment tools and scales to predict future suicide or repetition of self-harm," instead advocating to "focus the assessment on the person's needs and how to support their immediate and long-term psychological and physical safety" (1.65).

NICE (2022) stresses the importance of establishing a safety plan, which is often the overall approach taken by counsellors when working with survivors of domestic violence, and safety has been emphasised as the first step in recovery from trauma by Herman (2015). NICE (2022) encourages collaborative and compassionate working with the client in "shared decision making," which is in alliance with principles of client-centred therapy. It further recommends (1.11.6): "Work collaboratively with the person, using a strengths-based approach to identify solutions to reduce their distress that leads to self-harm," which is supported by research on resilience training (Padesky & Mooney, 2012). However, NICE guidance to work collaboratively with family and other support systems may not be possible because of the abuse survivor's isolation.

Psychotherapists should tread carefully and respectfully when helping clients to change their behaviours to more adaptive ones as if the therapy is paced too quickly, clients may become overwhelmed by the powerful and extremely painful feelings underlying the protective behaviours. For example, although self-harm is distinct from suicidality, it is important for psychotherapists to continue their assessments of suicidality especially if the person is cutting and over time may begin to cut more deeply, accidentally putting their lives in danger. There have been reports in clinical practice of perpetrators of domestic violence mocking their victims and "goading" them to engage in self-harm behaviours, including cutting, withholding food, addictive behaviours, and parasuicidal or suicidal behaviours, and the therapist should work towards establishing a safe therapeutic space where clients might feel free to reveal such painful and shameful experiences.

Supervision can help practitioners to explore their own painful reactions to working with client self-harm. In the United Kingdom, the NICE guidelines (2022, 1.15.1) recognise the impact that working with clients who self-harm can have on professionals and recommend that supervision should include reflective practice and "promote the delivery of compassionate care." Working with survivors of domestic violence who self-harm can truly pose challenges of practicing compassion towards clients as well as self when it may be so difficult to remember the protective function of the self-harm behaviours.

Reflection: How can a psychotherapist reconcile the BACP ethical values of protecting the safety of clients and alleviating symptoms of personal distress and suffering with the ethical value of autonomy: respect for the client's right to be self-governing when working with clients who self-harm?

Returning to the Abuser

Ambivalence and self-harm are both embroiled in the actions of a domestic violence survivor who then paradoxically returns to the abuser, and it is this very pattern that is most bewildering to those who are unfamiliar with the concepts of coercive control and trauma-coerced attachment. It is of upmost importance for the practitioner to have a deep understanding of these dynamics so that they can maintain unconditional positive regard and help clients to develop insights into their destructive patterns of returning to the abuser.

SafeLIves (2015) reported that in a survey in the United Kingdom, victims lived with their abusers an average of two to three years before getting help, with 68% of high-risk victims attempting to leave an average of two to three times in the year before they were effectively helped and 78% of them having reported the abuse to the police. Twenty-three per cent of high-risk victims had been to accident and emergency in the prior year, many of them more than once. Leaving the abuser is clearly a process that is riddled with obstacles and the answer to why a person has not permanently left a relationship may be that they have already tried but were unsuccessful or the abuse may have escalated after they had left in post-separation abuse (Spearman et al., 2022).

Doychak and Raghavan (2020) have described trauma-coerced attachment in victims of sex trafficking which is also applicable to victims of domestic violence as coercion and abuse exist side by side with intimacy and affection. They describe how victims deny and minimise their abuse and even take personal responsibility for it, something perpetrators encourage as they deny and minimise and blame their victims for their abusive behaviour.

It is important to remember that the abusive partner may be or may deliberately be manipulative in appearing to be very sincere in apologising for their behaviours that temporarily gives the partner hope that that the abuse will not reoccur. The abusive partner may have reinforced victim fears about not being able to survive on their own, and may have removed resources and capabilities to prevent them being able to do so. The desire to believe the partner's apologies should not be underestimated in understanding the trauma bond/attachment.

Furthermore, the concepts in "totalistic identity theory" (Dubrow-Marshall, 2010) add another layer of understanding to the tendency of victims of abuse to return to the relationship by describing the process through which multiple identities that the person may have had prior to the relationship (e.g. mother, daughter, nurse, volunteer) become subjugated and replaced by the dominant identity of being the partner in an abusive relationship where abiding by the wishes and whims of the perpetrator is the only thing that matters (see also chapter 3). Dubrow-Marshall (2010) describes this as a process of

> how normal cognitive processes of categorisation can go awry; of how the normal formation of psychological groups and movement between them in terms of psychological salience can become restricted and dominated on one specific identity that is extreme within the frame of reference. (p. 12)

He has applied this to intimate partner relationships where the partner becomes the entire existence of the person and the focal point around which everything else revolves. This is also akin to the "dispensing of existence" in Lifton's (1961) theory of "thought reform."

> Reflection: What are some of the internal (psychological) and external obstacles to leaving an abuser and how do these interact? How can the therapist both accept the ambivalence about the relationship and help the client to move towards safety?

Addiction

Some clients will present with addictive issues which will require therapeutic attention in addition to the issues of being in an abusive relationship. The aetiology of the addiction is important to assess in devising the treatment approach, for example, was the person addicted before the relationship or is it part of the process of being in the relationship? If the client's partner has been involved in the development of the addiction, it is important to determine if the influence to become addicted was direct or indirect, forcibly accomplished or through persuasion, as these have different implications. If the partner actively forced the client to abuse substances, it may be easier for them to recover as it was not something that they ever thought they wanted. If the primary mechanism for becoming an addict was due to coercive persuasion, such as "Come drink with me, get high with me, don't spoil my fun, come on relax, isn't this better now," the pressures may have been internalised and the client blames themselves. If the perpetrator is an active addict, they may want their partner to be in the same position and may fear that they will lose control if not and so the pressure to stay an addict will intensify if the victim is attempting to abstain from substances or at least minimise the harmful behaviours associated with their addiction.

It may also be useful to use the lens of addiction to view the relationship that both the perpetrator and victim of abuse have with each other in terms of understanding the dynamics and *addictive processes* that may be present. Caution must be observed in order not to label the client as an addict, which could be stigmatising and shaming and alienate the client from engaging in the therapeutic relationship. The World Health Organization (WHO, 2022) gives criteria for disorders due to substance abuse or addictive behaviours (including gambling and gaming disorders) which include increased use to obtain the same effect, cravings, and withdrawal. Addictive behaviours are described as repetitive behaviours over which there is little control; giving increased priority to the behaviour over other aspects of their life; and continuing the behaviour even when there are negative consequences. This description can be mapped against Walker's (1979) model of the cycle of domestic abuse and the addictive lens adds appreciation for how the violence in the relationship escalates over time. The controlling and coercive behaviours are no longer enough to produce the same effect, so they are intensified. The victim of these behaviours becomes increasingly dependent on their partner and attempting to please the abuser takes over their lives, mimicking how other addictive and compulsive behaviours (including eating disorders) increasingly dominate more energy, time, and resources, and ultimately steal from the person their personal integrity, dignity, sense of self, restrict their emotional and cognitive functioning, and cause increasing amounts of despair and impairment.

Recovery principles that have been proposed for "love addiction" may be helpful to incorporate into the therapeutic process, including identifying peer support and possibly group recovery meetings, and adding a spiritual component for those who are open to such an approach. The term "codependency" is also sometimes welcomed by people in abusive intimate relationships, although we prefer the term prodependency (Weiss, 2018) which is less stigmatising and recognises the good qualities of the desires to please one's partner, emphasising the pro-social aspects of the behaviours rather than just focusing on pathological behaviours. Weiss (2018) recommends that: "We can simply acknowledge the trauma and inherent dysfunction that occurs when living with an addict, and then we can address that in the healthiest, least shaming way" (p. 72).

This can be seen as a metaphor for living with someone who is compulsively controlling of their partner who may or may not also be addicted to substances.

> Reflection: What did you previously know about addiction? What is your own relationship with addiction? Consider how the answers to these two questions might impact on your practice?

Summary

In conclusion, it is helpful to view behaviours exhibited by survivors of domestic violence including ambivalence, self-harm, returning to the abuser, and addictions as having a meaning and purpose which can be gently explored with the client in an empathetic and compassionate manner which will aid their recovery much more than labelling the behaviours as pathological and self-destructive.

Key Learning Points

1 Client ambivalence about the relationship, situation and events can show in counselling. Careful exploration of the ambivalence in a supportive and caring way can help the client to understand what is going on for them.
2 There are many different ways to self-harm and many reasons for this to happen. Exploring the underlying feelings relating to the behaviour can be helpful for the client.
3 Returning to the abuser is documented as a factor in domestic abuse which can be frustrating for those trying to help. Understanding the psychology behind this can help counsellors to empathise more with the client.
4 Understanding the background to how any addiction came into being can provide helpful pointers in how to work with the client.

References

Boyle, A., Jones, P., & Lloyd, S. (2006). The association between domestic violence and self harm in emergency medicine patients. *Journal of Emergency*, *23*, 604–607. 10.1136/emj.2005.031260

Courtois, C., & Ford, J. (2015). *Treatment of complex trauma: a sequenced, relationship-based approach*. Guilford Press.

Doychak, K., & Raghavan, C. (2020). 'No voice or vote': trauma-coerced attachment in victims of sex trafficking. *Journal of Human Trafficking*, *6*(3), 339–357.

Dubrow-Marshall, L. (2013). Curiosity and willingness to learn. *Therapy Today*. May 2013, p. 22.

Dubrow-Marshall, R. (2010). The influence continuum – the good, the dubious, and the harmful – evidence and implications for policy and practice in the 21st century. *International Journal of Cultic Studies*, *1*, 1–12.

Festinger, L. (1957). *A theory of cognitive dissonance*. Stanford University Press.

Freyd, J. (1996). *Betrayal trauma*. Harvard University Press.

Hartman, D., & Zimberoff, D. (2004). Existential resistance to life: ambivalence, avoidance and control. *Journal of Heart-Centered Therapies*, *7*(1), 3–63.

Herman, J. (2015). *Trauma and recovery*. Basic Books.

Johnstone, L., Boyle, M., Cromby, J., Dillon, J., Harper, D., Kinderman, P., Longden, E., Pilgrim, D., & Read, J. (2018). *The power threat meaning framework: towards the identification of patterns in emotional distress, unusual experiences and troubled or troubling behaviour, as an alternative to functional psychiatric diagnosis*. British Psychological Society.

Levinger, G. (1957). Kurt Lewin's approach to conflict and its resolution: a review with some extensions. *The Journal of Conflict Resolution*, *1*(4), 329–339.

Lewin, K. (1935). *Dynamic theory of personality*. McGraw-Hill.

Lifton, R. (1961). *Thought reform and the psychology of totalism*. W.W. Norton.

Mind (2020). *Self-harm.* Mind.org.uk. https://www.mind.org.uk/media-a/5783/self-harm-2020.pdf

Monckton-Smith, J. (2022). *In control: dangerous relationships and how they end in murder.* Bloomsbury Publishing.

National Health Service, United Kingdom (n.d.). https://www.nhs.uk/conditions/self-harm/

National Institute for Health and Care Excellence (2022). *Self-harm: assessment, management and preventing recurrence* (NICE guideline NG225). https://www.nice.org.uk/guidance/ng225/chapter/Recommendations#interventions-for-self-harm

Olson, M., & Hergenhahn, B. (Eds.). (2015). *Introduction to theories of learning* (9th ed.). Routledge.

Padesky, C., & Mooney, K. (2012). Strengths-based cognitive behavioural therapy: a four-step model to build resilience. *Clinical Psychology and Psychotherapy, 19*, 283–290. 10.1002/cpp.1795

Pickard, H. (2015). Self-harm as violence: when victim and perpetrator are one. In Maraway, H., & Widdows, H. (eds.) *Women and Violence: the agency of victims and perpetrators.* pp. 71–90.

Rousseau, D., Tomprou, M., & Montes, S. (2013). Psychological contract theory. In E. Kessler (Ed.). *Encyclopedia of management theory*, pp. 635–639. SAGE Publications.

SafeLIves (2015). *Insights IDVA national dataset 2013–14.* Safe Lives.

Spearman, K., Hardesty, J., & Campbell, J. (2022). Post-separation abuse: a concept analysis. *Journal of Advanced Nursing, 00*, 1–22.

Walker, L. (1979). *The battered woman.* Harper Collins.

Weiss, R. (2018). *Prodependence: moving beyond codependency.* Health Communications.

World Health Organization (WHO) (2022). *International classification of diseases* (11th Revision). WHO. https://icd.who.int/en

Chapter 8

Understanding Complex Trauma

Jeannette Roddy

Learning Objectives

1 Exploration of trauma and how we define it, diagnosis and issues
2 Understanding the effects of trauma on physiology, brain function, and response at the time of the incident(s)
3 Review of tried and tested models for trauma work
4 How to work within the "Window of tolerance"
5 Using metaphor to explore situations
6 When to refer on to other services
7 Using exercises to better understand trauma

Context

Many survivors of domestic abuse report high levels of anxiety, suicidal ideation, and intrusive memories (see also chapter 6). Part of the therapeutic process may be to help the individual to explore what is happening to them as these symptoms can relate to a traumatic response to a threatening (often life-threatening) experience. As a therapist, it is helpful to understand the process of trauma from the client perspective, as well as to understand some of the helpful ways to work with a client who is presenting with such symptoms.

What Is Complex Trauma?

Complex trauma is a relatively newly defined type of trauma. When the DSM 5 (American Psychiatric Association, 2013) was being discussed between 2010 and 2013, there was heated debate about whether complex trauma should be included, ultimately with a decision against inclusion. By the time ICD11 was being discussed between 2017 and 2019, the argument for complex trauma had strengthened and diagnostic criteria were included as part of the diagnostic framework available to mental health professionals (World Health Organisation, 2022). This shift in opinion within a period of five years is significant and driven by extensive research showing that complex trauma

DOI: 10.4324/9781003253266-8

was both real and different to other traumas, requiring a different approach. It is to be hoped that when DSM6 is discussed, complex trauma will form a part of this framework too.

There are three main types of trauma:

Category 1 – defined as acute trauma, caused by a single incident which someone may witness or be affected by, resulting in death (to other) or near death (to self or other) or serious or life-changing injury (to self or other). The trauma may be the result of an accident or natural disaster, but the important aspect of this is that it occurs only once. Whilst the incident is distressing and can lead to the individual experiencing memory flashbacks to the event and potentially leads to changes in behaviour to avoid a recurrence, the memory is generally detailed and can be recounted in full, allowing the memory to be processed effectively in therapy. There are a variety of therapies, such as EMDR, which can be particularly effective in treating such trauma (Marzillier, 2014).

Category 2 – defined as chronic trauma, is a series of less serious incidents repeated over an extended period of time. These incidents are difficult for the individual and may involve, for example, emotional or psychological abuse, or low-level physical abuse. It may include living in a domestically abusive house, but without the threat of serious physical harm or death. However, the relentless nature of the incidents can cause significant emotional and psychological distress, which can continue beyond the timeframe of the incidents.

People who have experienced domestic abuse may exhibit chronic trauma, resulting from shameful, threatening and/or degrading experiences over time. Here, the individual may find the events difficult to remember and be unable or unwilling to recall the incidents in detail. A key element of working with these clients is to provide a non-judgemental and positive space for the client to explore and work through their experiences and what they mean for them in their life today. Memories are highly subjective and from the perspective of the client, laid down in a particularly challenging environment. As such, we can say that the memories brought forward are the client's truthful recollection. Difficulties in the client's current life may be related to those memories and how the client perceives them. As therapists, we are not seeking the truth as others might perceive it, we are working with the client and their perspective. Appropriate challenge may be made as the events become clearer, but only in service of the client.

Sometimes, as therapy progresses and the client begins to feel safe in the relationship, memories start to re-emerge which can be shocking for both client and therapist and can feel like an untapped source of pain and distress. Whilst the client may want to stop therapy at that time, as they may feel that this part of the work is harder to cope with than they expected, it is usually more helpful to support the client to work through the memories to a conclusion. Once the rawness and newness of the disclosure is over, the processing of the memories appropriately brings lasting relief rather than temporary relief of attending therapy for a few sessions.

Category 3 – defined as complex trauma, is a combination of acute and chronic trauma, where the individual has been subjected to both low-level and life-threatening events over an extended period. This sort of trauma can be seen in people living in war zones, where the threat of death is constant and the incidents relating to immediate danger fewer but ongoing. Judith Herman (1992) clearly showed that in particularly abusive relationships, the threat of death through unwittingly "getting something wrong" was constant and required the individual to focus only on the abusers needs as a means of survival. The stress of living under such conditions for years can provoke long-term health conditions, such as those relating to the stomach, bowel, or heart, which may mean that clients have many doctor and hospital appointments alongside therapy.

In addition, multiple incidents may have caused alterations in consciousness during attacks for the individual which can result in memory problems when these are recounted. For example, specific sounds, smells, or images may be associated with the event, but these may be "unrelated" i.e. they were present at the time but not specifically related to the incident, such as remembering barking, when the next-door dog barked at a neighbour walking past but was not directly involved in the incident. The barking may have heightened the anxiety or stress of the moment or provided a focus away from what was happening and therefore became a part of the memory of what was happening at that time.

For those of you interested in the current requirements for diagnosis of complex trauma, please see the new ICD-11 definitions (World Health Organisation, 2022) which specifically mention domestic abuse as a possible cause. The diagnosis indicates the presence of PTSD plus specific problems with managing emotions, sustaining relationships and with feelings of guilt and shame in relation to the incidents leading to a sense of worthlessness or defeat. You can see from the preceding chapters why these issues are likely to be seen when working with domestic abuse clients, hence understanding and being able to respond to complex trauma are important aspects of this work.

Reflection: Think about your own life experiences and those of people you know well. Can you place any of the experiences you know of in any of these categories? Do these definitions help you to understand trauma experiences better?

A Model for Trauma Work

Understanding trauma as a therapist helps us to support the client as they review or relive memories which can be terrifying, shameful, and/or guilt-provoking. Having a good understanding of the impact of trauma on the body and how we can support clients to manage their distress are both important features of trauma work. For example, being able to monitor the client for any changes in voice tone, pallor, bodily movements, as well as hearing any nuanced changes in a story already told can help us prepare for a significant disclosure as well as assessing whether they will need support with emotional regulation during the session. In this section, we will talk about session management, with the following section suggesting that the creative exploration of trauma, rather than recounting the detail of the trauma, can be much more helpful to some of the clients (see also chapter 13).

There are many models for trauma work and, depending on your interests and experiences, you will be aware of some more than others. Practices based on polyvagal theory (Dana, 2020), bodywork (Rothschild, 2017), sensorimotor psychotherapy (Ogden, 2021), and visualization (Glouberman, 2022; Sieff, 2015) can all be helpful. However, to understand and utilize these concepts and techniques fully requires additional training. Here we are going to introduce you to some key concepts which will allow you to work with trauma to a limited extent, recognizing that this work should be done in conjunction with a trauma-trained supervisor and with completion of the exercises in this chapter within an educator space. Further training is, of course, essential.

The model of trauma recovery that is most closely related to the counselling model is that of Judith Herman (1992). This seems to fit the experience of domestic abuse survivors most closely, as it is based on a healing relationship with the therapist. This is consistent with the model, particularly in terms of the advanced therapeutic skills discussed in chapters 3 and 4. The first stage in Herman's model is based on creating a safe space which equates to Step 3 of the model described in chapter 2. More medicalized models may call this stage stabilization. The key aspect of this stage is to create a safe space, a trusting relationship, and a clear understanding that the client can bring whatever they need to bring into the space.

Once the client feels safe, the second stage of Herman's (1992) model (called remembrance and mourning) can begin. Within this stage Herman suggests that the client tells the story of the trauma, at a pace to suit them, in depth. This may be called memory integration in more medicalized models. See chapter 9 of Herman's (2001) edition for more detail in what this section entails. Where the model in this book differs from Herman's model, is that it comprises two parts rather than one, that is, working through the trauma and settling down to explore other aspects of the client's life (Steps 4 and 5 in Stage 2, see chapter 2). Rarely will a client come in specifically to deal with the traumatic experiences to the exclusion of everything else. Instead, the client will often talk about their most difficult experiences when the rest of their life is quiet and about what has happened in life when things are more complex again. Being in constant touch with the abuser through child custody, court cases or sometimes through friends and family means that not all therapy time will be taken up processing trauma. Hence the remembrance may at times be delayed or deferred as other aspects of the client's life take priority. For some clients working through the story of their trauma in detail can be very difficult and using creative methods (see working with metaphor in this chapter and also chapter 13), where the client is happy to do so, can provide some relief and assistance.

One of the key aspects of the therapist's role in conducting this work is to gain an understanding of what happened from the client's perspective and to assist the client in understanding what actually happened, rather than what they were led to believe happened by their abuser. It is also important to help the client to understand fully how they had protected themselves and helped themselves to survive. Whilst the therapist must not construct an alternative happy ending, they can usefully challenge thinking that shows that the client does not fully understand the whole situation (see also chapters 6 and 7) to enable them to take any credit for their actions previously withheld. Processing the hidden or suppressed memories of their experiences so that they become memories that can be accessed with compassionate understanding takes away the pain of shame and guilt and allows the memories to become factual stories rather than highly emotional and painful memories. Much as processing the death of loved one is helped by talking through painful memories, so is processing trauma.

The second element of Herman's (2001) stage 2 is that of mourning what has been lost as part of the trauma. The realization of the cost to the client of living with the abuser can be overwhelming and clients will need support to process the grief associated with this. For example, being unable to contact family members due to the abuser's restrictions may have resulted in the loss of family memories and support at births, marriages, and deaths. Work, career, and friendships may have suffered for many years. Often, the loss of the person they were, in comparison to the person they had become in the relationship, can be hard to bear. Being able to confront these losses, just as in bereavement work, allows the client to let go of what they have been holding on to and start to move on with their life.

Whilst the client can never go back to who they were before because they have had many more experiences since then, they can integrate what they have learned post-abuse with the things they admired about themselves prior to the relationship, to create a stronger version of the self they had once valued. This is the final stage that Herman (1992, Chapter 10) calls "Reconnection." Other models may call this stage "reintegration" as the trauma memories become a part of the client's history rather than a disruption of the present. Whilst this part of the process is important for the self, the other part of the reconnection and reintegration is about the client in conjunction with other people in their life. The ability to trust people and to actively seek out and enjoy their company, allowing some dependence on others once more, is the final step in the process. Often this is a result of the therapeutic relationship healing some of the relational wounds and allowing the client to try out other relationships, now that they have one that seems to have been successful. Once a client has other supportive relationships in their life, the requirement for therapy becomes much less and the client begins to move towards stage 3 (chapter 2) where they begin to consider leaving. Seeing steps 6 and 7 as part of the ending of trauma work allows the client to make their own choices about ending (where there are sufficient sessions to do so). This helps to create a lasting change in their life as they decide that they are now self-supporting and fine to be their own.

One of the problems with models which promote a very strong sense of self, without then looking at community and relationship, is that the individual can cope with life again but without the richness of companionship and support that can change an existence into a full life. Surely, after all that has happened, our clients deserve to live fully again. These additional few sessions to reconnect can make all the difference to clients as they leave.

The Effects of Trauma

Trauma affects the way the brain responds to frightening situations both at the time and potentially also at future times when the danger is gone. This can seem a strange concept to people who have not studied trauma and it is helpful to understand why this happens if we are working with people who have experienced trauma. Part of the answer lies in the way that the brain has evolved to protect us from the dangers our ancestors faced.

Initially, the alert system was contained only within the brain stem, which is at the back of the head near the neck. Known as the reptilian brain, its function was to keep humans alive by responding quickly to stress situations or sudden changes in environment (startle response). This allowed the person to respond to danger by fleeing, fighting or freezing. In days where danger lurked around every corner, this was a highly effective system for maintaining human existence.

As time went on, the brain developed the limbic system, that part of the brain which sits in the middle of your head. This developed the ability to retain long-term memories and sensations (hippocampus) together with the emotional content of those memories and whether action needed to be taken (amygdala). This helped humans to learn which situations were likely to be more threatening than others and allowed them to take preventative rather than reactive measures for safety.

Eventually, the frontal part of the brain developed the neocortex. This allowed the brain to process memories and reflect on what was most important in terms of safety, learning, and so on. Being able to assess situations and prioritize our responses to those meant that there would be fewer false alarms. When everything is working well, this part of the brain manages our response to situations and assesses whether any action is required. In our day-to-day life, we assume that we, and those around us, will be able to manage our stress and fear by using our neocortex appropriately.

However, when something very threatening happens to us, the brain responds in the best way possible to help us to survive by instigating a physiological response. This means making more use of the early warning signals of the reptilian brain, rather than the more complex functions of the neocortex.

Exercise: It can be helpful to think of Siegel's hand model when thinking about how memories are laid down (Siegel, 2009). Holding your hand out in front of you, your wrist is the reptilian brain, your palm and thumb your limbic system and your fingers your neocortex. If you place your thumb in your palm and close your fingers over the top, then the neocortex and limbic system are in close contact and monitoring the situation. However, if the neocortex is overloaded, the fingers and thumb fly out and contact between the three parts is diminished or lost. You may now move your fingers and thumb into and out of the fist, making and breaking contact with the other parts of the hand, which is how trauma affects the way the brain works. If you try this out whilst looking around the room, think about the times that your fingers touch your hand and those times where they are not touching, and then try to reconstruct your image of the room using only those images that involved your fingers touching your hand. If your fingers were in contact a lot of the time, much of the detail will be there. However, if your fingers were separate for many and longer periods, it may be harder to make sense of the fragments. In the absence of information, you may relate these to other memories of the room you already have or earlier events in a similar room to understand this better (fill in the blanks). Where there are no similar memories, there are only blanks. This is the effect of trauma on the brain and why there can be disruption or fragmentation of memories.

It can also be useful to understand what is specifically happening in the brain to cause this response and the impact of this more widely on the body. When the brain perceives threat, it provides messages to other parts of the body depending on which safety system is enacted, which then influences how connected and in control of the situation the person feels. In the reptilian brain, which responds to large and present threats, this is primarily to help the body into fight or flight. This requires the creation of energy to flood muscle groups, which enables the person to respond to the trauma to some extent. This energy is created when the brain perceives fear and the amygdala sends a message to the hypothalamus, which in turn activates the Autonomous Nervous System (ANS) and the Sympathetic-Adrenal-Medullary (SAM) system. This floods the body with adrenaline, creating a state of high alert (characterized by the dilation of pupils, fast breathing, pounding heart, tense muscles, and sweating palms) but also has the effect of slowing down the digestive system and increasing the glucose production from the liver to support the increased energy needs of the body.

Where the stress response is required over a longer period of time, perhaps due to difficult living conditions, the Hypothalmic-Pituitary-Adrenal (HPA) system is also activated, releasing cortisol and allowing the body to remain in a state of high alert. Where the body is in continual alert mode, there is not enough time for the adrenaline and cortisone to be metabolized before the next release. Over time, the body moves into a dominant SAM state which has a negative impact on blood pressure, kidney function, bone density, and the immune system, as well as continuing to over produce glucose leading to higher blood sugar levels. Hence the stress response creates the potential for serious longer term health conditions. This continued state of alert (hyper-vigilance) relies on the amygdala rather than the hippocampus (which could shut off the stress system) and the focus is on whether to take action at any given time, rather than laying down longer-term memories. This can result in fragmented memory and, in children, having ongoing higher levels of adrenalin and cortisol due to a difficult home environment can also lead to lower cognitive functioning (see chapter 9). Experiencing childhood domestic abuse can therefore result in issues for adult survivors.

Sometimes, the brain recognizes it is unsafe to fight or to leave the situation. This can be the case with children, where they have nowhere to go other than the family home, as well as with adults, for example, in cases of sexual assault. This freeze response, also known as tonic immobilization, can occur where the threat is seen as overwhelming and occurs when the parasympathetic branch of the ANS is activated. Here, the person's breathing becomes very shallow, or they may hold their breath, and become very still. Often the person's heart rate will go down and the person will become cold. Hearing and sight senses become more acute to help assess the situation, whilst the ability to talk may disappear during the event. When processing this in later years within therapy, the client can move back into the physiological state they were in at the time of the incident which may restrict the ability of the client to communicate verbally. Keeping blankets in a therapy room and offering them to a client when they are cold can be helpful, both physically and emotionally. Creative options for working may also be effective for such clients (see chapter 13) as they may find it easier to write about or draw, rather than talk about, their experience.

It can be possible for someone to move from fight or flight into immobilization/freeze if they become overwhelmed by the hyper-arousal experienced in recounting the trauma. Slipping into hypo-arousal (a form of dissociation) instead can be an easier option for survival (see section below on the window of tolerance) and this can happen in the therapy room. Alternatively, someone who has had many traumatic experiences as a child may go straight to freeze, repeating the best and safest option in an environment where they perceived there was no option for fighting back or leaving. This may become a dissociative coping mechanism, allowing the person to detach from what is going on around both physically and emotionally. Whilst this response may have been very helpful to the individual in the past, it may not serve the client as well in adulthood, for example shutting down when completing a presentation in front of colleagues at work. Within the therapy room, the client may appear to have glazed eyes, appear to be zoning out and unresponsive. Within life more generally, they may report feeling cut-off or shutdown when with others, may be avoidant of places and feelings, seem very serious and sad, and have poor sleep and energy levels.

Finally, there is another category that has been recognized as an outcome from traumatic experiences, that of fawning. This is the survival technique of meeting the wishes, needs, and demands of the threatening other at the expense of ourselves. This is often presented in domestic abuse counselling when the client tries to guess what the therapist wants them to say or tries to gain favour by being very complimentary about their counselling skills for example. Whilst this trauma response is not embedded in physiology, it is embedded in the individual's psychological response to trauma as they have been trained (unconsciously) to behave in this way by the abuser (see also chapter 3). This can be the result of emotional neglect or living with a narcissistic powerful other either as an adult or child. People who tend towards fawning as a coping mechanism often apologize and struggle to state what their own thoughts and feelings are, instead focusing on the needs of others. When working with trauma clients, it is important to recognize these factors as it can make therapy much less effective if this is not addressed. In these circumstances, it would also be useful to read chapter 5 on attachment and transference.

Managing Trauma Responses in the Therapy Room – Working within the Window of Tolerance

Helping clients to process what has happened to them can be helpful, but it can also be quite a difficult and intense experience. A key element of successful therapy is to create an environment for exploration that the client can tolerate. The Window of Tolerance (Rothschild, 2017) is an important trauma model for assisting us with this task. In simple terms, it means that if a client is too hyper-aroused (panic) or too hypo-aroused (dissociation) then they are unable to process material. However, if they are not fully engaged in the material, they are unlikely to be able to recall it in the detail required to process the experience. Hence the skill of the therapy is to work with the client to ensure they can approach the material they need to, without becoming highly distressed or dissociative. In part, this is by being very aware of the physiological changes in the client, such as through their increased agitation, rapid breathing and heart rate, or sudden reduction in movement and heart rate, shallow breathing and lack of psychological contact. It may also be through more rapid speech or your own felt sense in your own body, which you can check out with the client. Being aware of these physiological changes means that you can track the client and assist in maintaining contact and safety for the client during a session. As clients are helped to manage their trauma response in sessions, they can also start to use it in their lives too, and as they become more confident in being able to cope with sudden changes in how they feel, their window of tolerance expands.

In general, it is useful to think of trauma responses as providing either an external or internal response within the client. That is, if the client is highly aroused and agitated and is looking for danger outside themselves, they might need help to bring them back into their body and into the therapeutic relationship again. If they have moved into their body (as a form of dissociation) to take themselves away from the external environment, they may then need help to bring them back into the room and reconnect with the therapist. There are different approaches to managing these responses and it is important to use the most appropriate one for the client at the time of their distress.

When a client is hyper-aroused, anxious, agitated, highly alert, perhaps angry, or out of control if they have been hyper-aroused for a while, it is useful to have grounding exercises that you can use with the client, such as breathing exercises or safe-place imagery (see chapter 10) or encouraging the client to focus on touching the chair, feeling their feet on the floor, their back against the chair. It can also be useful to have them focus on one thing quite close to them, for example if you have shells or buttons close by, to ask the client to select one of a specific colour and describe how it feels. If you are working online you might ask the client to focus on things within their own space and describe them. This encourages focus away from the memories and onto something quite safe. Whilst some practitioners focus on breath control, this will generally only work if the client has some level of body control. It is sometimes easier to start with physical grounding first to bring them into their body, before attempting breathing exercises. If you have a client presenting with trauma, it is useful to start these grounding exercises with them from the first session, so that if you need them within session, the client is used to the exercise and can very quickly adapt to the change of focus in the session. If the client finds it difficult to do these grounding exercises or chooses not to, then it may well be inappropriate to continue to work with the trauma, and referral for specialist trauma therapy may be required.

Where a client is hypo-aroused and is withdrawn and disconnected from the session, the focus is on establishing psychological contact with the client as quickly as possible. If the client becomes frozen and immobile, assure the person they are safe by using a gentle, slow voice at a reasonably deep pitch, much as you would soothe a baby or a pet who is distressed. Talk about what is happening in the present moment, for example, what time it is, where they are right now and that they are in a therapy session. If you have previously agreed with the client that you can touch their hand, you may consider doing so as this can have a positive effect. A client who is highly dissociative is not a good fit for online trauma work and should only be seen by a trauma-trained therapist face-to-face.

As you establish some psychological contact, ask them to move their head and neck from side to side and look around the room to find something specific such as something green or three objects they can see or just to look around and find something that is interesting to them, which they can then describe. Finally, a quick exercise that engages each of their senses, sight, smell, sound, touch, taste to describe their experience now ensures they are fully back with you in session.

A client who has become hypo-aroused but is still in contact with you during the event can be asked to move their head and neck and then focus on things around the room. Catching the dissociation early and helping the client to process it can help the client to become more aware of their own bodily process which can help them to manage their trauma symptoms outside of therapy too.

Exercise: Work with a partner. Take it in turns to be counsellor and client.

As client, first of all imagine a highly anxiety provoking situation, one that makes you feel panicky. Start to tell your partner about the situation (as happening now, in the moment) so that you have feelings of anxiety. The counsellor can then start to use the techniques suggested for hyper-arousal to assist you with calming down. Once you have calmed down, change over as counsellor and client and repeat the exercise. Debrief with each other after the session as to what was helpful, what was not, how you feel now.

As client, now start to focus deeply within yourself, perhaps thinking about a particularly difficult issue you have. As counsellor, note how you feel as the client goes deeper into their own world. Once you feel psychological contact is ceasing, use the techniques for hypo-arousal to bring the client slowly back into the room. Once the normal connection between you is established, change over as counsellor and client and repeat the exercise. Debrief with each other after the session as to what was helpful, what was not, how you feel now.

It is important that you both try hard to create these spaces as client. The need to act as a counsellor in these situations is immediate and confident action (with something you have already tried successfully) is more likely to bring a good client outcome.

When a client becomes hyper or hypo aroused, the memory shuts down and it can become difficult to remember or discuss what had seemed quite easy only a few seconds ago. If we can catch the client before they become fully aroused in their telling of the story, once brought back into the room they can continue with the story as the trauma as experienced in the moment has receded. This can help significantly in recounting and reprocessing those memories that are accessible.

Using Metaphor to Help Process Memories

Sometimes, memories are not fully accessible because of the way that the memories have been laid down. They are fragmented and appear to make little sense, a bit like looking at painting by numbers before the paint has been applied. However, the memories may be accessible by looking at what comes up for the client when they start to explore those topics within their body or within their imagination. For example, a client may have a sense of heaviness in their body as they talk which they cannot explain. Careful exploration of that feeling and what that is "like" for the client as a metaphor can often bring unexpected and rapid understanding to the client. Working with the image to a positive end point can help the client to process the trauma without having to remember the detail of the event (which may be beyond the client in any case).

Metaphor is not a new idea for working with trauma, but it can be effective if used with a competent practitioner. The important aspect of this is that metaphor can be used with any client in an appropriate situation and so there is plenty of scope for practitioners to hone their skills in how to work with metaphor with fellow students and general counselling clients, with appropriate supervision. Once confident and fluent in how to work with metaphor, this can be reasonably applied with domestic abuse clients.

Working with Metaphor

Metaphor in this context is about the image the client either has or can bring into awareness of an event or situation or person. Any imagery should be driven by the client as this will be very meaningful to them and will relate strongly to things in their life. For example, young people and old people may see different images of a similar situation, perhaps one involving video games and the other a movie. There will also be cultural contexts to consider (see also chapter 11). It is important to take the image presented and work with the client on the image. This can help to challenge assumptions by the counsellor and client and introduce new frames of reference. Sometimes a counsellor will offer an image and the client will take it and expand upon it. This is fine if the counsellor can let go of the image introduced and start to explore the one the client now sees. Done well, there is a significant feeling of teamwork between therapist and client and there can be a significant strengthening of the therapeutic relationship. However, imposing your own image, trying to interpret the image for the client or not spending enough time immersing yourself in what is going on for the client (leading to misunderstandings) can have detrimental effects. Getting the exploration process right is key to this work. For a particularly good explanation of how to work in the moment with client imagery see chapter 4 of Glouberman (2022).

When you are working with metaphor, try not to lead the client by assuming anything. For example:

Client: I have this feeling in my chest.
Counsellor: And what is that like for you?
Client: It feels like a really heavy boulder is laying there.
Counsellor: How big is the boulder?
Client: It's really big – it comes from my neck right down to my pelvis and lies across my arms too.
Counsellor: How heavy is it?
Client: It's quite heavy, it's difficult to move.
Counsellor: What happens when you try to move?
Client: It wobbles a bit, then these two green shoots come out and stop it from wobbling.
And so on … … .

By the counsellor simply being curious about the feeling in the chest, we now have an image of a heavy boulder with some resources built in to keep it in place. This could be a very useful image to explore further which may reveal a number of things about the client's past experience that they are continuing to hold onto, despite now having the resources to move on. Working with the imagery will provide the client with the opportunity to move or have a relationship with or find the motivation for the boulder being there.

As you explore the image, it is useful to think about the context of the image (what is also around there), size, colour, texture, weight, whether it will engage in conversation, how long it has been there, how it helps the client, what its needs are, how it hinders the client, and so on. Surprisingly perhaps, when asked how long the (image) has been there, most clients can state straight away how many years, months, weeks, or days it has been there, sometimes then linking it to a past memory or person that suddenly has much more significance than previously.

One of the key things to remember in doing this work in trauma is that it is important to keep the client safe within the image, to allow the image to progress at the client's pace, and to process and transform the image into something easier or more manageable as a result of the work. Taking the example above, we might explore this a little further, such as:

Counsellor: Tell me a bit more about the green shoots, they sound interesting.
Client: I have only just noticed them. They are quite thin and now I see them they are doing a lot of balancing work all the time, in and out.

Counsellor: Do you feel scared by them?

Client: Actually no, they are just doing a job. They are not interfering with me, they are just propping the boulder up.

Counsellor: What do you think would happen if they weren't there?

Client: I think the boulder would roll off eventually, because every time I move it seems to unbalance.

Counsellor: Do the green shoots have to be there?

Client: No, I don't think so. They seem tired, like they want to stop. It's the boulder that wants them to carry on.

Counsellor: Can you talk to them, perhaps give them permission to stop?

Client: Yes. (client has internal dialogue). Yes, they are happy to stop, they are tired and want to recover.

Counsellor: What about the boulder now?

Client: The boulder seems much lighter now. If I wiggle around a bit I can see it start to fall. Oh, it's gone, it's lying beside me.

Counsellor: How is that for you?

Client: I feel so much lighter. I feel better that I have managed to push it away. I can't tell you how good that feels.

Counsellor: And what about the boulder now? What would you like to happen to it?

And so on ….

The key to metaphor is to keep a clear vision of what is happening, focus in on different aspects, make sure the client is safe. If the client is scared, either move away from the image to safe distance, or ask the client what they need to feel safe and introduce that into the image. For example, a very thick acrylic wall to stand behind can often be helpful in the client continuing to explore the image, but without the fear of what might happen next in front of them.

When the client wants to stop, or the image has been processed, find a safe way to come back into the room and leave the image behind. It is important that the client has the option to leave anything they want to leave in the counselling room. In the example above, the counsellor may provide the opportunity to keep the boulder on behalf of the client, until they want it back. Of course, they may never want it back and as a counsellor, you will need to have your own process to find a different home for the boulder in due course.

There are several helpful authors on metaphor if you are interested in reading further (Gladding, 1988; Glouberman, 2022; Hartley, 2012).

Additional Resources

There are many texts on trauma which will explain these concepts in much more detail. A small section of a chapter in a book is only going to present the main ideas helpful to working in this area. For those of you specifically interested in this area of work, please do follow up with the leading authors in this area, such as Dana (2020), Kepner (2013), Ogden (2021), Porges and Dana (2018), Rothschild (2017), and van der Kolk (2014). For accessible and helpful resources relating to working with trauma, see Carolyn Spring of PODS.

Summary

New definitions of complex trauma have helped those who have experienced domestic abuse to find a description of their experiences. The nature of complex trauma means that it will not necessarily respond to traditional trauma treatments. New ideas on trauma, such as polyvagal theory and bodywork, are showing good results in this area. Understanding how trauma impacts the memory and the individual can help therapists to work more clearly and compassionately with this client group. Simple techniques for grounding and exploring imagery and body sensations can prove valuable for clients who have experienced multiple traumas in their lives.

Key Learning Points

1. Complex trauma is a relatively new trauma classification which shows the impact of severe and long-term exposure to fearful and life-threatening situations.
2. Domestic abuse can sometimes prompt symptoms of complex trauma due to the impact of the trauma response on the brain and nervous system responses.
3. Many of the symptoms reported by people who have experienced domestic abuse in terms of high anxiety and dissociation can be explained as a trauma response that has become embedded as a response to incidents, even those with a lower trauma content.
4. Understanding the effects of trauma in a client can help therapists to work with them more effectively. Having a clear idea of a trauma model to work with clients will help to ensure that appropriate interventions happen at appropriate times.
5. Managing hyper- and hypo-arousal using exercises to reduce the felt stress of traumatic memories can help clients to self-regulate in session and to use those skills in their life outside too.
6. Using creative imagery, such as metaphor, can be very helpful in processing trauma without specifically retelling the story of the event.
7. Any trauma work should be supervised by someone experienced in trauma.
8. Therapists should undertake additional trauma training before working with clients.

References

American Psychiatric Association (2013). *Diagnostic and statistical manual of mental disorders: DSM-5* (5th ed.) [Non-fiction]. American Psychiatric Association.

Dana, D. (2020). *Polyvagal exercises for safety and connection*. W. W. Norton & Company Ltd.

Gladding, S. T. (1988). *Uses of metaphor's and imagery in counseling: An instructor's manual*. American Association for Counseling and Human Development Foundation. https://eric.ed.gov/?id=ED321194.

Glouberman, D. (2022). *ImageWork*. PCCS Books Ltd.

Hartley, T. (2012). Cutting edge metaphors. *Journal of the Association of Surgeons of Great Britain and Ireland, 37*(Sept 2012), 26–29. https://cleanlanguage.co.uk/articles/articles/325/1/Cutting-Edge-Metaphors/Page1.html.

Herman, J. L. (1992). *Trauma and recovery*. Pandora.

Kepner, J. I. (2013). *Healing tasks: Psychotherapy with adult survivors of childhood abuse*. Gestalt Press.

Marzillier, J. (2014). *The trauma therapies*. Oxford University Press.

Ogden, P. (2021). *Sensorimotor psychotherapy in context*. W. W. Norton & Company Ltd.

Porges, S. W., & Dana, D. (2018). *Clinical applications of the polyvagal theory: The emergence of polyvagal-informed therapies (Norton series on interpersonal neurobiology)*. WW Norton & Company.

Rothschild, B. (2017). *The body remembers volume 2: Revolutionizing trauma treatment*. W. W. Norton & Company Ltd.

Sieff, D. F. (2015). *Understanding and healing emotional trauma*. Routledge.

Siegel, D. J. (2009). *Mindsight*. Random House.

Van der Kolk, B. (2014). *The body keeps the score: Mind, brain and body in the transformation of trauma*. Penguin UK.

World Health Organisation (2022). 6B41 Complex post traumatic stress disorder. In *ICD-11 for Mortality and Morbidity Statistics*. World Health Organisation. https://icd.who.int/browse11/l-m/en#/http://id.who.int/icd/entity/585833559.

Chapter 9

Understanding the Developmental Impact of Domestic Violence and Adverse Experiences in Childhood across the Life-Course

Celeste Foster and Leigh Gardner

Learning Objectives

1. Use a developmental approach to understand the broad-ranging impacts of experiencing domestic abuse in childhood, across the life course.
2. Recognise the relationship between developmental disruptions precipitated by adverse childhood experiences and mental distress in adolescence and adulthood.
3. Appreciate that surviving adverse experiences can also produce extraordinary strengths and skills.
4. Understand the influence of formative attachment relationship experiences upon patterns within the therapist-client relationship; consider what this means for your own practice development.
5. Explore creative and expressive-play-based strategies for engaging children, young people, and the adults they become.

Context

For the purpose of this chapter children and young people (CYP) refers to ages 0–18. Working with CYP requires additional training and is covered by BACP (2019) and other regulatory body guidelines and standards. However, all practitioners have a responsibility to be aware of the signs and impacts of abuse on CYP, and how to signpost to effective forms of help (Bickham, 2017). Here we introduce you to some key concepts which will increase your awareness of the needs of CYP and support you to work with young adults and adult clients who have survived domestic violence in childhood, recognising that this work should be done in conjunction with an appropriately trained supervisor.

Around one in five children has been exposed to domestic abuse. Domestic abuse is one of the most common forms of adverse or traumatic experience to

DOI: 10.4324/9781003253266-9

which CYP are exposed today (Geldard et al., 2019). Children who witness violence experience the same fear, intimidation, and threat to their safety as the adults, and can be witnesses to, or experience violence, and/or be co-opted into perpetrating violence.

Domestic violence is one of ten identified Adverse Childhood Experiences (ACES). These are experiences related to family life in childhood that have been shown, by repeated large-scale research studies, to significantly increase the risk of physical and mental illnesses, poor psychosocial outcomes, such as substance misuse and incarceration, and suicide across the life course (Hughes et al., 2017). Domestic violence within the family is a statistical risk factor for the likelihood of children being subject to other forms of abuse such as neglect, physical and sexual maltreatment. Domestic abuse has been found to be a factor in over half of serious case reviews in England (Sidebotham et al., 2016). This is important, because ACES research has demonstrated that the more ACES experienced, the more likely negative health and well-being outcomes are experienced in adulthood. People who have survived four or more ACES are 14 times more likely to attempt suicide and four times more likely to develop long-term physical and mental health conditions (Hughes et al., 2017).

Positive attachment relationships with primary carers and wider family/community members serve as a protection against the impact of some ACES, helping children to feel safe, bounce back, and to understand what has happened to them. Most children will experience emotional/psychosocial difficulties at some point in their childhood; but they will develop and grow through these difficulties, as they draw on the support of good enough-parents/carers, wider social support, and their own internal resources, to overcome or resolve any problems life throws their way.

For some CYP this is not the case. Their primary carers, on whom they rely to mitigate stress, help them cope with difficult circumstances and develop emotional regulation skills that can protect against the effects of frightening life events, are either the target of violence or a perpetrator of violence. This means the usual ways in which a child is protected from harm are disturbed and the effects of the harm are therefore often amplified. Research has highlighted that it is not just the actual episodes of violence that impact on the child's development. Day-to-day parenting styles of those who perpetrate intimate partner violence have been shown to range from authoritarian, uninvolved, irresponsible, to self-centred (Bancroft et al., 2012), further shaping up difficulties in how the child develops, sees themselves, and learns about relationships. It is essential when working with older adolescents and adults who have survived domestic abuse in their childhood, that practitioners have a detailed understanding of how these lived experiences can affect all aspects of the individual's psychosocial and relational functioning in adulthood.

Perhaps not surprisingly, studies of population statistics indicate that those who have experienced domestic abuse in childhood are at greater risk of being in adult relationships characterised by coercive control and violence. When working with adults who have survived abusive adult relationships, it is therefore important to keep in mind that for some, this will have come on top of the impacts of surviving domestic abuse during childhood. It must also be remembered that hidden within the statistics are also all the people who have experienced domestic abuse in childhood who have managed to grow and thrive, through great tenacity, adaptability, and survivorhood.

Already we can start to see the importance of understanding and responding effectively to the impact of domestic violence in childhood: it is relatively common; comes with a significant risk of disrupting ordinary childhood development, future relationships, and of the emergence of mental and physical illnesses that persist into adulthood; and contributes to the intergenerational transmission of domestic abuse over time. At the same time research, clinical evidence, and experiential expertise of survivors demonstrates that relationships which support development of emotional regulation, resilience, self-worth, and a sense of belonging within one's community can positively mitigate the relationship between ACES and poor health outcomes at all stages of the life course (Callaghan et al., 2015; McLeod & Flood, 2018).

We will explore some of the complex mechanisms that underpin the statistics and outcomes summarised in this section and show how understanding the experience of witnessing domestic abuse in childhood as a developmental trauma can equip helping professionals to engage adult clients effectively and with sensitivity.

Introducing a Dynamic Developmental Framework of Understanding

Through a developmental lens, trauma is a relative concept. The earlier in our life traumatic experiences occur, the smaller they need to be and the bigger/ more harmful the impact may be. Young children are at high risk, due to their not-yet-developed ability to understand what is happening and why, or how to regulate their own emotions.

Garland (2018) defines trauma as an event or series of events that overwhelm our existing defences and confirm something of our worst fears or deepest anxieties. Using this definition, we can see that for a baby, who is entirely dependent on its carer for survival and cannot even regulate its body temperature or heart rate independently, the experience of being left cold and hungry for an extended period may leave the baby's defences temporarily overwhelmed and activate an anxiety about being left alone. However, with the return of a carer to provide warmth, food, and comfort, this is a temporary ordeal with little lasting effect and one that can actually contribute to the development of resilience through the building of frustration tolerance. If the baby is repeatedly left cold, hungry and with no one to soothe its distress for extended periods, and its only defence of being able to cry for help does not work, the impact on the baby will be much more serious. As the baby's body is overwhelmed by physical stress, a dysregulated heartbeat, temperature, and hunger, worst fears of abandonment and death may start to come to life alongside the emergence of a realisation that one is powerless. In this instance, we can start to see that the baby's experience begins to approach something traumatic, with lasting consequences.

> Reflection: Consider the two descriptions of a baby waiting to have its cries for help met by a carer. Now think about what the experience and learning might be for a baby whose cries for help are met with anger, aggression, and retaliation. What might be the impact on the way baby relates to itself, its carers, and the world around them? How might these changes affect the child's development and relationships as it grows?

Developmental trauma is used to describe the cumulative impact of early, repeated abuse, neglect, separation, and adverse experiences upon the child's physical, psychological, social, and emotional development, and on the adult they become (van der Kolk, 2015). It parallels the diagnosis of complex trauma discussed in chapter 8. Unlike complex trauma it is not a formal diagnosis. It is a label used to distinguish the impact of experiencing complex trauma within primary-care relationships in childhood, in terms of the interaction with usual physiological and psychological developmental processes and the long-lasting global impact on the person's future development. A dynamic developmental framework seeks to locate the person's difficulties in context, understanding them as a function or outcome of how their experiences have impeded or enhanced usual development, rather than seeing them as symptoms of illness. Observational and neurodevelopmental research illuminates how people who have been subject to repeated interpersonal stress in childhood:

- develop a range of coping strategies which helped them survive at one point in their life, but which may now be problematic;
- do not always develop the cognitive tools that are essential for daily living skills, such as being able to manage impulses and solve problems.

This way of understanding ACESs also highlights their cumulative nature: disruption in one stage of development can result in gaps in the skills and knowledge needed to make achieving the developmental tasks of the next stage, and so on.

For CYP, domestic abuse is almost always enacted within primary-carer attachment relationships. Chapter 5 has laid out how being in controlling and abusive adult relationships can alter the victim's behaviour within relationships: developing more preoccupied and fearful attachment behaviours and resulting in corrosion of confidence and trust in others and one's own mind. The magnitude of experiencing domestic abuse in childhood is amplified. Our primary attachment relationships are not only a source of comfort, pleasure, and security; they are the most important source of growth and learning in childhood, setting the foundational templates we use for making sense of all future relationships. This includes how we think we deserve to be treated by others, the ability to name, understand and regulate changes in our emotions, guess the feeling of others, and adapt to our surroundings (Bowlby, 1988). These are skills that are essential for understanding what is happening in our body, treating ourselves with appropriate care, and navigating future relationships, including being able to notice and protect oneself from abusive behaviour within intimate relationships. In secure attachments, our carers do these things for us whilst teaching us how to do it. It is easy to forget that being able to do this for ourselves is not a given that comes with age, but rather, a maturational achievement that requires certain conditions to foster it (Winnicott, 1984). These conditions come from relational environments that confer safety, belonging, and legitimacy and that work to keep stress hormones at bay, supporting neurological development and understanding of our self and others (Sunderland, 2016). Maintaining an attachment with an unavailable, unpredictable, rejecting, invalidating or harmful primary-carer, to survive, can produce anxious, ambivalent, avoidant, and disorganised attachment patterns in future relationships (Bowlby, 1988).

Fear within primary attachment relationships can disrupt development of the person's capacities to forge, make use of, and learn from future helpful interpersonal relationships, which are key to recovery from ACEs, including professional therapeutic relationships. This phenomenon has been coined "double deprivation" (Williams, 2005). Attachment styles remain in adulthood: clients will still be carrying their own attachment styles and working with a therapist will give cause for transference and projection as an adult client, just like a child, tries to find out if they can trust this relationship. With survivors of childhood domestic violence, it can be helpful to recognise that being preoccupied with what the therapist is thinking and feeling, in order to protect oneself from what is coming next, is a very functional response to the client's experiences. Providing information and commentary about your own thinking processes as you go along, can create predictability in the relationship for the client. It helps lessen their need to preoccupy themselves with what might be going on in your mind, allowing them to relax and focus on their own processes in the moment.

> Reflection – think of a client that has difficulty in trusting you as a therapist, what is it like for you, what is it like for them? What factors that you know of in their childhood may have led them to feel like this and what might you both need to build this relationship?

Survival of difficult experience can also produce resilience, skill, and strength. Children who have acted as young carers may develop a range of life skills much earlier than would be expected; those living in unpredictable environments may have honed skills of people management and conflict mediation well beyond their years. Children can show enormous adaptability and tenacity in the face of adversity – thriving at school, creating functional relationships with other adults in their network, hiding their difficulties. Winnicott (1971) described the concurrence of areas of vulnerability with areas of unexpectedly well-developed skill that comes from surviving adverse experiences, "Islands of competency." This is an important concept in therapeutic work with people of all ages, as otherwise, we may make sweeping assumptions based on one part of a person's functioning that blind us to a person's strengths or vulnerabilities in other areas that can be harnessed in the service of recovery.

A developmental model reminds us that at any point in the life cycle, the availability of helpful, attuned, consistent adults, who can give us space to validate and work through our experiences can help assuage our distress, reduce vulnerability, and address gaps in our skill development. The past informs the present and the future, but it is never too late to intervene.

Recognising the protective and growth-promoting role of adults in children's lives requires us to acknowledge and give value to the protection conferred by many parents who are the victim of domestic abuse, who may not be able to escape what is happening to them, but who commit themselves to limiting the impact upon their children in whatever ways they can (Haight, 2007). Demonstrating an understanding of this in the therapy room can go a long way to promote the client's engagement, as they begin to realise that the therapist does not have an over-simplified view of the complex but important relationships with their childhood carers.

A dynamic developmental approach demands that we ask and understand: what was happening? when was it happening? what were the developmental tasks of the child at that point? how were those tasks affected? who was around to help? how did they help (or not)? what went before and what came after? In other words, the impact of domestic abuse is a process, not just an event or experience. Therefore, anyone working with a client who experienced domestic abuse in their childhood needs to have a basic appreciation of child development, including developmental tasks and milestones, social learning and attachment theory and cognitive development. It can help to contextualise how the client has made sense of their experiences and alert the counsellor to possible differences and challenges in the client's cognitive and emotional processing, which may need attending to in the relationship.

The Developmental Impact of Experiencing Domestic Violence in Childhood

In chapter 8 you were introduced to the key concepts and approaches to working with complex trauma which are highly relevant for working with survivors of domestic abuse in childhood. However, when we apply this to childhood trauma, we must remember that children are in the process of building the cognitive, emotional, and neurological building blocks of resilience. The effects of trauma are therefore built into the neuropsychological architecture of their emotional, cognitive, autonomic, social, and relational systems, in just the same way as the positive growth-promoting effects of love and good-enough care. It is the relative balance of these two forms of experience that we can come to call vulnerability and resilience.

The effect of overwhelming traumatic events can be the loss or shattering of any internalised resilience, acquired by the child up to that point. It can mean that we go back to having to rely on others to regulate our emotions for us, until we can do it for ourselves again. This can be temporary or can take a long time to recover, depending on the nature, severity, and chronicity of the trauma and can persist into adulthood, meaning that therapy may need to integrate help to learn regulation skills. If there are pre-existing difficulties and deprivation in early experience of care, then our resilience and defences will be more vulnerable to being overwhelmed at later stages of the life course. Poor professional understanding of this phenomenon is often at the root of negative attributions made about adolescents and adults who have histories of complex childhood trauma, due to the tendency to appraise people's coping style and skills against expectations for their chronological age.

Neurobiological Impacts

It is now well understood that key aspects of neurological development in infancy and toddlerhood are dependent on and shaped by the quality of our relationships and events in the external world (Gerhardt, 2014). In the first four years of life, our bodies build the foundational blocks of the:

- Autonomic nervous system (e.g. basal heart rate, temperature, and metabolism)
- Hypothalamic-pituitary-adrenocortical axis (HPA)
- Myelination (wiring and insulation) of neural circuits in the Right Brain and limbic system.

Chapter 8 provides a detailed outline of how these parts of the brain develop, their function, and what happens in adulthood if they are subject to high levels of threat and stress. This information also applies to children. However, there is a very important difference. In adulthood, these neurological systems have already been built and are then subject to injury. When children experience trauma, it directly affects how these neurological systems are built, meaning that some differences can be "hardwired" into the system. Whilst change and recovery is always possible, realistic understanding of the extent of challenge a survivor of childhood adversity is facing, and level of tenacity and persistence needed to bring about change can significantly enhance one's empathy and therapeutic connection with the client.

From birth up to three years of age the right brain is more dominant, for facial recognition and pattern recognition. This is an essential part of development of capacities for communication and social bonds. In later childhood, the development of executive cognitive functioning – working memory, problem-solving, self-control, flexibility of thought (Diamond, 2013) – is promoted by increasingly complex educational and social experiences but built on these early foundations. In periods of stress the body is flooded with the stress hormone cortisol. Cortisol breaks down fat and protein to generate extra energy and draws the body's attention and resources away from the building and maintenance of essential structures, to manage immediate threats (Gerhardt, 2014). In short bursts, cortisol is extremely helpful, but when children's bodies are bathed in it, on a chronic basis, essential neurobiological developments are stalled, distorted, or corroded.

It is often not the conscious memory of traumatic events in childhood or the resultant thoughts and feelings, that are so impactful, as these may not even be available. Forgotten trauma lies in our nervous system, as the biological centres for threat perception are over-activated and the centres for emotional regulation and thinking are under-activated (Gerhardt, 2014).

Work to support healing from trauma must then seek to appreciate and address the essential role played by the body. (Van der Kolk, 2015). One way this can be implemented in therapeutic practice is to provide clients with accessible information about the bodily impacts of ACES (see resources).

Psychological Impacts

There is no one profile for the sequelae of childhood traumatic experience. However, there are some commonly experienced psychological effects which can be helpful to keep in mind when working with survivors.

People can struggle with hypervigilance as body and mind become permanently "on-guard" for signs of danger, leading to misinterpretation and exhaustion. It can be very hard to let go of behaviours that helped once but don't anymore. These behaviours are defence mechanisms that keep overwhelming anxiety at bay. Work in therapy must be slow, respectful and value the importance of these behaviours in the person's life.

Learning from one's experiences means that intimacy can feel dangerous and it is difficult to have faith in carer's capacities for "good-enough" protection and care. This can lead to very high levels of self-reliance and distrust of others. To protect themselves people can adopt a practice of self-constraint, managing what they say and do to avoid being noticeable (McLeod & Flood, 2018). At the other end of the continuum, individuals can find it hard to regulate their own emotional states leading to unpredictable, rapid, and intense changes in mood, in response to seemingly small triggers.

The ability to think about one's own thoughts and feelings can be negatively affected. It is hard to think about and attach meaning to traumatic experiences as the hurt may be too painful to bear, particularly if the development of emotional regulation skills has been disrupted. This can lead to avoidance of anything that symbolically represents traumatic experiences and unconscious repetition of difficulties. It can be difficult for individuals to imagine how others may feel or to name and express feelings directly, leading to powerful non-verbal communication that is outside of their awareness. For others, the opposite may be true, as becoming supremely skilled at reading imperceptible cues to predict the mental state of people around them may be lifesaving (Callaghan et al., 2015). Congruence and unconditional positive regard become so important here alongside the use of metacommunication, to ensure that the dialogue is continuously open about what is happening in the relationship, in the here and now.

Survival Behaviour and Coping Strategies

Expressing emotional upset and worry through challenging or changed behaviour is the developmentally normal way for CYP to communicate and cope with their difficulties, as they do not have fully developed language for emotional expression, or the cognitive skills needed to manage the stress they are experiencing. Problematic behaviour should be seen as holding information about how the child is feeling; seen in the context of what is happening in their life; and understood as functional (i.e. serving a purpose). When understood in this way, it becomes much easier to engage with CYP, and the adults they become, and to help them think about alternative ways of managing their distress.

Common coping behaviours that can challenge us as professionals often centre around the use of the adolescent body. Adolescence is a time of ordinary preoccupation with the body in the context of puberty. It is usual to use it as a site for acting out, communicating, or getting rid of complex and powerful feelings (Waddell, 2018). Examples include aggression towards others or self-harm. When young people are overwhelmed in the face of traumatic experiences, their sense of body and mind can become disconnected (Lemma, 2014). This unconscious split allows the body to become a site for angry, self-hateful impulses to be projected, which in turn can relieve internal conflicts, temporarily at least allowing enabling mental survival and a sense of control or mastery. Adolescent states of mind are often seen in adult survivors and are worked with very much in the same way, that is enabling mastery and choice wherever possible, not judging, being alongside and risk-assessing behaviour with no sense of control over the client.

Self-harm, aggression, and other acting-out behaviours should always prompt careful risk assessment, supervision, and where appropriate multi-professional liaison. However, this should not be at the expense of taking the time to work collaboratively with the person to develop a shared understanding of the meaning and function of their behaviours in the context of their biography and developmental stage.

Impact on Mental Health across the Life Course

Adolescence and Young Adulthood

Before accounting for the impact of any ACEs, the uncertainty of the physical changes of puberty along with the increased social and educational demands and responsibilities makes adolescence a time of higher risk of onset of mental health problems. However, significant mental distress in CYP is most commonly a response to what is happening within the systems in which they live. A study by Sidebotham et al. (2016) found almost two-thirds of the young people aged 11–15, and 88% of the older adolescents who had experienced domestic abuse, had mental health problems. The impacts of domestic abuse can make some tasks of ordinary adolescent development additionally complex. These include:

- Mourning of one's childhood and re-negotiating dependency relationships with adults, to move toward independence
- Identity development, including gender identity
- Psychosexual development, including how one relates to one's own body and perceives how it should be held and treated by others
- Managing the increased intensity of emotional and aggressive impulses that come with puberty, within a body that has newly developed power to act on them

Common mental health difficulties with onset in adolescence and associated with domestic abuse include:

- Low self-esteem/worth, guilt, and self-blame
- Anxiety
- Depression
- PTSD
- Suicidality
- Acute emotional dysregulation
- Displaying aggressive and/or socially challenging behaviours
- Medically unexplained physical health problems.

Associated difficulties with problem-solving skills, concentration, and memory can also impact on academic performance, which further exacerbates the above problems.

It cannot be stated strongly enough, that despite the risks outlined, adolescence is a uniquely important time of opportunity for intervention that can bring about long-lasting change. Adolescents are naturally primed by the neurobiopsychosocial changes of puberty for re-working what has gone before, in the service of growth and change. It is therefore important that the therapist has a good understanding of these impacts and is able to work with clients holding this knowledge and acceptance.

Into Adulthood

Adolescence is the gateway to adulthood. If young people are not offered opportunities and support at this point, then difficulties can follow into adulthood and become more fixed. Whilst it is never too late to help, the pace of work and of change in adulthood can be slower.

The neurodevelopmental impacts of traumatic experience in childhood are associated with a greater risk of major depressive disorder, anxiety, schizophrenia, and complex PTSD in adulthood. The cluster of symptoms under the psychiatric diagnoses known as personality disorders is directly associated with experiences of childhood trauma. These diagnoses indicate high, persistent, and complex need, and yet they are also labels that attract high levels of stigma or are used to exclude people from services (Lamb et al., 2018). Early intervention wherever possible is therefore essential. As is an understanding of the effects that childhood trauma can have on adults who do not receive this early intervention.

Implications of Providing Effective Psychological Approaches to Recovery for Survivors of Childhood Domestic Abuse

Understanding the developmental impacts of surviving violence and control leads to a recognition of four important dimensions that must be considered in therapeutic work:

1. The usual course of child development has been altered in ways that are complex and unique to each child/adult and their biography,
2. Surviving repeated potential and actual frightening events in childhood wires our bodies to be on-guard for even the smallest signs of danger, and prone to surging physiological sensation and emotion,
3. Clients may have very good reason to be distrustful of others, whilst also longing for a safe, trusting relationship with a helpful and attuned other,
4. The therapeutic relationship will inevitably evoke attachment behaviours that the client has used to survive in previous attachment relationships.

These challenges and the opportunity for growth and repair in the therapeutic relationship are two sides of the same coin.

Recognising that therapeutic work always evokes the person's experience of early care, and addressing the challenges that come with this, actively supports the development of a more compassionate and accepting sense of self for the client (Winnicott, 1971).

Rogers (in Kirschenbaum & Henderson, 1990) explains the organismic valuing process, where a baby can distinguish its likes, dislikes by itself with no outer influence, relying on its own locus of evaluation. Rogers' "locus of evaluation" simply means the place (locus) from where a value judgement is coming from. In babies the judgement is from their organismic self as there is no other "concept" of self. This changes over time, due to influence or "introjects" of the carers affecting the development of the self-concept. If a child grows up without unconditional positive regard or being loved for exactly who they are, there will be an incongruence between the self-concept and the organismic self, as the child tries to form themselves into a being that is acceptable to the carers or other voices of authority. An understanding of how to work with the child within the client (or the inner child) will be useful in most adult therapeutic relationships.

For this, therapists need to be aware of the acute stage of development adolescents are at in the transition to adulthood. The work of the self-concept and how it is forming at this stage is important as the young person tries to find their own way in the world or "individuation" (Geldard et al., 2019). Recognising the need for help at a time when you are trying to master the idea of independence can be difficult for all teenagers, and ambivalence about therapy is to be expected. For CYP and adults who are functioning with an insecure attachment style, seeking help can be a time of even greater distress and disorder and can engender shame and resistance in the therapy room.

Accepting that the client may need to keep "one foot in and one foot out" of the therapy room, especially at the beginning, can enable them to take a chance on work that could otherwise feel too intrusive. Building a relationship may be slow and gentle work and involve ways of communicating that allows the client to feel as if they are valued and respected in the relationship and, as part of humanistic counselling, that they are the ones directing the therapy.

Power dynamics are of extreme importance here as there is an immediate power difference between adults and CYP. Whether this is actual, in the case of CYP, or perceived in the case of adult survivors. therapists must balance this to reduce power over the client (Proctor, 2017).

Receiving good-enough care in the future can bring the realisation of what one has not had and can stir up intense feelings of anger towards the primary-carer who is not there. The current carer or therapist can find themselves on the end of very raw and powerful feelings. This means that the therapist needs to continuously reflect, work on self-awareness, think about their scope of practice, use clinical supervision to carefully work through their experiences in the therapeutic relationship and above all prioritise self-care (see also chapters 5 and 14).

Use of Play and Expressive Approaches

The central tenant of counselling, building a therapeutic relationship, is often forged with children through play. Play is an important factor when working with children as it is the medium through which they learn and make sense of the world around them (Axline, 1981; Jennings, 2017).

Where an adult's difficulty can be traced to a childhood period, it can also be helpful to explore this through play, helping the client to access and reflect on experiences, thoughts, and feelings which may never have been encoded into adult language or verbal expression. Play, such as sand tray work, can be highly effective with adults as well as children and allow both to explore and "act out" events in a safe and controlled way (Lowenfeld, 2005).

The walls of the sand tray (a rectangular box, often blue in colour to represent water under the sand) literally contain the action and help the client to explore in a safe way, some deep and troubling emotions. All sorts of enactments can happen in the sand tray – battles, fights, reconciliations. The sand allows for tactile and sensory motion allowing connection of both body and mind, where not only stories are built, but memories can resurface. See chapter 13 for an example of sandtray work.

"*Play is to the child what verbalisation is to the adult*" (Landreth, 2012) and often in survivors of childhood trauma, a part that may have been missing in their lives due to the circumstances they have been in can be accessed. Play is an essential part of socialisation, that needs to happen throughout childhood, into adulthood, to encourage imagination, creativity, and development of self (Winnicott, 1971). Playing is communication and as part of therapy, helps to build trust in both the therapist and the client themself. It also helps clients gain some element of control (or mastery) over events that can be deeply traumatising. Creative play encourages the development of the right brain to process and integrate feelings and memories (Siegel, 2012).

If the therapy room has creative materials in it a client may reach out for them without thinking and start to use what is available. For instance, picking up coloured pens to doodle with as they talk or even, eventually, use as a conversation between two people as in Winnicott's squiggle game (Winnicott, 1971); reaching their hands into the sand tray and touching the sand; picking up miniatures, gently starting to explore with sensory motion to help tap into emotion. Emotion/feelings cards or symbols/archetypes (Jung, 1991) can be useful for both CYP and adults (age appropriate for each) and encourage collaborative working. See chapter 13 for more on creative interventions

Useful Resources

Child Development

Bee, H, L. & Boyd. D.A., 2011. *The Developing Child.* London: Pearson Education Limited.

Attachment Theory

https://learning.nspcc.org.uk/child-health-development/attachment-early-years

Complex Trauma

Blue Knott foundation: National Centre of Excellence of Complex Trauma, Australia: https://blueknot.org.au/

Key Learning Points

This chapter outlines a dynamic developmental approach to working with clients who have experienced domestic abuse in childhood. The key elements are:

1. The usual course of child development has been altered in ways that are complex and unique to each person and their biography.
2. Take the time to come to a detailed understanding of the specifics for each individual, and to meet clients where they are developmentally speaking, rather than based on expectations related to their chronological age.
3. Develop a foundational understanding of child development and the impact of ACES upon neuro-psycho-social development.
4. Focus on supporting clients with getting back on track with their developmental trajectory.
5. Forging therapeutic alliances that create the conditions for growth and reparation is at the heart of supporting people who have survived ACES.
6. ACES do not only produce vulnerability, but also resistance and skill. Use a strengths-based approach, based on deep respect and appreciation for the client's coping strategies and survivorhood.
7. Work with all ages needs to integrate the usual ways that CYP communicate and learn, through play, creative, and expressive activities.
8. Working within competency as a therapist and knowing when they need to refer on is an important part of this complex work.
9. Using supervision to develop self-awareness, appreciation of the transference dynamics and prioritising self-care are central components to develop practice in this area.

References

Axline, V. M. (1981). *Play therapy*. New York: Ballantine Books.

BACP (2019). Children and young people competence framework. https://www.bacp.co.uk/media/5863/bacp-cyp-competence-framework.pdf

Bancroft, L., Silverman, J., & Ritchie D. (2012). *The batterer as parent: Addressing the impact of domestic violence on family dynamics* (2nd edition) Thousand Oaks, CA: Sage.

Bickham, V. (2017). Focus on families: Risk, threat and toxic trio. Safe Lives. https://safelives.org.uk/node/1058

Bowlby, J. (1988). *A secure base: Parent-child attachment and healthy human development*. New York: Basic Books.

Callaghan, J., Alexander, J., Sixsmith, J., & Fellin, L. (2015). Beyond "witnessing": Children's experiences of coercive control in domestic violence and abuse. *Journal of Interpersonal Violence, 33*(10), 1551–1581.

Diamond, A. (2013). Executive functions. *Annual Review Psychology, 64*, 135–168. doi:10.1146/annurev-psych-113011-143750

Garland, C. (2018). *Understanding trauma: A psychoanalytical approach*. London: Routledge.

Geldard, K., Geldard, D., & Foo, R. Y. (2019). *Counselling adolescents: The proactive approach*. London: SAGE.

Gerhardt, S. (2014). *Why love matters: How affection shapes a baby's brain*. London: Routledge.

Haight, W., Shim, W., Linn, L., & Swinford, L. (2007). Mothers' strategies for protecting children from batterers: The perspectives of battered women involved in child protective services. *Child Welfare, 86*(4), 41–62.

Hughes, K., Bellis, M. A., Hardcastle, K. A., et al. (2017). The effect of multiple adverse childhood experiences on health: A systematic review and meta-analysis. *The Lancet Public Health, 2*(8), e356–e366.

Jennings., S. (2017). *Creative play with children at risk*. London: Routledge.

Jung, C. G. (1991). *The archetypes and the collective unconscious*. London: Routledge.

Kirschenbaum, H., & Henderson, V. L. (1990). *The Carl Rogers Reader*. London: Constable.

Lamb, N., Sibbald, S., & Stirzaker, A. (2018). Shining lights in dark corners of people's lives: Reaching consensus for people with complex mental health difficulties who are given a diagnosis of personality disorder. *Crim. Behav. & Mental Health, 28*, 1.

Landreth, G. L. (2012). *Play therapy: The art of the relationship*. 3rd edition. Abingdon-on-Thames: Routledge.

Lemma, A. (2014). Trauma and the body. In: *Minding the body: The body in psychoanalysis and beyond*. Routledge. 10.4324/9781315758824.

Lowenfeld, M. (2005). *Understanding children's sandplay. Lowenfeld's world technique*. Eastbourne: Sussex Academic Press.

McLeod, D., & Flood, S. (2018). Coercive control: Impacts on children and young people in the family environment: Literature Review (2018). Dartington: *Research in Practice*.

Proctor, G. (2017) *The dynamics of power in counselling and psychotherapy*. Monmouth: PCCS Books Ltd.

Sidebotham, P., Brandon, M., Bailey, S., Belderson, P., Dodsworth, J., Garstang, J., Harrison, E., Retzer, A., & Sorensen, P. (2016). *Pathways to harm, pathways to protection: A triennial analysis of serious case reviews 2011 to 2014: Final report*. University of East Anglia & University of Warwick for the Department of Education. ISBN: 978-1-78105-601-1

Siegel, D. J. (2012). *The developing mind: How relationships and the brain interact to shape who we are, second edition*. New York: The Guildford Press.

Van der Kolk, B. (2015). *The body keeps the score*. UK: Penguin, Random House.
Waddell, M. (2018). *On adolescence: Inside stories*. Routledge, Karnac Books. ISBN: 1782205268.
Williams, G. (2005). Double deprivation. In M. Bower (Ed.), *Psychoanalytic theory for social work practice, thinking under fire*. London: Routledge.
Winnicott, D. (1971). *Playing and reality*. London: Tavistock Publications.
Winnicott, D. W. (1984). *The maturational processes and the facilitating environment: Studies in the theory of emotional development*. Routledge.

Chapter 10

Compassionate Mind Training

Elaine Beaumont

Learning Objectives

1. To explore the theoretical underpinnings of the compassionate mind model
2. To examine how cultivating compassion can help people who have experienced DA
3. To develop an understanding of the threat, drive, and soothing systems
4. To develop an understanding of some of the competencies that support engagement with distress and key areas for action
5. To use practical exercises to gain an understanding of some of the key skills of compassion
6. To create a Pre, During, and After Plan

Overview

The cultivation of compassion has been found to be a significant factor in client recovery from domestic abuse (DA), both in receiving compassion from the therapist and in offering compassion to themselves and others (Roddy, 2014). Whilst there are elements of how compassion can be developed, used, and applied throughout this book, this chapter aims to help practitioners develop knowledge regarding some of the core theoretical elements of Compassionate Mind Training (CMT) and Compassion Focused Therapy (CFT). This can then provide a core model for compassion in work with survivors: including exploration of the evolved nature of the human mind, how a sense of self is created through an interaction between genetics and social experience, and how cultivating compassion for one's own suffering can help people who have experienced DA. Symptoms of trauma include shame, self-criticism, self-blame, and guilt, which can have a debilitating impact on people who have experienced DA (see also chapters 6 and 7).

Experiential and reflective exercises are incorporated either the chapter to help facilitate learning. The chapter focuses on how people can respond to suffering with a compassionate motivation.

DOI: 10.4324/9781003253266-10

Working with people who have experienced trauma can also have an impact on practitioners (see also chapter 14). Therefore, this chapter also aims to help practitioners reflect and cultivate compassion for their own struggles, which in turn may help build resilience, and reduce self-critical judgement.

Rationale

CFT and CMT were initially designed to help people who experienced high levels of self-criticism and shame by responding to their self-critic with self-supportive inner voices (Gilbert, 2009; 2010; 2014; 2020). With roots in attachment theory (Bowlby, 1973), Buddhist philosophy, neuroscience, and evolutionary psychology, CFT is a psychotherapy used in therapeutic settings, which includes using CMT. CFT and CMT use contemplative, imaginal, and body-based practices to help people cultivate compassion (Beaumont, Bell, McAndrew & Fairhurst, 2021; Gilbert, 2009; 2020).

Survivors of DA often experience shame, guilt, and high levels of self-criticism (Buchbinder & Eisikovits, 2003) (see also chapter 3) and struggle to show compassion or kindness to themselves. Some people who have experienced DA may use self-blame (e.g. "it's my fault") as a coping protective strategy, believing that self-blame will not trigger the perpetrator. While self-blame may be seen as an effective tool to decrease conflict by reducing the perpetrators abusive behaviour, it can have a negative impact on well-being, and is associated with increased risk of post-traumatic stress disorder (PTSD) and symptoms of depression and anxiety (Tesh et al., 2013).

There has been an increase in research studies in recent years, which focus on exploring whether individuals can learn to cultivate compassion for self and others by engaging in CMT. Cultivating compassion for one's own suffering has been found to help people who have experienced trauma (Beaumont et al., 2012; Beaumont et al., 2016; Karatzias et al., 2019; Lawrence & Lee, 2014; Leaviss & Uttley, 2015; Lee & James, 2012). Compassion training has been found to have a variety of benefits including; improving mood, levels of compassion, and general well-being (Beaumont, Irons & McAndrew 2022; Irons & Heriot-Maitland, 2021; Neff 2009; Neff et al., 2007; Neely et al., 2009; Seppälä et al., 2017; Van Dam et al. 2011), reducing symptoms associated with depression, anxiety, and stress (Gilbert, 2017; 2019; Kelly & Tasca, 2016; Kirby 2016; Kirby et al., 2017; Macbeth & Gumley, 2012; Seligowski et al., 2014) and reduced psychiatric symptoms, interpersonal problems, and personality pathology (Schanche et al., 2011). These are all symptoms that people experiencing DA can experience.

Compassion training has also been linked to positive changes in the functioning of the autonomic nervous system, particularly the vagus nerve (Di Bello et al., 2020) and has been found to lead to changes in neurophysiological responses in the brain (Kim et al., 2020). People with higher levels of self-compassion are also more likely to reach out for social support, which is important for people experiencing DA (Heath et al., 2016).

The Three Emotional Systems

Gilbert's (2009; 2010) model proposes that CFT and CMT can bring balance to our three emotional systems: the *threat, drive,* and *soothing systems* (see Figure 10.1).

The threat system is motivated to protect, detect and respond to losses. This system alerts and directs attention to things that are threatening (Gilbert, 2014) by activating the fight-flight system, triggering a freeze, faint, or play dead response or shutting down – a demobilisation (helplessness) (Gilbert & Simos, 2022). The threat system responds by triggering physiological changes in the body and brain. This stress response prepares the body for danger by activating the sympathetic nervous system and hypothalamic-pituitary adrenal axis (see also Chapter 8). Rumination, "what if" thoughts, threat-based images, flashbacks, fear, anxiety, anger, and disgust can trigger the threat system.

The drive system is activated when joy and/or excitement are experienced. Its function is to energize and to pursue resources that are advantageous; food, social status, relationships, and sexual partners (Irons & Beaumont, 2017). When activated we experience positive emotions, which reinforce behaviour.

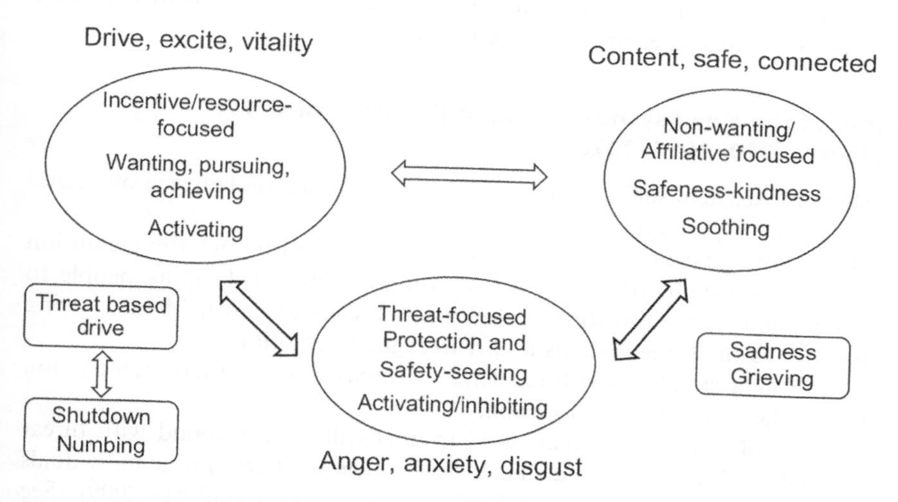

Figure 10.1 The three functions of emotion: Adapted from Gilbert 2009 © Paul Gilbert. Figure 10.1 From Gilbert (2022). An evolution-informed, biopsychosocial approach to psychotherapy: history and challenges. Adapted from Gilbert (2009) The Compassionate Mind with permission from Little, Brown Book Group.

Both the threat and drive systems are essential for survival and reproduction, but if over activated can impact negatively on well-being and mood.

The soothing system helps to bring balance to the three systems and helps us to rest, slow down, and recuperate. This system is linked to the parasympathetic nervous system, which plays an important role in calming and regulating the threat and drive systems (see also chapter 8).

Asking people to draw their three circles at the beginning of therapy is really helpful. The threat system would probably be the largest system and the soothing system the smallest. The aim is to bring balance to all three systems.

Reflection: Use the worksheet to help you explore what triggers your threat, drive, and soothing system.

How often is each system triggered?
What tends to trigger each system?
How long does each system stay activated for once triggered?
How powerfully do you experience this system when triggered? (if 1 is weakly, and 10 powerfully)
What type of thoughts do you have when in this system?
What do you want to do when this system is triggered?

From Irons & Beaumont, The Compassionate Mind Workbook: A step-by-step guide to cultivating your compassionate self (2017), reprinted with kind permission from Little, Brown Book Group

Some of the Key Psycho-Education Elements of CMT (Gilbert, 2010; 2014; 2020)

- How our sense of self is created through the interaction between our genes and social experiences.
- Discussion regarding evolution and the role played by our three emotion regulation systems (threat, drive, soothing) is crucial. Helping people to understand that cultivating a compassionate mind can help them bring balance to the three systems and help regulate emotion.
- That compassion flows in three ways – compassion for others, compassion from others, and self-compassion.
- That people who have experienced trauma will often respond with threat emotions, self-criticism, and shame. Self-critical or shame prone individuals are sensitized towards having a dominant threat system (Gilbert, 2009). (See also chapter 6).
- That much of what goes on in the mind is "not our fault." People who experience traumatic events are vulnerable to a variety of problems that impact on well-being (e.g. fear arousal, rumination, self-criticism, shame).

- Fears, blocks, and resistances (FBRs) are important aspects of the model. Fears of compassion relate to compassion being seen as weak, self-indulgent, or self-pitying. Blocks to compassion relate to situational factors or time pressures, whereas resistances occur when people do not want to engage in compassion, maybe because they do not think they deserve it (Gilbert & Mascaro, 2017; Irons & Beaumont, 2017; Steindl et al., 2022) or they find it difficult to relate to their experiences.

Three Core Qualities of Compassion

According to Gilbert (2014) compassion is "*a sensitivity to the suffering in self and others, with a commitment to try to alleviate and prevent it*" (p. 19). There are three core qualities of compassion:

1. Wisdom – the compassionate self is wise and has an understanding about the nature of suffering. They understand the difficulties you experience in life and are able to offer helpful perspectives on those difficulties.
2. Caring-commitment – the compassionate self has a caring motivation and commitment to you. It does not criticize; it wants to support you and help you take responsibility for your difficulties.
3. Strength and courage – the compassionate self is strong and courageous and has a sense of authority and confidence. They are able to tolerate distress and difficulties and will always be there to support you.

Competencies that Support Engagement with Distress and Key Areas for Wise and Courageous Actions

Figure 10.2 examines Gilbert's (2022) domains for therapeutic engagement. Gilbert suggests that there are six competencies that support our engagement with distress (the inner circle: *sensitivity, sympathy, distress tolerance, empathy,* being *non-judgemental* and demonstrating *care for well-being)* and six key areas for wise and courageous actions (outer circle: *attention, imagery, reasoning* and *thinking, behaviour, sensory focusing* and *feeling*). Together the domains for therapeutic engagement give rise to commitment, courage, and wisdom to acknowledge and address suffering. Previously Gilbert (2009) referred to these competencies as the "first psychology of compassion" (inner circle) and "second psychology of compassion" (outer circle).

You can see here a clear overlap of the skills and qualities of CMT and CFT with the competency framework developed for working with DA clients (Roddy and Gabriel, 2019). The ability to offer a compassionate space is both helpful and important to working with this client group.

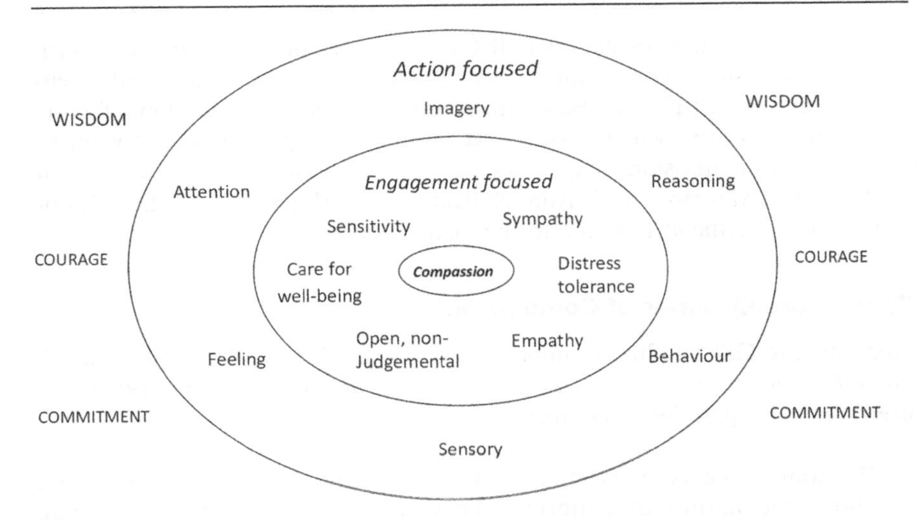

Figure 10.2 From Gilbert (2022). In, P. Gilbert & G. Simos. (eds). Compassion Focused Therapy: Clinical practice and applications (p. 243-272). London Routledge. Adapted from Gilbert (2009) The Compassionate Mind with permission from Little, Brown Book Group.

Both CMT and CFT aim to develop the skills required using a variety of exercises, which include:

- Breathing exercises, which aim to activate the parasympathetic nervous system (e.g. Soothing Rhythm Breathing)
- Attention and mindfulness training (e.g. mindful listening, mindful walking, and mindful eating)
- Using memory (e.g. remembering times when we have been in receipt of compassion or showed compassion to another being)
- Imagery (e.g. creating a calm, soothing place in the mind)
- Experiencing compassion as a flow (e.g. cultivating self-compassion, receiving compassion from others, and offering compassion to others)
- Developing the compassionate self by using method acting techniques and by working with the body, senses, and breathing (e.g. using the mind, body posture, voice tones, and facial expression to cultivate compassion)
- Creating an "Ideal Compassionate Other" (e.g. a compassionate image of another being, animal or part of nature – someone or something that has our best interests at heart)
- Compassionate letter writing
- Exploration of our multiple selves and bringing compassion to self-criticism

In the next sections, we will practice and reflect on some of the skills of compassion (for a comprehensive overview of exercises, practices, theory, worksheets, and case studies see Irons and Beaumont, 2017 and for a comprehensive overview of the clinical practice and applications of compassion see Gilbert and Simos, 2022).

Attention

We can train our attention – it can be moved just like a spotlight. Strengthening "our attention muscles" can lead to benefits both for physical and mental health (Beaumont & Welford, 2020; Irons & Beaumont, 2017). When we train our attention, we begin to realize that our minds easily wander and when we notice this happening, we can gently re-focus our attention using our breath, sound, and our body as an anchor for our mind. Using exercises such as mindfulness of sound may help people who have experienced DA dampen down some of the effects of trauma and hyperarousal. The following example demonstrates how we can use sound as the anchor for our attention.

Mindfulness of Sound

From Irons & Beaumont, The Compassionate Mind Workbook: A step-by-step guide to cultivating your compassionate self (2017), reprinted with kind permission from Little, Brown Book Group

Find a comfortable place to sit and adopt an upright posture. For 30 seconds or so, just become aware of your body sitting in the chair, and for a moment or so, become aware of your breath as it moves in and out of your body.

When you feel ready, see if you can slowly allow your attention to broaden away from your body. Start to become aware of the sounds that you can hear around you. To start with, try not to reach out to the sounds, but rather be receptive as they arise and disappear around you. Let them come to you – you are in this moment, just paying attention to the sound as it arises. Become aware of the direction they arise in, and their nature – what their character is, volume, tone, pitch or whether they are constant or intermittent. Try to notice when your mind has become distracted. This might be by thoughts or concerns that pop into your mind or emotional reactions to the sounds – try, to the best of your ability, to bring your mind back to noticing the sounds around you again.

For 60 seconds or so, see if you can focus your attention more purposefully on one sound that you can hear around you. Really try to use this as an anchor for your attention. Notice with curiosity the nature and characteristics of this sound and return to the sound if your mind wanders.

After a while try to pull back from focusing on this sound and see if you can split your attention and notice or become aware of all of the sounds you can hear around you, so that no sound is paid more attention to than others. Repeat this process, focusing on just one sound for a period, and then pulling the focus back to become aware of all sounds.

Reflection: How did it feel to use sound as an anchor for your mind and attention? If you noticed your mind wandered, were you able to bring your attention back to the sounds around you? How could you use this with a client? What would you need to consider? Remember when we do notice our mind has wandered this is helpful because we develop an understanding that this is what minds do (attention drifts away). The key is to just kindly and gently return the focus to the exercise without judgement.

Compassionate Sensory Focusing

Focusing on senses (e.g. touch, sound, smell, sight, and taste) can help stimulate the soothing system and slow our minds and bodies down. Using our senses and bodily focus can be helpful in regulating distress as we connect with our soothing system. The way we breathe, for example, has a powerful impact on our well-being because it can help our bodies and mind slow down. Actors, singers, and people involved in sports use their breath and bodies in a way that helps them deliver their best performance.

The way we breathe influences our nervous system triggers a variety of emotions and impacts on our behaviour and thinking patterns. When we create a soothing breathing rhythm our parasympathetic nervous system is triggered, which helps regulate heart rate and slow down our mind and body. Using this exercise with people who have experienced DA can be beneficial, especially if they present with high levels of anxiety.

Have a go at the next exercise, which aims to help slow down your breathing.

Learning to Slow Down – How to Slow Your Breathing

From Irons & Beaumont, The Compassionate Mind Workbook: A step-by-step guide to cultivating your compassionate self (2017), reprinted with kind permission from Little, Brown Book Group

Find a quiet and comfortable place to sit. Take a moment to embody a grounded, upright, confident posture. If you feel comfortable, close your eyes. If not, rest your gaze directly ahead of yourself, with your head in an alert, upright position.

Begin by bringing your attention to your breathing in a mindful way. Notice the sensations present as you breathe in and out. If you notice that your attention becomes distracted, and moves away from your breath, just observe this, and gently try to bring your attention back to your breath, without judging or criticizing yourself that this has happened.

Now, as you're gently holding your attention in the flow of your breath, gently try and bring a soothing or calming rhythm of breathing to your body. This is likely to be a slower and deeper rhythm than usual, but one that feels comfortable and natural to your body. Try if you can to breathe in a smooth, even way. If you notice your attention moving away from your breath, or that you become distracted in any way, gently bring your attention back to your breath and tune back in to the calming or soothing quality of your breathing rhythm.

Now, see if you can slow your breathing down a little further. Sometimes it can be worth counting your breath to start with. For example, try breathing in for a count of five, with each count representing a second. Once you've got to five, hold for one second before breathing out for five seconds (again counting to five as you do so). Hold for the count of one, before breathing in again to the count of five.

Out-breath 1 – 2 – 3 – 4 – 5
Hold 1
In-breath 1 – 2 – 3 – 4 – 5
Hold 1
Out-breath 1 – 2 – 3 – 4 – 5
Hold 1
In-breath 1 – 2 – 3 – 4 – 5
Continue – roughly in this rhythm – for another two or three minutes, staying connected with your soothing rhythm breathing.

When you're ready, widen your awareness to the room around you … notice the sounds in the room and bring yourself to the present moment.

Reflection: What was your experience of slowing down your breathing rhythm? What did you notice about your thoughts, physical sensations and feelings? What future stressful situations could be helped by doing this exercise? How could you use this with a client? What would you first need to consider? For example, you may need to check in regarding their physical health. Do they have a breathing condition (e.g. asthma).

The aim is to engage the soothing system to help us be alongside difficult experiences when they arrive. However, it is always worth practising these exercises when we are OK as this can help us prepare for stressful or difficult situations. Repeating phrases in the mind such as "mind slowing down" and "body slowing down" can also help people find a steady, calm breathing rhythm.

Many people find it helpful to use their phones or computers to help them with these types of exercises. It may be useful for you to record this type of exercise for clients to use outside of therapy. Alternatively, many people find breathing apps useful in helping them slow down. The Self-Compassion App https://www.selfcompassion.me/ is a 28-day app that focuses on the techniques, theory, principles, and practices of CFT and CMT (Beaumont, Irons & Psychological Technologies, 2020).

Imagery

Creating a calm, peaceful place in our mind can help slow down and potentially soothe the traumatized mind. Have a go at the next exercise that focuses on creating a calm, peaceful, relaxing, or soothing place.

My calming, peaceful, relaxing, or soothing place

From Beaumont and Welford, The Kindness Workbook: Creative and Compassionate Ways to Boost Your Wellbeing (2020), reprinted with kind permission from Little, Brown Book Group

1. Once you've found somewhere to sit and have settled your mind and body, gently bring your attention to your breathing, becoming mindful of it. Notice the sensations as you breathe slowly in and slowly out. Feel your body begin to relax slightly as you breathe a little slower and deeper than usual. Let your shoulders drop and your jaw loosen.
2. Allow an image to form that's calming, peaceful, relaxing, or soothing in some way. You may have been to this place, but it doesn't matter if you haven't – it can be somewhere you've created in your mind or that you've seen in magazines or on TV.
3. Don't worry if no image comes to mind straight away. Just gently try and allow an image to form that's special to you.
4. When your mind has settled on an image, spend a couple of minutes paying attention to what you can see.
5. Now spend some time noticing what you can hear in your special place. Notice the different qualities of the sounds and how they make you feel.
6. Are there any soothing or comforting smells present?
7. Spend some time noticing any physical sensations. Is there anything in your image that you want to touch? You may wish to feel sand, super-soft carpet, water, or grass under your feet. You may notice the warmth of the sun on your face or a gentle breeze blowing through your hair.
8. Now notice whether you're on your own in your calming, peaceful, relaxing, or soothing place. Would you like to have somebody or something (perhaps an animal) with you?

9 Imagine that this place has an awareness of you. For a few moments, just imagine that the place you have chosen is really delighted to see you. How does it feel to know that this is your very own place and its only purpose is to help and support you?

10 Is there anything else you would like to do? You may want just to be still, or you may imagine you're walking or swimming. You may want to have fun on a swing, play a game or just relax in a hammock. This is your special place and you can use it in any way that helps you to feel at ease.

With the knowledge that you can return to this exercise and experience your calming, peaceful, relaxing, or soothing place at any time, gently bring the exercise to a close and widen your awareness to the chair that's supporting you and the room that you're in. If your eyes have been closed, open them: lift your gaze. Take some calming breaths and maybe have a stretch before moving on to the reflective exercise.

You will find a recording of this audio in the download resources section on *The Overcoming Website* https://overcoming.co.uk/678/The-Kindness-Workbook

Reflection: What was it like to create an image of a calm, relaxing, peaceful or soothing place? What could you see, hear, touch and smell? What physical sensations did you notice? What did you do? What was it like to be welcomed by this place? How could you use this with clients? What would you need to consider and how could you address any concerns? For example, research suggests that between 2% - 5% of the population experience aphantasia (are unable to visualise images in their mind) and therefore this exercise could trigger a threat response rather than soothing system response.

Compassionate Thinking and Reasoning

When we worry or ruminate our threat system is activated. This often involves self-critical judgement rather than self-compassionate inner self-talk. Therefore, it can be useful to help people who have experienced DA generate supportive and compassionate statements. Have a look at the examples which focus on learning to demonstrate empathy for distress, compassionate attention, compassionate thinking, and compassionate behaviour:

It's understandable that I'm finding change difficult. Other people have experienced this type of situation and have also found it difficult.

It is understandable that I feel like this (e.g. sad, angry, afraid, disgusted).

I'm proud of myself for noticing when my threat system is activated. When it is activated, I'm likely to have self-critical thoughts and potentially biased 'all or nothing' thoughts.

There are people who are trying to support me and do care about me and want to help me.

Reaching out to friends, people at work or family members may help me or may help me come to terms with this situation.

Body language, voice tone, and inner dialogue (supportive inner voice) can also have an impact on well-being. Changing our body posture for example can have an impact on our feelings and can either stimulate the threat system (e.g. folded arms, shoulders in a crunching position), which can increase anxiety and tension. An open, upright body posture and even a friendly facial expression, on the other hand, can help you feel more confident and grounded. Asking clients to think about what they would say to a friend or someone they cared about who is in a similar situation may encourage them to learn to be kinder to themselves.

Compassionate Feelings

In chapter 4, we talked about how helpful it can be to name feelings for a client when they appear unaware of them. As therapy progresses, or if the client is already aware of their own feelings, helping the client to notice, identify, and name their emotions can help us both to understand:

1. How the body responds to different emotions (e.g. our heart rate may change, our fists may clench, our voice tone may change, or we may feel sick)?
2. How often do we experience particular emotions (e.g. do we experience one emotion more than another or notice that we do not experience a particular emotion)?
3. What happens to thought processes when we experience difficult emotions (e.g. thoughts may include *"It's my fault," "what will other people think,"* and/or *"nobody cares for me")*?
4. How we behave or what we want to do or not do (e.g. anxiety may cause someone to hide away, fear might mean we avoid situations, anger may cause someone to lash out or hurt themselves)?

Reflection: Noticing and naming emotions can help us to learn to regulate and express how we feel. It could be helpful to explore the following:

- Imagine you are at your compassionate best. How could your compassionate self, help you express how you feel?

- Would it help to write about how you feel, record a video diary, use music or art to help you express emotions?
- Would it help to practice talking about how you feel out loud whilst looking in the mirror?
- How can you show compassion to the part of you that is struggling? What do you need in this moment?

If people struggle to express their feelings, they may find it helpful to observe how others communicate and express their emotions. For example, perhaps your client could observe the body language, voice tone, and the facial expression of other people who they believe are compassionate (e.g. this could be a character from TV, a friend, or colleague). Clients may also learn from you when you share congruently the emotions you experience from listening to their stories.

Preparing for Challenging Situations – Pre, During, and After (PDA) Plans

PDA plans (not to be confused with public displays of affection) are often used in sports to help people prepare for an event, game, or match. For example, footballers prepare for matches by taking penalties over and over again, and tennis players practice serves and winning shots before a match. Pre the event, an athlete would eat certain foods, create a plan, warm up, and stretch their body, and they may also imagine or visualize themselves crossing the finishing line of the race in first position.

We can use PDA plans to help prepare ourselves for challenges (Irons & Beaumont, 2017). For example, before anxiety-provoking situations we can use exercises that slow down our mind and body, we can be mindful of our self-talk. Using supportive inner dialogue, such as "you've got this" or "you're doing the best you can right now" can also be helpful. In relation to DA, PDA plans could be used to help people plan for difficult situations such as meeting with ex-partners to pick up or drop off children, preparing for court hearings, or having difficult conversations with ex-partners about finances.

Creating a soothing rhythm breathing rate, imagining a calm, relaxing, or soothing place, and/or creating a list of supportive statements after the challenge can also help as it gives us an opportunity to reflect on things that went well. This also gives us the chance to ask "what would I like to try in the future."

The PDA plan Table 10.1 could also include holding a soothing object (e.g. shiny stone or something comforting), writing a compassionate letter, or looking at photographs of loved ones that boost mood before, during, or after the challenge. Just like in sport, people may not always get the desired outcome, but the act of preparation is important in itself. Regardless of the outcome it is important to recognize good intentions. Remind your client (and yourself) that you tried. It takes courage when we face challenges.

Table 10.1 A Pre, During, and After (PDA) Plan

Difficult situation	*Pre*	*During*	*After*

Summary

In this chapter we have explored strategies that aim to cultivate compassion. You have been introduced to some of the practices and skills used in CFT and CMT and you have had the opportunity to practice and explore some of the techniques and skills aimed at cultivating a compassionate mind. Providing a secure base in counselling and psychotherapy fosters the conditions needed to help people who have experienced DA bring balance to their threat, drive, and soothing systems.

You have also spent time reflecting on how you can cultivate a compassionate mind. As you move forward, hold in mind the importance of practitioner self-care and self-reflection. People working in the helping professions often have very high levels of compassion for others, which is essential in our line of work, but it is also important to focus on self-care and compassion for self (Beaumont & Hollins Martin, 2016). We will explore this further in chapter 14.

Key Learning Points

In this chapter we have explored how we can help clients cultivate compassion for their own suffering. Some of the key elements of the CFT model we have explored are:

1 The theoretical underpinnings and philosophy of the model
2 Understanding the threat, drive, and soothing systems and how DA impacts on the three systems
3 The competencies that support our engagement with distress which include sensitivity, sympathy, distress tolerance, empathy, being non-judgemental, and demonstrating care for well-being
4 The three core qualities of compassion – wisdom, caring commitment, and strength and courage

5 The key skills of compassion which include compassionate attention, imagery, reasoning, behaviour, feeling, and sensory focusing
6 Experiential exercises including attending to sound, creating a calm place, focusing on a slower breathing rhythm, and creating a PDA plan
7 Being mindful of your own well-being and cultivating compassion for your own struggles and challenges.

References

Beaumont, E, Bell, T, McAndrew, S, & Fairhurst, H (2021). The impact of compassionate mind training on qualified health professionals undertaking a compassion-focused therapy module. *Counselling and Psychotherapy Research*, 21, 910–92210.1002/capr.12396.

Beaumont, E., Durkin, M., McAndrew, S., & Martin, C. (2016). Using compassion focused therapy as an adjunct to trauma-focused CBT for fire service personnel suffering with trauma-related symptoms. *The Cognitive Behaviour Therapist, 9*, e34, 1–13. 10.1017/S1754470X16000209

Beaumont, E., Galpin, A., & Jenkins, P. (2012). 'Being kinder to myself:' A prospective comparative study, exploring post-trauma therapy outcome measures, for two groups of clients, receiving either Cognitive Behaviour Therapy or Cognitive Behaviour Therapy and Compassionate Mind Training. *Counselling Psychology Review, 27*, 31–43

Beaumont, E., & Hollins Martin, C. J. (2016). A proposal to support student therapists to develop compassion for self and others through compassionate mind training. *The Arts in Psychotherapy, 50*, 111–118

Beaumont, E., Irons, C., & McAndrew, S. (2022). A qualitative study evaluating the impact The Self-Compassion App has on levels of compassion and wellbeing. *OBM Integrative and Complementary Medicine*. 7(3), 23. https://www.lidsen.com/journals/icm/icm-07-03-045

Beaumont, E., Irons, C., & Psychological Technologies (PSYT) (2020). The Self-Compassion App. https://www.selfcompassion.me/

Beaumont. E. & Welford, M. (2020). *The kindness workbook: Compassionate and creative ways to boost your wellbeing*. London: Little, Brown Book Group

Bowlby, J. (1973). *Attachment and loss, vol. II: Separation* (Vol. 2). New York: Basic Books.

Buchbinder, E., & Eisikovits, Z. (2003). Battered women's entrapment in shame: A phenomenological study. *American Journal of Orthopsychiatry, 73*(4), 355–366. doi: 10.1037/0002-9432.73.4.355

Di Bello, M., Carnevali, L., Petrocchi, N., Thayer, J. F., Gilbert, P., & Ottaviani, C. (2020). The compassionate vagus: a meta-analysis on the connection between compassion and heart rate variability. *Neuroscience & Biobehavioral Reviews, 116*, 21–30.

Gilbert, P. (2009). *The compassionate mind: A new approach to facing the challenges of life*. London, UK: Constable Robinson

Gilbert, P. (2010). *Compassion focused therapy: Distinctive features*. Hove, UK: Routledge

Gilbert, P. (2014). The origins and nature of compassion focused therapy. *British Journal of Clinical Psychology*, *53*(1), 6–41
Gilbert, P. (Ed.). (2017). *Compassion: Concepts, research and applications*. Taylor & Francis.
Gilbert, P. (2020). Compassion: From its evolution to a psychotherapy. *Frontiers in Psychology*, *11*, 3123
Gilbert, P. (2022). Introducing and developing compassion functions and competencies. In Gilbert, P., & Simos, G. (eds). *Compassion Focused Therapy: Clinical practice and applications*. pp. 243–272. London: Routledge.
Gilbert, P., & Simos, G. (2022) (eds). *Compassion Focused Therapy: Clinical practice and applications*. London: Routledge.
Heath, P. J., Brenner, R. E., Lannin, D. G., & Bogel, D. L. (2016). Self-compassion moderates the relationship of perceived public and anticipated self-stigma of seeking help. *Stigma and Health*, 1–5. doi: 10.1037/sah0000072
Irons, C., & Beaumont, E. (2017). *The compassionate mind workbook: A step-by-step guide to developing your compassionate self*. London: Little, Brown Book Group
Irons C., & Heriot-Maitland C. (2021). Compassionate mind training: An 8-week group for the general public. *Psychol Psychother*, *94*, 443–463.
Karatzias, T., Murphy, P., Cloitre, M., Bisson, J., Roberts, N., Shevlin, M., ... & Hutton, P. (2019). Psychological interventions for ICD-11 complex PTSD symptoms: Systematic review and meta-analysis. *Psychological Medicine*, *49*(11), 1761–1775.
Kelly, A. C., & Tasca, G. A. (2016). Within-persons predictors of change during eating disorders treatment: An examination of self-compassion, self-criticism, shame and eating disorder symptoms. *International Journal of Eating Disorders*, *49*, 716–722. doi: 10.1002/eat.22527
Kim, J. J., Cunnington, R., & Kirby, J. N. (2020). The neurophysiological basis of compassion: An fMRI meta-analysis of compassion and its related neural processes. *Neuroscience & Biobehavioral Reviews*, *108*, 112–123.
Kirby, J. N., Doty, J. R., Petrocchi, N., & Gilbert, P. (2017). The current and future role of heart rate variability for assessing and training compassion. *Front Public Health*, *5*, 40
Kirby, J. N., Tellegen, C. L., & Steindl, S. R. (2017). A meta-analysis of compassion-based interventions: Current state of knowledge and future directions. *Behavior Therapy*, *48*, 778–792. 10.1016/j.beth.2017.06.003
Lawrence, V. A., & Lee, D. (2014). An exploration of people's experiences ofcomp assion-focused therapyfor trauma, using interpretative phenomenologicalanalysis. *Clinical Psychology & Psychotherapy*, *21*(6), 495–507.
Leaviss, J., & Uttley, L. (2015). Psychotherapeutic benefits of compassion-focused therapy: An early systematic review. *Psychological Medicine*, *45*(5), 927–945.
Lee, D., & James, S. (2012). *The compassionate mind approach to recovering from trauma: Using compassion focused therapy*. Hachette UK.
MacBeth, A., & Gumley, A. (2012). Exploring compassion: A meta-analysis of the association between self-compassion and psychopathology. *Clinical Psychology Review*, *32*(6), 545–552.
Neely, M. E., Schallert, D. L., Mohammed, S. S., Roberts, R. M., & Chen, Y. J. (2009). Self-kindness when facing stress: The role of self-compassion, goal

regulation, and support in college students' well-being. *Motivation and Emotion, 33*(1), 88–97.

Neff, K. D. (2009). The role of self-compassion in development: A healthier way to relate to oneself. *Human Development, 52*, 211–214.

Neff, K. D., Kirkpatrick, K. L., & Rude, S. S. (2007). Self-compassion and adaptive psychological functioning. *Journal of Research in Personality, 41*(1), 139–154.

Roddy, J. K. (2014). A client informed view of domestic violence counselling. [PhD, University of Leeds]. Leeds: University of Leeds.

Roddy, J. K., & Gabriel, L. (2019). A competency framework for domestic violence counselling. *British Journal of Guidance & Counselling, 47*(6), 669–681. https://doi.org/10.1080/03069885.2019.1599322

Schanche, E., Stiles, T. C., McCullough, L., Svartberg, M., & Nielsen, G. H. (2011). The relationship between activating affects, inhibitory affects, and self-compassion in patients with Cluster C personality disorders. *Psychotherapy, 48*(3), 293.

Seligowski, A. V., Miron, L. R., & Orcutt, H. K. (2014). Relations among self-compassion, PTSD symptoms, and psychological health in a trauma-exposed sample. *Mindfulness, 6*, 1033–1041. doi: 10.1007/s12671-014-0351-x

Seppala, E. M., Simon-Thomas, E., Brown, S. L., Worline, M. C., Cameron, C. D., & Doty, J. R. (Eds.) (2017). *The Oxford handbook of compassion science*. Oxford University Press.

Steindl, Stan, Bell, Tobyn, Dixon, Alison, & Kirby, James N. (2022). Therapist perspectives on working with fears, blocks and resistances to compassion in compassion focused therapy. *Counselling and Psychotherapy Research*. https://doi.org/10.1002/capr.12530

Tesh, M., Learman, J., & Pulliam, R. M. (2013). Mindful self-compassion strategies for survivors of intimate partner abuse. *Mindfulness*. doi: 10.1007/s12671-013-0244-4

Van Dam, N. T., Sheppard, S. C., Forsyth, J. P., & Earleywine, M. (2011). Self-compassion is a better predictor than mindfulness of symptom severity and quality of life in mixed anxiety and depression. *Journal of Anxiety Disorders, 25*(1), 123–130.

Chapter 11

Different Clients, Different Contexts

Jeannette Roddy, Laura Viliardos, Mark Widdowson, Rod Dubrow-Marshall, and Keelan Donohue

Learning Objectives

1 Understand that the experience of abuse is unique to the individual
2 Recognise that the tools of the abuser are related to the context of the relationship and the abuser's access to resources and knowledge of the client
3 Learn how abusers can use the client context to gain control of the relationship
4 Be aware of the cultural context in abusive relationships

Context

The language used throughout this book is neutral, as far as possible, around gender, sexuality and culture. It recognises that domestic abuse can happen irrespective of the community in which the relationship developed. However, the context of the client is important in understanding what the abuser used to exert control and the client's history and upbringing may helpful in understanding what was particularly difficult about the experience for the client. These factors may also impact on how they feel about accessing support, what they need from a counsellor and how they feel about working with you (see also chapter 5).

In this chapter we look at some of the differences between male and female counselling needs as well as the needs of clients from an LGBTQI+ or faith community. There may also be specific challenges for people who have relocated to the UK which can be important to explore. Whilst this chapter is too short to answer all questions or tackle all inequalities or power dynamics in relationships, the sections are designed to help you to think about what may be important for the client within their life context, rather than simply working with the experience of abuse as defined in chapter 3. You are also invited to explore your own life experiences and how these may be similar to or different from your clients.

Privilege, Culture, and Class

One of the myths about domestic abuse is that it only happens in the poorer sections of the community. It is certainly true that being poor can create

DOI: 10.4324/9781003253266-11

tension in a family and that, in turn, can lead to abusive behaviours born out of frustration and helplessness. However, it is the impact of the environment on, rather than the characteristics of, people in poverty that can result in violence and abuse. Hence any relationship which is subject to external stress could become abusive wherever and however that stress is generated. In this sense domestic abuse happens irrespective of one's economic position, it is about the requirement of one partner to have control over another, perhaps due to the lack of control they have in other areas of their life. The means of control may be financial, emotional, physical, sexual, or psychological but is nevertheless still domestic abuse (see chapter 3 for more details).

As a counsellor, it is important to acknowledge one's own position of privilege, not only as we might see ourselves, but as others might see you. One useful tool to look at privilege is the privilege walk (McIntosh, 1990) (just type "privilege walk" into a search engine and you will see many exercises freely available for you to use). In this, the participants are asked to assess themselves on a range of topics from ethnicity to parental encouragement, from disability to sexuality by taking steps forward or backward depending on the question. By doing this as a group, it becomes clear which members are more privileged (according to the measure) than others and a facilitated discussion on that experience can be very helpful. As an individual, it is also helpful for us to engage with these societal constructs and see where we fit. It is sometimes surprising to see how privileged we may appear to others yet still have difficulties, or how few privileges we seemed to have yet still succeed. Sometimes success or failure is determined by the expectations of others, rather than us. Examining privilege may also help us to understand some of the difficulties our clients may have in a world that is different to the one that we inhabit.

> Reflection: Investigate the Privilege Walk and go through it as an exercise. What have you learned about yourself in doing so? What have you learned about others that you perhaps work or socialise with? What might you take with you into your counselling work as a result of this exercise?

We may also relate economic wealth, education, and privilege to class. The wealthier, more educated and more privileged someone is, the higher the class that can be associated. This is a very western construct valuing education, employment position and wealth. The UK has seen an increase in individuals being classified as "middle-class" over the last 30 years, linked to higher living standards and increased access to education (Arnett, 2016). If domestic abuse were linked to class, rates would have diminished over the last 20 years, yet they have not, suggesting class is not specifically a factor in abuse.

However, it is also important to recognise that there are many other cultures within our society that we come across in therapeutic work with different systems of valuing or classifying a person, such as the family someone marries into or their links to the community, which will be discussed in more detail later. Not meeting the expectations of whatever our cultural norms are provides the potential for anxiety, stress and hopelessness.

The type of abuse perpetrated is likely to have cultural context and we cannot estimate the impact of whatever has been said to the client based on our own cultural norms. For example, a Jewish female married to a doctor may find it hard to seek help, as her society may see only a good marriage. The abuser can use coercive control and gaslighting to undermine confidence that the victim would ever be believed and to remind them of the shame that would come with the breakdown of marriage. Within a closed society that looks up to medical professionals, where is there to go?

Reflection: Thinking about western society as working, middle and upper class, what sort of abuses of power do you think might be most effective in each of these classes? How might a client see these and what might be difficult for them?

When working with clients, it is important to understand their stories from their own cultural context, what matters to them and their family, what it is that makes it so especially difficult to make a change in their life. Sometimes these issues are intractable, and therapy is about understanding and managing the situation more comfortably and constructively, sometimes it is about challenge and change. In this unknown world, we must hold our client's objectives for counselling clearly and visibly and not be tempted into working from our own views and values.

The situation can become more complex still where we are working with clients who have recently relocated. This can be as simple as from London to Manchester or from Scotland to England, or it could be more complex and involve moving across continents, with or without the support of family. It is, perhaps, surprising how many cultural differences there are, even when moving a short distance. Things from children's birthday parties to eating out with friends will have their own dynamic of "the way we do things around here" which must be learned.

When considering that isolation from friends and family is a key element of abuse (see chapter 3) the potential for experiencing abuse and being unable to call for help due to relocation increases. Often families have warned the person not to move and then, when things become difficult, it is more difficult to go back home. Compassion and understanding about such difficulties are vital as the individual needs to develop trust in someone. This allows them to look at their partner more objectively as they no longer depend on them for everything – they now have someone else to share things with.

Reflection: What is your experience of relocating? What was easy and what was difficult? How would you have felt if your family was unsupportive at this time? If you have never relocated, think about people who have moved into your area and how you responded to them? What have you noticed about how they 'settle in' or not? What was helpful to them in settling and what caused difficulties?

An additional complication can sometimes be seen when working with people who have moved from a different culture as they may have assimilated the new culture to a greater or lesser extent. You may find someone caught between the old culture they came from and the new culture they have moved to (Cromby et al., 2013). Here the work is to help them to establish what is right for them and what is not. Again, we can only work with the client's worldview and help them to reach their own conclusions about how they want to be in the world and what they are prepared to tolerate and what they are not. We can certainly offer observations about what and how things seem to affect the client for them to determine what that means and where that can be placed in their new construction of their environment. However, the western-centric view of supporting individual autonomy may not always be the best option for everyone. It may be helpful to share, but we must also be respectful of other cultures' requirement for community over individualism, and the different ways that such communities may resolve difficulties that can be just as effective.

Reflection: Think about your own family and any disagreements you might have had with parents or siblings about how you live your life compared with how they would prefer you lived your life. How did it feel? What did you do or want to do? What stopped you or drove you on? If you have ever engaged with a family from a different culture, how did that feel? How did you come to terms with the differences? What did you like and dislike about the differences?

Age and Disability

Often when we consider domestic abuse, we think about young heterosexual adults, with the male dominating the female. As the new definition of domestic abuse indicates, domestic abuse is much wider than that. As more research has been completed, new groups previously excluded from the definition have appeared. People may now be in their 70s and 80s and still be in an abusive relationship. Individuals may require care from partners or family members such as their children, which can also lead to abuse (Brandl & Meuer, 2000). This may be due to, for example, the stress of caring; the lack of love felt by the carer for and/or from the individual; or the carer's desire to control finances with minimal care provided. The individual does not want to get the carer arrested or sent to prison, as they could be "punished" by being sent to a care facility and may feel they have few options to seek help. Neglect is a common outcome. When working with our clients, we must not make any assumptions about what home life is like, we must explore each situation and look at the client experiences, even if they do not necessarily first see this as abuse.

Just as the elderly may need to depend on others, so may people with disabilities. A recent study in New Zealand (Fanslow et al., 2021) of people from across the population who had physical, emotional, and intellectual disabilities found that those with disabilities were much more likely to experience domestic abuse than the general population. Those with psychological and intellectual disabilities experienced higher levels of abuse than those with physical disabilities. Psychological and physical abuse were most reported, with psychological abuse highest. Men with disabilities were more likely than women to report physical abuse.

> Reflection: When considering working with vulnerable groups such as the elderly and those with disabilities, think about your own views of these groups. What are your pre-conceptions about abuse? Did anything surprise you about the types of abuse presented? How could you work with cases like this, where there may be no immediate opportunities to leave?

When listening to stories from vulnerable people about the abuse they have received, be open to the potential for the abuse to be ongoing and prepared to refer into frontline services in their local area for support and options if necessary. Also be aware of the impact on you, as a therapist, as the abuse of vulnerable people can be difficult to understand and can cause emotional responses in us, such as anger, disbelief, and wanting to act on behalf of the individual. Remember our role in this is to support and facilitate client action, in whatever way works for and helps the client.

Working with Men

Due to the gendered nature of domestic abuse, male victims have often been overlooked when it comes to the research literature and service provision. Early research theorised that domestic violence is a consequence of men's desire to control and dominate, rooted in historically and socially constructed gender norms, with patriarchal values facilitating male privilege (Hines et al., 2020). Research has tended to focus exclusively on women as victims and men as perpetrators of domestic violence (Barber, 2008) and there are several books on how to support women in counselling which still have relevance today (Dutton, 1993; Walker, 1979; Sanderson, 2008). The experiences and needs of women are expressed in the NICE guidance for domestic abuse, published in 2014. Few studies have explored the experiences of male victims and there are limited specialist counselling services (Roddy, 2015) and support organisations available for men. Given the lack of available information on the male experience, this section will focus on men.

Despite the lack of research and support available, the prevalence of domestic violence perpetrated against men is arguably high. For every three victims of domestic violence, two will be female and one will be male (ONS, 2020). Further evidence has suggested that one in six to seven men will experience domestic abuse in their lifetime, compared to one in four women (ONS, 2020). The limited studies which have explored the prevalence of domestic violence perpetrated by females towards males have noted significant physical aggression towards men, including kicking, biting, choking, scratching, and the use of weapons (Drijber et al., 2013; Hines et al., 2007). Further, it is estimated that one-third of male victims abused by females sustain serious injury (Hines & Douglas, 2010). A study by Bates (2020) reported that men frequently experienced verbal and sexual aggression, including being forced to penetrate their partner. Sexual aggression and forced penetration have been known to result in significant psychological distress (Hines & Douglas, 2016).

As the experience of domestic abuse is considered to be more prevalent for women than men, theories of domestic abuse have derived from research on women's experiences. As such, there is a limited understanding around the long-term impact on male survivors (Sita & Dear, 2021). As well as physical injuries, male domestic violence survivors can experience low self-worth, suicide ideation (Tsui, 2014), anxiety, post-traumatic stress disorder, substance misuse, feelings of isolation and loneliness, and physical health problems (Hines & Straus, 2007; Hines & Douglas, 2016). A further legacy of domestic abuse is the impact on forming and maintaining future relationships, due to the inability to trust future partners (Bates et al., 2019). For men with children, domestic abuse can have a negative effect on the relationship with their children due to parental relationship disruption, alienation, and legal proceedings. Involvement in family courts can also have an overwhelming impact on mental health (Berger et al., 2016). These are all issues that may be brought into therapy.

> Reflection: Just as with women, the psychological harm men experience can last well after injuries have healed. Given the extensive prevalence in the UK of teaching about the male abuser, what difficulties might you experience in working with a male victim who describes his female partner as behaving in a similar way to a male perpetrator?
>
> [Female counsellors please note: "I would just work from his frame of reference like I would anyone else" is not a good answer here. Think about the cultural and societal pressure which women feel differently.]

Domestic violence against male victims will often go unrecognised. It is considered that men are less likely than women to report abusive experiences due to fear of embarrassment and ridicule and the lack of support services available for men (Barber, 2008). It is also argued that professionals offering support to male survivors should consider and address the influence of domestic abuse on the victims' sense of masculinity (Sita & Dear, 2021). It could also be argued that domestic abuse is thought to be experienced more commonly in women because male victims of partner abuse are far more likely than women to perceive what happened to them as not being domestic abuse (ONS, 2020).

> Reflection: Men may not perceive domestic abuse or perhaps they may not want to consider that they have been abused due to the way society may view them. What impact might this have on exploring and/or naming the abuse in therapy?

Studies have reported that a recurring fear for male victims is losing custody of children. Furthermore, the fear around the breakup of a family often leads men to remain in an abusive relationship (Hines & Douglas, 2010; Simmons et al., 2016). Although fear is a common response to domestic abuse reported by both men and women, a recent small-scale case-based study by Sita and Dear (2021) found a notable difference in the type of fear experienced by men compared to women. Whereas female victims will typically express a fear for their life, the men in the study had a profound fear of what the abuser could do to their lives; some examples included financial abuse, restricting access to children, and damaging their reputation and social relationships.

The needs of male victims are often neglected compared with women (Huntley et al., 2019). When it comes to fleeing a domestic abusive relationship, there are a minority of refuges, safe houses, and supported housing available for men in the UK. Although there are few refuges, domestic abuse victims are legally classified as a "vulnerable adult" and local authorities have an obligation, under the provision of the Housing Act 1996 (part V11) and Homelessness Act 2002, to ensure that male victims have access to emergency housing. According to Routes to Support (2019) only 12% of refugees in the UK will house men and there were only a total of 171 bed spaces available to men across all services, of which just 23 were reserved for men only (Women's Aid, 2019). Research with male victims suggested that some begin living in their cars, whilst others have to seek refuge with family members (Roddy, 2014).

Many organisations supporting survivors of domestic abuse are grounded in feminism (see also chapter 12), offering services targeted towards women, with predominantly female staff. The gendered language and terminology used by services, for example, "Women's Aid," can serve as a significant barrier for men accessing support. Men can experience "invisibility" within domestic abuse services. Studies have found that men can often be unaware that services are available to them or can perceive services as inappropriate (Bacchus et al., 2018; Frierson, 2014; McCarrick et al., 2015). The "shop front" of services can pose as a barrier to help seeking for men. As the depiction of services being a space for women only can prevent men from accessing support, there is an increasing need for a gender-aware culture within domestic abuse services and separate male services (McCarrick et al., 2015).

> Reflection: Thinking about your own practice, how welcoming might men or women who have experienced domestic abuse find it? What colours do you use on your website? What image is construed when entering the counselling room? Is it gendered in any way? Have you checked this out with colleagues or clients?

The gendered landscape of domestic abuse services has the potential to perpetuate the societal perception of domestic violence being mainly a female issue. In addition to female-focused services and feminist paradigms in the theoretical understanding of domestic abuse, public awareness campaigns, policy, and portrayals of domestic violence in the media are often centred around the male perpetrator and female victim dyad (see also chapter 12). Hence a much greater need for understanding in society of what it means to be a male victim of domestic violence.

Sexuality

The past 30 years have seen enormous social change in relation to attitudes and acceptance towards LGBTQ+ people. This includes, but is not limited to, legal equality for same-sex relationships. Yet, access to services or support for those seeking help from interpersonal violence (IPV) within same-sex relationships is extremely poor, or non-existent in many areas. The widespread perception that IPV is primarily a male perpetrator – female victim phenomenon has contributed to a relative invisibility of IPV within same-sex relationships in policy and practice (Donovan & Barnes, 2019). Indeed, IPV occurring in same-sex relationships has only relatively recently been recorded separately by many police forces, with Greater Manchester Police force being the first in the UK to formally do so (BBC News, 2017).

The LGBT pride movement and the growth of allyship mean that it is not uncommon to see statements on social media such as "love is love" and "gay people are just the same as heterosexual people." Whilst these statements are correct, same-sex relationships do have different dynamics to heterosexual relationships. For example, same-sex relationships are generally more egalitarian with balanced shared decision-making and division of domestic tasks (Nichols, 2021). Research indicates that couples in same-sex relationships are better at defusing conflict and are more likely to use humour to manage and reduce emotional tensions in conflict situations than heterosexual couples (Gottman et al., 2003).

Despite this, research indicates that the prevalence of IPV amongst same-sex relationships is as common as it is amongst heterosexual couples.

Research conducted by Stonewall (2018) found that 11% of LGBT people had experienced IPV in 2017–2018. Shockingly, this further rose to 15% for disabled LGBT people, 17% for LGBT people from ethnic minorities, and 19% for transgender or non-binary people. Moreover, although same-sex relationships have different dynamics to heterosexual relationships, research in IPV has identified similar risk factors between heterosexual and LGBT relationships. Risk factors have been identified as a potential influence to IPV for victims and perpetrators of abuse, such as perpetrators or victims of abuse experiencing domestic violence during childhood, mental health problems prevalent amongst parents, and history of substance abuse (DeKeseredy & Dragiewicz, 2009; Whitfield et al., 2003; Wolfe & McIsaac, 2010, as cited in Lorenzetti et al., 2017).

> Reflection: What's your experience of same-sex and heterosexual relationships? Have you noticed differences in other relationships that contrast with your own? How do you consider relationships different from your own (in terms of gender and/or sexuality)?

Although research into IPV in same-sex relationships has increased in recent years, a clear understanding of same-sex IPV dynamics still remains poorly understood. During the past two decades, factors unique to same-sex relationships have been identified to play a significant role; understandably contributing to further complexity in our understanding of same-sex relationship experiences of IPV. Lorenzetti et al. (2017) propose several factors, some of which consider the experiences and impacts of heterosexism (the presumption that people within society are heterosexual (Mule, 2008, as cited in Lorenzetti et al., 2017)); social exclusion and isolation; and lack of accessible support services for LGBT victims and perpetrators of IPV.

> Reflection: Social isolation has already been raised as an issue in domestic abuse. What might be the additional factors in same-sex relationships that create even more difficulties for the client?

Further barriers to seeking support are identified amongst research, for instance, the process of help-seeking is not solely limited to official services of support, in fact, family and friends can offer a crucial source of help for victims of IPV (Peraica, 2020). However, victims have experienced troubled family relationships due to disclosing their sexuality and were unable to rely on emotional or practical support in times of need; challenges may be experienced when approaching their heterosexual friends (Donovan & Barnes, 2019). The extent to which an individual's sexuality is known by their family or friends is often referred to as "outness or closetness" and presents an additional factor to consider amongst LGBT victims and perpetrators of IPV (Longobardi & Bardenes-Ribera, 2017).

Alcohol and drug use may be a factor in same-sex IPV, with LGBT people being seven times more likely to have drug or alcohol problems than heterosexual people (Stonewall, 2018). Internalised homophobia/transphobia and a strong sense of shame may be factors which can generate feelings of self-loathing (Longobardi & Badenes-Ribera, 2017).

Past experiences of discrimination and negative stereotyping can result in stigma consciousness, which describes the extent to which LGBT groups anticipate being stereotyped and shamed by others because of these instances (Longobardi & Badenes-Ribera, 2017). This can result in internalised homophobia (Miltz et al., 2019). Shame has been identified as a barrier to disclosure, especially amongst men, who may feel emasculated or not taken seriously if they report IPV from their male partner. Whilst research into help-seeking and LGBT victims remains poorly documented, Huntley et al. (2019) highlight how male victims of IPV (a minority group themselves) can experience a challenge to their masculinity. Often avoidance of seeking help is likely due to male victims potentially perceived as weak or feminine, thus resulting in further challenges and negative consequences of disclosing such as processing internal feelings of shame and denial.

Greater attention into IPV amongst LGBT relationships has challenged previous perceptions of IPV, consequently a shift has been witnessed amongst research and has offered new theory to this discussion. Arguably the most dominant theory is the minority stress hypothesis (Miltz et al., 2019; Barrett, 2015; Sylaska & Edwards, 2015) which considers the unique factors identified amongst sexually diverse relationships and specifically explores the exposure of additional stress experienced by individuals belonging to this specific minority group (Meyer, 2003, as cited in Longobardi & Badenes, 2017).

Very little research has focused specifically on counselling consideration with supporting LGBT victims or perpetrators of IPV, which provides opportunities for future research. Banks and Fedewa (2012) emphasise the importance for counsellors to take greater responsibility in raising awareness within communities and directly attend to the challenges identified within this field, in the hope of encouraging victims to disclose their abuse and seek help: whether that be from services or their social network.

Faith and Belief

Domestic abuse and coercive control have been repeatedly reported as occurring across cultures (Schechter, 1982) and this in part reflects the hegemony of patriarchal power relations which infuse much of the abuse that takes place in family and intimate relationships (Stark, 2007; Walker, 1979). Furthermore, abuse takes place within a context of faith and belief which may incorporate personal spiritual beliefs as well as expectations and rules from a faith community/religious group/extremist or cultic group. An understanding of the layer of coercion that is added through some faith and belief systems is critical in helping practitioners to work with survivors of domestic abuse and will help to deepen an appreciation of potential obstacles to recovery.

> Reflection: What is your experience of faith? How easy is it for you to understand and/or work with someone who has a strong faith? In what ways could expectations from a faith community make it easier to stay in a domestically abusive relationship? What might you need to be aware of in your own process to do this work?

Fortune et al. (2010) argue that religion, alongside ethnicity and cultural background, can be both a pathway and barrier to recovery from domestic abuse (referred to as "roadblock" and "resource" by Fortune & Enger, 2005). The beneficial aspects include the potential support of the faith community and religious beliefs which can bolster courage and strength in making difficult decisions. Barriers can include a "misinterpretation and misuse of religious texts and traditions" which intensify suffering, including self-blame, and can help perpetrators to make excuses for their abusive actions. The authors, who are Jewish, Christian, and Muslim, point out the need to address existential issues around the meaning of the experience of domestic violence and from a spiritual perspective make the point that: "Sometimes, people try to explain suffering by saying that it is 'God's will' or 'part of God's plan for my life' or 'God's way of teaching me a lesson.' These explanations assume God to be stern, harsh, even cruel and arbitrary. This image of God runs counter to a Biblical image (and a Qur'anic image) of a "kind, merciful and loving God" (p. 5). They share the insight that in advanced stages of recovery, the person may recognise that their suffering led to personal growth, an idea that is sometimes referred to as post-traumatic growth (Tedeschi et al., 2018).

Truong et al. (2022) conducted individual interviews and focus groups with members of various faith groups in Australia and concluded that even though participants understood that their faith did not condone domestic violence, there were "cultural structures related to their faiths that enabled and ignored abuse against women" (p. 1), and undoubtedly these structures would be further bolstered within a patriarchal society and cultural beliefs that violence is sometimes necessary to control people, counsellors should examine all these layers as these can influence the meaning that their clients make of their experience of violence and abuse.

Counsellors may be comfortable talking with clients about their religious and spiritual beliefs, but they may feel less comfortable in involving a faith leader. Fortune et al. (2010) stress the importance of including faith leaders as an adjunct to other interventions. If a client would like to include their religious leader, consent can be obtained for some collaborative work, similar to the need to sometimes involve a medical professional or social worker in the overall recovery approach.

Ethnicity

Ethnicity can include religious beliefs but is also used more broadly to refer to culture, language, race, and other shared characteristics that may lead to identification with a social group. In the UK, ethnic groups are categorised as anything other than white British and include Asian or Asian British; Black, Black British, Caribbean, or African; Mixed or Multiple Ethnic Groups; White; and Other Ethnic Groups, but it is recognised that this is not an all-inclusive list (Gov.UK, n.d.).

When working with survivors of domestic abuse, it is important to consider how much of a role a person's ethnic identity may be playing in influencing their perceptions and interpretations of the domestic abuse. Truong et al. (2022) noted in their qualitative research study that ethnicity and cultural practices were cited by faith leaders and community members as being more influential than faith and religion in understandings of domestic abuse. They quoted one of their interview participants who said: "Because that's their culture and it's not their religion. Religion does not sanction this [violence] but certain culture, they bring from the village" (p. 8).

Honour-based abuse, sometimes more accurately referred to as "so-called honour-based abuse," has been criminalised in England and Wales as examples of domestic abuse as reflected in the Domestic Abuse Act (Home Office, 2022) and other laws, and includes female genital mutilation, forced marriage, and "honour" killings. The Home Office (2022) has reported 2,383 "honour"-based abuse-related offences, 78 female genital mutilation offences, and 125 forced marriage offences in the year ending March 2021. They state that: "This type of abuse can happen to anyone. It has in cases been identified with close-knit or closed communities with a strong culture of 'honour' and 'shame', such as some minority groups, or closed ethnic/religious groups and other particularly isolated social groups" (p. 42). They further reported that reproductive coercion including forced abortion for "honour-based" practices is more common for Black, Asian and minority (BAME) defendants.

The Home Office (2022) have cited specific reasons that BAME people will face additional barriers to identifying, disclosing, seeking help, or reporting abuse, including distrust and suspicion towards the police, fear of racial stereotyping, fears about immigration status, language and cultural barriers, being disproportionately impacted by "honour"-based abuse, shame and fear of their family finding out, and fear of rejection by the wider community. The assumption is therefore made that domestic abuse in minority communities is under-reported. They recommend (p. 69) that: "Professionals working with minority communities should be aware of barriers and actively seek to ensure the right support is made available to overcome them, including appropriate interpretation and translation support where this may be needed. There are distinct structural barriers that minority communities face in accessing support." This recommendation should be given full attention by psychotherapists working with BAME clients and openly discussed.

Enabling Change Rebuilding Lives (2009) have recommended in a training toolkit that health professionals have an awareness that Asian women experiencing domestic abuse are abused twice – once by the perpetrator – or perpetrators if multiple family members are involved, such as in honour-based abuse – and then by their community. They explain that family honour is known as "izzat" and that women are held responsible for maintaining it and for avoiding "sharam" or shame, and that this occurs in a conventional gender-stereotyped community where women may be considered as "property."

Bhandari and Sabri (2020) interviewed twenty South Asian women living in the United States and reported that factors that helped them to leave their abusive relationships despite the cultural barriers against doing so were: an increase in the severity of the abuse; children witnessing the abuse; deception; and being forced to leave. They stress that practitioners should be aware of these factors and help their clients to recognise warning signs earlier. They called for cultural competency training and for "culturally appropriate interventions" to be provided to victims of abuse. Therapists could then facilitate referral to appropriate support.

Counsellors and psychotherapists who are trained in active listening and providing reflective summaries and affirmations of clients are well placed to help clients facing ethnicity and cultural barriers to their recovery and ability to access help, but they would also be expected to improve their effectiveness by being sensitive to cultural and ethnicity issues. The counselling field would benefit from additional training resources and research in this area.

> Reflection: Imagine that a white client tells you that they are being abused by their partner and that they are afraid to call the police. How do you support your client? Now imagine that it is a BAME client telling you the same thing. Is there a different intensity to the fears of calling the police? What might be the impact of them having experienced racism more generally?

Summary

This section of the book was added to acknowledge that, because of our own histories, we may not immediately be able to acknowledge what it is like to be someone else, with a history very different to our own. In this section, we have explored culture, privilege, social class, age, disability, gender and sexuality, in the context of difference against a white, Christian, heterosexual female, that often forms the basis for domestic abuse research. The opportunities to reflect on your own beliefs and ideas throughout this chapter have hopefully provided some insight into any prejudices or preconceived ideas that until now have been hidden from view. Working with domestic abuse means being open to understanding the nuanced world of the client.

Key Learning Points

1. Domestic abuse can happen independent of privilege, class, or culture. The different aspects of these social constructs may inform the type of abuse perpetrated, but not the presence.
2. Vulnerable groups such as the elderly or those with disabilities are more susceptible to abuse than the general public. These are under-researched areas and could usefully be explored further.
3. The predominant theory of domestic abuse in the UK and other western nations is feminist, with a heterosexual male perpetrator and female victim. Whilst there is now more research on male victims and female perpetrators to help understanding of the similarities and differences within a heterosexual partnership, there is still a need to understand and research more on the types of domestic abuse perpetrated within same-sex partnerships.
4. Men have a different experience of domestic abuse compared with women, where they fear the power of their partner to undermine the life they have built socially, professionally and within the community. The potential loss of children should their partner gain custody is often a significant factor in remaining in the relationship.
5. Much of the literature on domestic abuse is about the experience of women, and that is woven into this book as well as the main domestic abuse training programmes in Western society, hence women were not highlighted specifically within this chapter.
6. Whilst faith communities may believe in a "merciful and loving god," abuse can be interpreted as a "punishment from god" which appears to contradict the faith philosophy. This can be explained as linked to the culture within the faith community.
7. It is believed that domestic abuse in non-white-UK communities may be underreported. This may be due to the local community culture or previous difficult experiences of seeking help in the UK. Counsellors should be aware of the potential for external sources of abuse that can also be directed at minority communities in the UK which can impact on help-seeking.

References

Arnett, G. (2016). UK became more middle class than working class in 2000, data shows. *The Guardian*. Published on 26 February 2016. Accessed on 27 August 2022. URL: https://www.theguardian.com/news/datablog/2016/feb/26/uk-more-middle-class-than-working-class-2000-data

Bacchus, L. J., Buller, A. M., Ferrari, G., Brzank, P., & Feder, G. (2018). "It's always good to ask": A mixed methods study on the perceived role of sexual health practitioners asking gay and bisexual men about experiences of domestic violence and abuse. *Journal of Mixed Methods Research*, *12*(2), 221–243.

Banks, J. R., & Fedewa, A. L. (2012). Counselors' attitudes toward domestic violence in same-sex versus opposite-sex relationships. *Journal of Multicultural Counseling and Development*, *40*(4), 194–205.

Barrett, B. J. (2015). Domestic violence in the LGBT community. In *Encyclopedia of Social Work*.

Bates, E. A. (2020). "Walking on egg shells": A qualitative examination of men's experiences of intimate partner violence. *Psychology of Men and Masculinities*, *21*, 13–24.

Bates, E. A., Klement, K. R., Kaye, L. K., & Pennington, C. R. (2019). The impact of gendered stereotypes on perceptions of violence: A commentary. *Sex Roles*, *81*, 34–43.

Barber, C. F. (2008). DV against men. *Nursing Standard*, *22*(51), 35–39.

BBC News (2017, 10 April). Greater Manchester police recording LGBT domestic abuse. Retreived 25th September from https://www.bbc.co.uk/news/uk-england-manchester-39551595

Berger, J. L., Douglas, E. M., & Hines, D. A. (2016). The mental health of male victims and their children affected by legal and administrative partner aggression. *Aggressive Behavior*, *42*, 346–361.

Bhandari, S., & Sabri, B. (2020). Patterns of abuse among South Asian women experiencing domestic violence in the United States. *International Social Work*.

Brandl, B., & Meuer, T. (2000). Domestic abuse in later life. *Elder Law Journal*, *8*(2), 297–336.

Cromby, J., Harper, D. & Reavey, P. (2013). Culture. In J. Cromby, D. Harper & Paula Reavey (Eds.). *Psychology, Mental Health and Distress* (pp. 55–74. Basingstoke: Palgrave Macmillan.

DeKeseredy, W. S., & Dragiewicz, M. (2009). *Shifting public policy direction: Gender-focused versus bidirectional intimate partner violence*. Toronto: Ontario Women's Directorate.

Donovan, C., & Barnes, R. (2019). Help-seeking among lesbian, gay, bisexual and/or transgender victims/survivors of DV and abuse: The impacts of cisgendered heteronormativity and invisibility. *Journal of Sociology*, *56*(4), 554–570. 10.1177/1440783319882088

Drijber, B. C., Reijnders, U. J. L., & Ceelen, M. (2013). Male victims of domestic violence. *Journal of Family Violence*, *28*, 173–178.

Dutton, M. A. (1993). Understanding womenas responses to domestic violence: A redefinition of battered woman syndrome. *Hofstra Law Review*, *21*(4), 1191–1242.

Enabling Change Rebuilding Lives. (2009). *Asian women domestic violence and mental health: A toolkit for health professionals*. Government Office for London.

Fanslow, J. L., Malihi, Z. A., Hashemi, L., Gulliver, P. J. & McIntosh, T. K. D. (2021) Lifetime prevalence of intimate partner violence and disability: Results from a population-based study in New Zealand. *American Journal of Preventive Medicine* *61*(3), 320–328.

Fortune, M., Abugideiri, S., & Dratch, M. (2010). *A commentary on religion and domestic violence*. Faith Trust Institute. https://www.faithtrustinstitute.org/resources/articles/Commentary.pdf

Fortune, M., & Enger, C. (2005). *Violence against women and the role of religion*. The National Online Resource Center on Violence Against Women.

Frierson. (2014). *The fear of being judged: African American gay men and intimate partner violence a qualitative study*. ProQuest Dissertations Publishing.

Gottman, J. M., Levenson, R. W., Swanson, C., Swanson, K., Tyson, R., & Yoshimoto, D. (2003). Observing gay, lesbian and heterosexual couples' relationships: Mathematical modelling of conflict interaction. *Journal of homosexuality*, *45*(1), 65–91
Gov.UK (n.d.). List of ethnic groups. https://www.ethnicity-facts-figures.service.gov.uk/style-guide/ethnic-groups
Hines, D. A., Bates, E. A., & Wallace, S. (2020). "I have guys call me and say 'I can't be the victim of domestic abuse'": Exploring the experiences of telephone support providers for male victims of domestic violence and abuse. *Journal of Interpersonal Violence*, 88626052094455–886260520944551. 10.1177/0886260520944551
Home Office (2022). *Domestic abuse statutory guidance*. Open Government License.
Hines, D. A., Brown, J., & Dunning, E. (2007). Characteristics of callers to the domestic abuse helpline for men. *Journal of Family Violence*, *22*, 63–72.
Hines, D. A., & Douglas, E. M. (2010). A closer look at men who sustain intimate terrorism by women. *Partner Abuse*, *1*, 286–313.
Hines, D. A., & Douglas, E. M. (2016). Relative influence of various forms of partner violence on the health of male victims: Study of a help seeking sample. *Psychology of Men and Masculinity*, *17*, 3–16.
Hines, D. A., & Straus, M. A. (2007). Binge drinking and violence against dating partners: The mediating effect of antisocial traits and behaviors in a multinational perspective. *Aggressive Behavior*, *33*, 441–457.
Huntley, A., Potter, L., Williamson, E., Malpass, A., Szilassy, E., & Feder, G. (2019). Help-seeking by male victims of DV and abuse (DVA): A systematic review and qualitative evidence synthesis. *BMJ Open*, *9*(6), e021960. 10.1136/bmjopen-2018-021960
Huntley, A. L., Szilassy, E., Potter, L., Malpass, A., Williamson, E., & Feder, G. (2020). Help seeking by male victims of domestic violence and abuse: an example of an integrated mixed methods synthesis of systematic review evidence defining methodological terms. *BMC Health Services Research*, *20*(1), 1–17.
Irving, P., & Dickson, D. (2006). A re-conceptualization of Rogers' core conditions: Implications for research, practice and training. *International Journal for the Advancement of Counselling*, *28*(2), 183–194. 10.1007/s10447-005-9000-3
Longobardi, C., & Badenes-Ribera, L. (2017). Intimate partner violence in same-Sex relationships and the role of sexual minority stressors: A systematic review of the past 10 years. *Journal of Child and Family Studies*, *26*(8), 2039–2049. 10.1007/s10826-017-0734-4
Lorenzetti, L., Wells, L., Logie, C., & Callaghan, T. (2017). Understanding and preventing DV in the lives of gender and sexually diverse persons. *The Canadian Journal of Human Sexuality*, *26*(3), 175–185. 10.3138/cjhs.2016-0007
McCarrick, Davis-McCabe, C., & Hirst-Winthrop, S. (2015). Men's experiences of the criminal justice system following female perpetrated intimate partner violence. *Journal of Family Violence*, *31*(2), 203–213
McIntosh, P. (1990). White privilege: Unpacking the invisible knapsack. *Independent School*, *49*(2), s. 31–36.
Miltz, A., Lampe, F., Bacchus, L., McCormack, S., Dunn, D., & White, E. et al. (2019). Intimate partner violence, depression, and sexual behaviour among gay, bisexual and other men who have sex with men in the PROUD trial. *BMC Public Health*, *19*(1). 10.1186/s12889-019-6757-6

Nichols, M. (2021). *The modern clinician's guide to working with LGBTQ+ clients*. Routledge.
Office for National Statistics (ONS). (2020). Domestic abuse victim characteristics in England and Wales: year ending March 2020. *Published online*: ONS.
Peraica, T., Kovačić Petrović, Z., Barić, Ž., Galić, R., & Kozarić-Kovačić, D. (2020). Gender differences among DV help-seekers: Socio-demographic characteristics, types and duration of violence, perpetrators, and interventions. *Journal of Family Violence*, *36*(4), 429–442. 10.1007/s10896-020-00207-8
Roddy. (2015). *Counselling and psychotherapy after domestic violence a client view of what helps recovery* (1st ed. 2015.). Palgrave Macmillan
Roddy, J. K. (2014). *A Client Informed View of Domestic Violence Counselling*. [PhD, University of Leeds]. Leeds.
Sanderson, C. (2008). *Counselling Survivors of Domestic Abuse*. Jessica Kingsley Publishers
Schechter, S. (1982). *Women and male violence: The visions and struggles of the battered women's movement*. South End Press.
Simmons, Brüggemann, A. J., & Swahnberg, K. (2016). Disclosing victimisation to healthcare professionals in Sweden: A constructivist grounded theory study of experiences among men exposed to interpersonal violence. *BMJ Open*, *6*(6), e010847–e010847.
Sita, T., & Dear, G. (2021). Four case studies examining male victims of intimate partner abuse. *Journal of Aggression, Maltreatment & Trauma*, *30*(1), 3–24.
Stark, E. (2007). *Coercive control: How men entrap women in personal life*. Oxford University Press.
Stonewall (2018). LGBT in Britain: Home and Communities. Retrieved 8 September 2021 from https://www.stonewall.org.uk/lgbt-britain-home-and-communities
Sylaska, K. M., & Edwards, K. M. (2015). Disclosure experiences of sexual minority college student victims of intimate partner violence. *American Journal of Community Psychology*, *55*(3), 326–335.
Tedeschi, R., Shakespeare-Finch, J., Taku, K., & Calhoun, L. (2018). *Posttraumatic growth: Theory, research, and applications*. Routledge.
Truong, M., Sharif, M., Olsen, A., Pasalich, D., Calabria, B., & Priest, N. (2022). Attitudes and beliefs about family and domestic violence in faith-based communities: An exploratory qualitative study. *Australian Journal of Social Issues*, *00*, 1–18. 10.1002/ajs4.21
Tsui, V. (2014). Male victims of intimate partner abuse: Use and helpfulness of services. *Social Work*, *59*, 121–130.
Walker, L. (1979). *The battered woman*. New York: Harper & Row.
Whitfield, C. L., Anda, R. F., Dube, S. R., & Felitti, V. J. (2003). Violent childhood experiences and the risk of intimate partner violence in adults: Assessment in a large health maintenance organization. *Journal of Interpersonal Violence*, *18*(2), 166–185.
Women's Aid (2019). Domestic Abuse Provision: Routes to support. Retrieved 25th September 2022 from https://www.womensaid.org.uk/domestic-abuse-provision-data-routes-to-support/#1552314575964-b31f3835-f2a1

Chapter 12

Understanding the Impact of Law and Ethics

Sarah Riding

Learning Objectives

1 To understand the key legislation that may impact on clients and their children
2 To recognise what clients may experience when social services are involved with their children
3 To recognise the impact of our own values and ethics on our practice
4 To explore how to support clients who are involved in child protection proceedings

Context

This chapter, written from a social work perspective, will consider how the law, particularly that relating to children, works to both protect and penalise victims of domestic abuse. The chapter will further explore how the value base of social work practitioners can have a significant impact on the way victims can be portrayed as "failing to protect" their child and not being "a good enough parent." The chapter will suggest that failure to understand the impact of perpetrator behaviour can lead to a second assault on the victim by those who are meant to keep them safe. Whilst counsellors and psychotherapists will not usually be involved with social workers, often clients will bring experiences of interacting with social workers and the court system. It is helpful for counsellors to understand the background to this, as the stories presented can otherwise, at times, feel strange and unusual to those not involved in these systems. This can assist in understanding and facilitating the client to tell their story in a compassionate and understanding environment.

Philosophical Base in Social Work

Dominant ideology about domestic abuse is still rooted in a family systems model (Kerr & Bowen, 1988) namely the idea of family dysfunction. This understands violence as being a result of a particular pattern of relationships

DOI: 10.4324/9781003253266-12

rather than arising from the behaviour of the individual. This explanation however places too much emphasis on family systems rather than societal factors or individual traits. It ignores the impact of partner behaviour within domestic abuse, often blaming the victim in the relationship for not doing more. It further works on gendered assumptions about roles within families, where the mother is blamed for not doing "her job" properly in keeping the children safe, or the father's experience of abuse minimised or discounted, with the emphasis being on their faults, not those of the perpetrator. While such an orthodox approach remains in practice and victims are seen as colluding or even to blame for the violence done to them, those supporting men, women, and children may be seen as part of the problem not a source of support.

Victims of domestic abuse and their children require their experiences to be validated and not to have shame reinforced. Indeed, social work responses to domestic violence have been described as using sanitised language rather than naming the level of violence and impact involved (Humphreys, 1999; Baynes & Holland, 2012). More often than not, other concerns such as alcohol use or mental health take priority as a focus of intervention rather than the impact of the violence (Humphreys, 1999). Interventions focus almost exclusively on children, often leaving the adult victim lost and alone, and perpetrators often disengage and disappear. Further it is important to note that men as both victims of domestic abuse and fathers are often ignored or not believed, as a dominant ideology that only women are victims of domestic abuse remains strong within social work. Practitioners need to be aware of the invisibility of male victims. Indeed, whilst 26% of victims of Domestic Abuse are male (Office for National Statistics, 2022), domestic abuse is predominantly taught on social work programmes as gendered violence perpetrated by males on females. There is often little attention paid to those in same-sex relationships or identifying as non-binary or transgender. Social work as a predominantly female profession can unwittingly perpetuate these stereotypes in practice. In 2018, The British Association of Social Work (BASW) published an article on its website entitled "Domestic abuse is everywhere in social work" with the author, despite the title, failing to identify the possibility that men may be victims of domestic abuse. BASW has since released new guidelines, published in April 2021, which form a useful guide for counsellors to understand the support offered through a variety of processes. Whilst the guide states its aim is to be inclusive of gender identities, it then states "we wish to acknowledge this whilst also recognising that most victims/survivors are in fact women –domestic abuse is a gendered crime" (BASW, 2021, p. 6). Social workers are therefore being trained to see a third of victims as somehow of less importance and indeed, whilst men are not the majority, there should not be a hierarchy of abuse. Failure to recognise that women and same-sex partners can be perpetrators of abuse can place both adults and children at risk and lead to unjust decisions being made.

The chapter will further demonstrate the emotional toll that court processes can have on victims and children and the need for those involved not to downplay the impact of emotional and psychological abuse. Findings from a "Costs of Freedom" study (Kelly et al., 2014) involving a hundred women and their children tracked over three years, identified that:

> Across all agencies domestic violence was still being reduced to incidents of physical assault, which led not only to an exclusion of some women from services and support when their abuse was more characterised by coercive control, but also a minimising of post-separation abuse. This misunderstanding also meant that many professionals underestimated the toll living with abuse had on women and children, expecting that separation, in and of itself, would not just create safety but also lift all the other burdens. Women may have moved on, but the shadow of domestic violence had not been rubbed out. (p. 7)

The above quotation can of course be applied to victims of any gender identity. The approach in this chapter is to draw on the above context and consider the impact of this thinking when using legal remedies and to make recommendations to improve practice based on the voices of survivors. The chapter will highlight the importance of services taking a domestic violence-informed approach in working with survivors and their children.

> Reflection: Clients who experience domestic abuse are sometimes working with social workers regarding care of their children. How might you feel if your client brought examples of being misunderstood or misjudged by the social worker? How might you respond to the client? What might you take to supervision?

Legislation and Domestic Abuse

According to Safelives (2014), 130,000 children live in homes where there is high-risk domestic abuse, whilst 62% of children living with domestic abuse are directly harmed by the perpetrator of the abuse, in addition to the harm caused by witnessing the abuse of others. Each year more than 100,000 people in the UK are at high and imminent risk of being murdered or seriously injured as a result of domestic abuse (Safelives, 2014). Since the COVID pandemic, the charity Refuge has reported a 25% increase in calls and online requests since March 2020, and visits to their helpline website have increased by 150%. The publication "Domestic abuse: Learning from Case Reviews" (NSPCC, 2020) highlighted that a dominant ideology in social work is still that mothers are responsible for the care and protection of their children and many practitioners did not fully understand the dynamics of domestic violence. The 2019 Triennial Analysis of Serious Case Reviews highlighted domestic abuse as prevalent amongst families where there had been a serious case review (now known as Safeguarding Practice Reviews). However domestic violence was only one factor amongst a range of family characteristics, the most prevalent being mental health, with substance misuse also more frequent than in the general population. This highlights the need for practitioners to understand the complexities of the lives of the families they work with to practice effectively.

Children Act 1989

The Children Act, 1989 remains the most important piece of legislation for social workers in safeguarding children. It is this legislation that allows social workers to support, intervene, and assess parenting capacity and as such it is important for counsellors to have knowledge of this given the implications this legislation can have on a client's life.

Under s1(1) Children Act, 1989 (CA, 1989),

> where the court is determining any issue relating to the upbringing of a child or the administration of a child's property, the child's welfare shall be the court's paramount consideration.

This paramountcy principle is the key consideration children and family social workers should be guided by alongside the welfare checklist set out in s1(3) CA, 1989. The factors listed in the welfare checklist are:

a the ascertainable wishes and feelings of the child concerned (considered in the light of his age and understanding).
b his physical, emotional, and educational needs.
c the likely effect on him of any change in his circumstances.
d his age, sex, background, and any characteristics of his which the court considers.
e any harm which he has suffered or is at risk of suffering.
f how capable each of his parents, and any other person in relation to whom the court considers the question to be relevant, is of meeting his needs.
g the range of powers available to the court under CA, 1989.

In considering both the paramountcy principle and welfare checklist it is not unreasonable to consider the welfare of the child as linked to that of the non-abusive parent and to understand that a strength-based domestic violence informed approach would recognise the need to support that parent as a priority to ensure the safety and well-being of the child. Too often children and families social workers appear to be forgetting that they are not only social workers to the child but to the family. This can result in an over harsh approach to the victim who is seen as failing as a parent and putting the child at risk by, for example, not leaving the relationship, without recognising how the perpetrator works to prevent this.

In understanding the harm domestic abuse has on children, not only does the social worker draw on the paramountcy principle but they need to understand the harm that is caused to the child. Social workers have a duty to investigate Under S47 of the CA, 1989, where they have reason to believe a child is at risk of suffering or has suffered significant harm and the harm is due to the care being given by the parent/carer. Under Section 31(9) of the Children Act, 1989, as amended by the Adoption and Children Act 2002:

> Harm means ill-treatment or impairment of health or development including for example impairment suffered from seeing or hearing the ill-treatment of another; Development means physical, intellectual, emotional, social or behavioural development; Health means physical or mental health; Ill-treatment includes sexual abuse and forms of ill-treatment which are not physical.

The Adoption and Children Act 2002 broadens the definition of Significant Harm to include the emotional harm suffered by those children who witness domestic violence or are aware of domestic violence within their home environment. This definition clearly recognises the harm domestic violence causes to the child, however, also highlights the role of the parent/carer as being responsible for harm. In the absence of a domestic violence-informed approach this can result in blaming the victim for "failure to protect the child," as Edleson (1999, p. 295) comments, "It is unfair to characterise our failure to rein in abusive men as battered mothers' failure to act."

However, this perception of failure on the part of the non-abusive parent remains a constant theme. It is not only that they are seen as failing to protect, but they are also re-shamed by professionals who focus on, for example, neglect in the home without recognising the paralysis to act that trauma can cause. It is important that counsellors understand that this process may be going on at the same time they are working with a victim to reframe their trauma and its impact as the approaches can contradict one another.

> after finally leaving and escaping to a refuge after years of abuse I was working with their counsellor on trying to put myself together, only for my children's' social worker to explain they were starting care proceedings as I wasn't a good parent because I used drugs, the drugs that helped me get through every episode of abuse I took to protect my children. (Survivor voice as told to refuge worker)

Assessments that are conducted most often focus on the mother and the child meaning the male parent, who may or may not be the perpetrator, is not assessed as part of the family. If a perpetrator, this means he does not have to take responsibility for his abusive behaviour. If he is a victim, he has no means of sharing his experiences or those of his children, leaving the mother to tell her version of events. Indeed, treatment by social workers can mean the toxic stress continues, even if they have been found sanctuary in a refuge, by being asked why they didn't leave and seeing any substance misuse as a choice rather than a way of managing the pain and trauma of the abuse.

Where contact with children has been granted to the perpetrator, victims require that recognition is given to the danger of on-going abuse and to the huge effects on children's well-being and mental health where they are forced into attending contact. Perpetrators have been known to seek contact with children solely to maintain contact with the other parent, rather than a desire to be a good parent.

Addiction must be seen as predominantly experience-dependent, not substance dependent. Social workers, together with other professionals, must change their approach and really understand what has happened during the abusive relationship to support the parent and thus the child. Failure to recognise the impact of abuse and the trauma can result in the removal of children as a result of parental substance misuse and then the abandonment of the parent by services.

If a social worker believes that the child has experienced harm and that harm is significant (and indeed no one would argue domestic abuse does not fall under significant harm) then to meet what is known as the threshold criteria for care proceedings to be started, not only has the harm to be significant it has also to be attributable to the parent/carer. This is a critical notion, as what is attributable to the parent in a domestic abuse scenario depends on an understanding of how perpetrators control their victims. Without this awareness and understanding of the impact of such control, social workers can see a parent: with neglectful home conditions; with mental health challenges; substance misuse; and as being responsible for harm that should be attributed to the perpetrator. However, being held responsible can re-traumatise the victim and this can have huge impact on counselling being undertaken. The implications of a victim of abuse being seen to meet the threshold criteria can be devastating as seen in the example from casework below:

> Following removal of a child from a parent, after the granting of a Care Order by the Court, the parent left a refuge upset and angry, still using substances to cope with the trauma of abuse and now of the court experience. When asked about support for her, the social worker involved remarked (unattributed):
>
> "I am the child's social worker; she has made her decision."

It appears a cruel system that would abandon a woman or man who has been a victim of domestic violence, that fails to recognise and understand trauma and that disregards the voice of the child who wants to remain with the parent.

> Reflection: What are your own feelings about the care of children? What are your experiences of childcare (as a parent and/or as a child)? How did the case study above affect you? How might this influence your practice?

This is not suggesting that if there is a risk of significant harm removing a child should not be considered. Indeed, the child protection system is complex, however, decisions must be made on reliable and verifiable evidence. The suggestion is rather that a domestic violence-informed approach would acknowledge the impact of trauma on the victim. Research by Allen and Riding (2018) looking at child protection social work has identified a lack of professional competence in working with Gypsy, Roma, Traveller families where pathologising a whole community as one where "domestic violence is in their culture" means children can be left in dangerous situations or removed without any actual evidence, based only on discriminatory judgements which are not challenged at any level of the child protection process including the judicial one. Cemlyn and Allen (2016) report that many Romani and Traveller families can be so intimidated, confused, and ashamed of child protection involvement that they significantly delay seeking independent advocacy and legal advice, sometimes until just before the final court hearing resulting in them being seen as uncooperative and uninvolved with their child.

The comments below demonstrate a prejudiced view of Traveller communities as ones where domestic violence is both rife and families are hard to reach. The result of such views is that the interpretation of the welfare of the child becomes linked to the social workers' own cultural bias where children are either to be rescued or left depending on whether the community is pathologised or there is a rule of cultural optimism in place, where children are fine as this is what they are used to. A social worker made the following comment:

> Domestic Abuse can be common in the Traveller culture. Statistics suggest that Traveller children are three times more likely to experience Domestic Abuse. They are also culturally close-knit, less likely to report Domestic Abuse or ask for help because of what will be felt within their communities. (South East: Focus Group 1) (Allen and Riding, 2018)

What is clear is that without any domestic violence informed assessment of the whole family these views will perpetuate to the detriment of children, families, and whole communities.

The Role of Mediation

Mediation requires both parties concerned to discuss the arrangements for children and is based on a belief that both of the parties involved have equal power. This is clearly not the case in terms of domestic abuse; however, parents are receiving notifications as to dates and times for mediation even when they are in a refuge having fled the violence. There is an assumption that holding mediation over a video link protects the victim, however, what is forgotten by professionals is that seeing the perpetrator or just hearing the voice, especially where there has been coercive control, can be re-traumatising. This has been recognised by the National Advisory Council on Violence against Women (2001):

> Women who are battered may be unable to participate fully or freely in mediation. They routinely assess the risks or costs of noncompliance with their abusive partner's demands, particularly related to disclosure of abuse. In mediation or in legal proceedings, battered women may not appear intimidated or fearful, but they may nonetheless be doing quick mental calculus to avert danger, achieve safety, and gain some authority to manage their lives. They may be weighing whether to assert their legal interests against the likelihood that doing so may compromise their safety. (2001, p. 14, ch. 3)

Where this is understood by those supporting victims, advice can be given for the victim to refuse mediation. The result of such a refusal is that CAFCAS (Children and Family Court Advisory and Support Service) will send an independent social worker to do fact-finding. This can involve getting information of previous convictions, for example, and building a picture of the abusive behaviour. Without this fact-finding process, the victim can be portrayed as merely being uncooperative. Should a counsellor discuss with a victim their desire to refuse mediation, this is not being obstructive as it may ensure that the process of fact-finding occurs and they can potentially keep the victim safe. It is critical therefore that professionals understand that whilst mediation might be a sensible solution for many, where there is domestic abuse, it can be abusive and dangerous.

Domestic Abuse Act 2021

The biggest change in legislation has come with the introduction of the Domestic Abuse Act 2021, which received Royal Assent of 29 April 2021. The aims of the 2021 Act are stated as being to:

- Raise awareness and understanding about the devastating impact of domestic abuse on victims and their families.

- Further improve the effectiveness of the justice system in providing protection for victims of domestic abuse and bringing perpetrators to justice.
- Strengthen the support for victims of abuse by statutory agencies.

The Act has been welcomed by those working with victims of domestic abuse, especially given the additional support it offers to victims through the court process. Where prior to this Act perpetrators could take their victim to court and cross-examine them themselves, recreating the trauma, the Domestic Abuse Act presumes victims be eligible for special measures in criminal, family, and civil courts. This can include giving evidence via video link. The Act further prevents the cross-examination of victims by their alleged perpetrator.

The Act creates the first statutory definition of Domestic Abuse and extends the definition of coercive and controlling behaviour by widening the parameters of "personally connected" to include ex-partners and family members who do not live together. This is important to victims who have previously had to fight for professionals to take their claims of ongoing abuse seriously when it has involved an ex-partner.

The Act places an onus on Local Authorities to develop and publish a Domestic Abuse Strategy for their local area. The duty requires the strategy to consider the support needs of victims of domestic abuse and their children in relevant safe accommodation. The Manchester City Council strategy, for example, includes the development of

> a coordinated Domestic Abuse Support in Safe Accommodation Pathway that allows for an integrated holistic assessment linked to a range of housing and support options that includes:
>
> - Integrated specialist front door and support planning which will combine domestic abuse and homelessness knowledge to best assess the suitability of various housing and support options
> - Enhanced safe accommodation and support offer, which will provide specialist support to adult and child victims of Domestic Abuse and include survivors with protected characteristics and/or complex needs. e.g. translators and interpreters, faith services, mental health advice and support, drug and alcohol advice and support, and immigration advice
> - Move on and recovery, to support victims/survivors of domestic abuse as they continue their recovery
> - Work with housing providers and private landlords/agencies to support victims.
>
> (Manchester Community Safety Partnership, 2021, p. 5)

The Domestic Violence Act 2021 gives the Police new powers to issue civil Domestic Abuse Protection Notices (DVPN). These provide victims with immediate protection from offenders and require them to leave the home for up to 48 hours. Magistrates' courts are now able to issue Domestic Abuse Protection Orders (DVPO) following an application by the police within two days of issuing the DVPN. This provides up to 28 days of protection from the offender returning to the home and/or re-abusing the victim. It is hoped both these orders will help in preventing domestic abuse by having the ability to force perpetrators to undertake mandatory support, for example, offender programmes and/or mental health support.

Where criminal charges are brought against the offender, victims report that they continue to struggle with the whole legal process, despite changes that have been introduced, as they can feel that they are kept out the loop as to Crown Prosecution Service charging decisions. For example, bail continuance can have a huge impact if bail is granted without a victim knowing: a protocol that requires them to be updated is called for. Victims have spoken of getting limited witness care especially if they have been coerced into a crime with the perpetrator. There is a requirement that they are treated as a victim.

Whilst the changes introduced due to the Act are warmly welcomed, there is still a need for professionals to have a domestic abuse/trauma-informed attitude. Without an understanding of the impact of abuse as trauma on the victim, professionals will still make assessments based on ill-informed assumptions that, for example, the victim has chosen to stay with the perpetrator and has failed to safeguard children and/or neglected the child because of their own mental ill health/substance misuse. The reinforcement of shame (see chapter 6) that can result from professional attitudes remains probably the most critical area of practice that needs to be changed and understood, given that social work is a profession founded on a social justice model.

Social workers must understand that living in an abusive relationship can lead to victims presenting in unexpected ways. How social workers interpret such responses and behaviours, especially those that are around survival, can lead to extreme difficulty for victims in disclosing abuse, particularly where there are children. The risk is to be labelled as an unfit parent who put their own needs first and who "choose" to stay with the perpetrator.

Reflection: The Domestic Abuse Act 2021 is an important milestone in working with domestic abuse. How might this affect any work you do as a counsellor? What might be useful for you to know?

The Safe and Together Model

It is important to recognise that work is being done to address some of the prejudiced behaviours and practices towards victims of violence, especially where children are involved. However, this needs to be a responsibility of all partner agencies, including the judiciary. The Safe and Together Model, developed by the Safe and Together Institute (2019) (see https://safeandtogetherinstitute.com/ for more information), aims to help child welfare systems become domestic violence informed. The model focuses on the patterns of behaviour of the perpetrator and uses the understanding of those patterns and their impact on the victim to work with the family. The key principle of the model is

> the concept that children are best served when we can work toward keeping them safe and together with the non-offending parent (the adult domestic violence survivor). The Model provides a framework for partnering with domestic violence survivors and intervening with domestic violence perpetrators in order to enhance the safety and well-being of children. (https://academy.safeandtogetherinstitute.com/course/intro)

The priority in the model is a focus on building the relationship with the victim to support them, whilst recognising that it is the behaviour of the perpetrator that is the source of harm. The model seeks to transform how practitioners view victims, not as willing participants in the family dynamic or as failing to protect, but as traumatised victims who use whatever they can manage the pain of the abuse. Several local authorities are now implementing to the Safe and Together Model which is an extremely positive move forward. The key features of the model are:

1. To keep the child together with the non-offending parent with services supporting the family to heal from the trauma and help provide stability and safety
2. Work with the non-offending parent as the default position and to keep a child focussed position
3. Intervention with the perpetrator and holding them accountable drawing on the full range of resources available (https://safeandtogetherinstitute.com/the-sti-model/model-overview/)

The Care Act 2014

Whilst a focus of domestic abuse has often been on the welfare of the Child, not all victims have children. In these circumstances, as adults, they should be afforded protection under the Care Act, 2014. The Care Act, 2014 places a duty on local authorities to promote individual well-being. The Care Act, 2014 is clear that well-being involves protection from abuse and neglect and the accompanying statutory guidance outlines that abuse takes many forms, hence local authorities should not be constrained in their view of what constitutes abuse or neglect. It includes psychological, physical, sexual, financial, emotional abuse and so-called honour-based violence, so it is clear domestic abuse is included. In situations in which domestic abuse is identified, social work practitioners must always consider raising a safeguarding concern. Further when any concern is raised about domestic abuse, or a disclosure is made, a Domestic Abuse Stalking and Harassment Risk Identification Checklist (DASHRIC) should be completed. Under the Care Act, 2014, if care and support needs are identified, a statutory assessment will be conducted where the adult will be considered as to whether they meet eligibility criteria for services. This is where the Care Act, 2014 can be limited as not all those being assessed will be identified as meeting the eligibility criteria for services. Should the adult be assessed as not meeting the eligibility criteria, but is still considered at risk, they can be assessed through a non-statutory inquiry. This can result in them being referred on to a range of services, for example, Women's Aid. Those deemed to be at high risk from domestic violence should be referred to a multi-agency risk assessment conference (MARAC). Whilst there is an acknowledgement that not all adults will of course require support under the Care Act, anyone undertaking assessment must have an understanding of how trauma impacts on Domestic abuse victims, something that is still missing from adult services.

> as we had been married for 40 years and had a circle of friends when I eventually left and asked for support I was on my own, I was referred to adult social services by the refuge and they told me that I basically had no needs even though I was traumatised and my mental health was shot, but it felt like no one cared, I was told that as I had friends I was lucky, I felt I was on my own. (reported to refuge worker by abuse survivor)

Too often the needs of adult victims of domestic abuse are downplayed as not important or that the individual has made a particular choice, which requires an understanding of how trauma can impact capacity. Domestic abuse training amongst adult social care staff is increasing and it is hoped that this understanding and awareness can lead to a domestic abuse-informed practice.

> Reflection: This chapter has shown a range Acts and acronyms. How comfortable do you feel with these? Where might understanding these details be helpful in your practice?

Summary

Whilst attitudes have changed significantly amongst professionals there still remain core beliefs based on longstanding stereotypes of the family and to the nature of domestic abuse itself. This results in an automatic prejudice, predominantly where the victim is a parent, especially with a presumption that they should be able to protect their child at all costs against violence being perpetrated. Given that the costs for many victims are so high, the only way to survive the level of trauma is often to use coping methods that may be detrimental to the child, for example using substances. Unless and until social work practitioners understand the nature of trauma and approach the victim with a trauma-informed, domestic violence-informed approach, victims will continue to be seen as failing as parents and the system will re-shame them. This can mean that children are removed, and victims abandoned.

This understanding needs to inform any therapeutic relationship being built with a victim, the recognition that the child protection system can re-abuse victims has to inform practice as there is a double abuse to be understood. It is good to see that changes are being made especially within children's social care with the introduction of models such as Safe and Together that clearly place responsibility on the perpetrator. However, such models need to be seen as the standard across all authorities. Adult social care further needs to recognise adult victims of abuse and understand the trauma, looking at thresholds for eligibility of services with a domestic violence-informed perspective. Without this, far too many victims are left without any support, vulnerable and alone.

It is sobering to note that when asked about what they would like from professionals, victims ask for little, far less than they should be given.

Key Learning Points

In this chapter the key legislation that impacts on victims has been considered, whilst this is by no means a substantive list, both The Children Act, 1989 and The Domestic Abuse Act 2021 can arguably be said to have a substantial impact on how both victims and perpetrators are perceived, with The Children Act, 1989 especially being impacted on where the social work practitioner views are underpinned by prejudice. This understanding and awareness is important for those who are involved in a supportive and therapeutic relationship with victims as it recognises several learning points:

The Key Elements Are

1. Recognition that where the victim is a parent, they may well have found themselves routinely blamed for the child being in a violent environment. Where victim blaming has been normalised there is deep shame to work with.
2. An understanding that use of alcohol and drugs for example is likely to be a method of coping with the deep pain of trauma being experienced, and the importance of not asking what is wrong with you but rather what has happened to you.
3. Encourage victims to have a voice. It is important to recognise that professional meetings where decisions are made about victims' children can replicate the power dynamics between the perpetrator and victim.

Victims may need advocacy support in the meeting and/or support prior to and after meetings.

4 There is a need for all professionals involved in work where domestic abuse is a factor to be familiar with their Local Authority's Domestic Abuse Action Plan and to ensure that the standards are upheld.
5 Where mediation is requested, it is important to be able to articulate on behalf of the victim the trauma that can be caused. Ensure that fact-finding is done prior to any mediation.
6 Where a victim has had children removed, they still remain a victim of domestic abuse and as such are required to be assessed for support under the Care Act, 2014. The abandoning of victims should never be an option and this may require advocacy in respect of the victim.

References

Allen, D., & Riding, S. (2018). The Fragility of Professional Competence: A Preliminary account of Child Protection Practice with Romani and Traveller Children. Project Report. Eurpoan Roma Rights Centre. http://www.errc.org/reports--submissions/the-fragility-of-professional-competence-a-preliminary-account-of-child-protection--practice-with-romani-and-traveller-children-in-england. (Accessed: 25 September 2022).

BASW England (March 2021). *Domestic abuse practice guidance: For both children and family/adult social workers*. BASW.

Baynes, P., & Holland, S. (2012). Social work with violent men: A child protection file study in an English local authority. *Child Abuse Review*, *21*(1), 53–65.

Care Act (2014). c.1.Available at https://www.legislation.gov.uk/ukpga/2014/23/section/1 (Accessed: 26 August 2022)

Cemlyn, S., & Allen, D. (2016). Outreach: care experiences amongst Gypsy, Traveller and Roma Families (P161–179). In C. Williams & M. J. Graham (Eds), *Social Work in a Diverse Society: Transformatory Practice with Black and Ethnic Minority Individuals and Communities*. The Policy Press.

Children Act (1989). c.1. Available at https://www.legislation.gov.uk/ukpga/1989/41/section/1 (Accessed: 26 August 2022)

Edleson, J. L. (1999). Children's witnessing of adult domestic violence. *Journal of Interpersonal Violence*, *14*(8), 839–870.

Humphreys, C. (1999). Avoidance and confrontation: Social work practice in relation to domestic violence and child abuse. *Child and Family Social Work*, *4*, 77–87.

Kelly, L., Sharp-Jeffs, N., & Klein, R. (2014). *Finding the costs of freedom: How women and children rebuild their lives after domestic violence*. Project Report. Solace Womens Aid, London.

Kerr, M. E., & Bowen, M. (1988). *Family evaluation: An approach based on Bowen theory*. W W Norton & Co.

Manchester Community Safety Partnership (2021). *Manchester community safety partnership domestic abuse strategy*. Manchester City Council. Available from: https://www.manchester.gov.uk/downloads/download/5643/domestic_abuse_strategy

National Advisory Council on Violence Against Women (2001). C.3.Enhancing the Response of the Justice System: Civil Remedies, in Toolkit to End Violence against

Women. https://www.ojp.gov/ncjrs/virtual-library/abstracts/toolkit-end-violence-against-women
NSPCC (2020). *Domestic abuse: Learning from case reviews*. London: NSPCC.
Office for National Statistics (ONS) (2022). Released 25 November 2022, ONS website, article, Domestic abuse victim characteristics, England and Wales: Year ending March 2022. https://www.ons.gov.uk/peoplepopulationandcommunity/crimeandjustice/articles/domesticabusevictimcharacteristicsenglandandwales/yearendingmarch2022
Safe and Together Institute (2019). Model Overview. https://safeandtogetherinstitute.com/the-sti-model/model-overview/
Safelives (2014). Getting It Right Everytime. https://safelives.org.uk/sites/default/files/resources/Getting%20it%20right%20first%20time%20-%20complete%20report.pdf

Chapter 13

Using Creative Arts Therapies to Work with Trauma Developed from Experiences of Domestic Abuse

Joanna Omylinska-Thurston and Leigh Gardner

Learning Objectives

1. Introducing creative arts therapies as a way of working with trauma developed from experiences of domestic violence
2. Highlighting ethical considerations when using creative methods to working with trauma
3. Working through the stages of trauma as defined by Herman (1992) and outlined in Chapter 2 including practical examples of using creative approaches
4. Introduction to Arts for the Blues to working with trauma

Introduction

The healing properties of the arts have been known for millennia but using arts with patients for trauma-related experiences became more prominent from the 1900s, when music was used as therapy to treat soldiers following WWI (Malchiodi, 2005). This was developed by Joseph Moreno (1932) who proposed action methods including the use of imagery and enactment for working with mental health problems. In other disciplines in 1942, Adrian Hill coined the term "art therapy" as he discovered that patients were able to express anxiety and trauma through painting which seemed helpful (Waller, 2015). Since then, the arts have been used more systematically in the UK especially with WWII veterans struggling with symptoms of trauma (Karkou & Sanderson, 2006). Arts therapies offer a good alternative, especially to verbal treatment for trauma where retelling traumatic experiences are often poorly tolerated (Schouten et al., 2019). Johnson et al. (2009) highlighted that the contribution of the creative arts lies in the use of the non-verbal and symbolic techniques related to specific artistic modalities. These modalities offer a protective shield through creating an aesthetic distance which allows clients to work with trauma while minimising the risk of being overwhelmed by traumatic memory.

DOI: 10.4324/9781003253266-13

Karkou et al. (2006) defined the use of "arts" in a therapeutic context as relating to activities such as music making, mark making, movement, and writing, where artistic value judgement is removed and the focus is on the process of art making, not the product. Working with arts modalities involves the whole person including sensi-motor, perceptual, cognitive, emotional, social, and spiritual aspects and relies on non-verbal communication. Creativity is a key aspect of arts therapies and involves discovering new connections, new relationships, and new meanings. Working with arts involves using imagery, symbols, and metaphors, thus externalising unconscious content making unknown known, through the mechanism of projection (see also chapter 8).

Many women's refuges and domestic violence support programs use creative arts as part of their offered activities which is different from offering creative or expressive therapies, but demonstrates the value of working with the arts for healing. Murray et al. (2017) devised workshops for survivors of intimate partner violence using several different kinds of arts modalities to reflect the unique needs and preferences of the clients and where they were in their individual healing process. The groups provided mutual support, with participants reporting feeling less alone in situations. An exhibition of the work produced helped to raise awareness of the effects of domestic violence in the community and gave the participants a sense of pride and purpose in what they had achieved.

Reflection: try to remember the last time you found yourself responding to a creative experience. It may have been a piece of music, an image, something you read or were making or a piece of nature. Note the feelings that come up for you.

Ethical Considerations When Using Creative Methods

Creative methods can be very powerful and often involve connecting and working with senses, the body and aspects of ourselves that are not usually accessed verbally via cognitive work. The strength of feeling elicited by working with the arts can be often underestimated and therefore this work requires preparation, training, and an ability to create an appropriate and safe space for the client.

Training for working creatively with trauma is essential to practice ethically. It is also essential to note the difference between being an arts therapist and using art in therapy. Some creative arts therapies mentioned in this chapter have professional registrations, for instance in the UK arts therapists (art therapy, music therapy, and dramatherapy) will be HCPC registered or linked with professional bodies such as Association for Dance and Movement Psychotherapy. If you are a therapist but not trained specifically in one of the arts psychotherapies, you will be using expressive activities in your practice, but you are not using "art therapy" or "drama therapy" unless you have the qualification for doing so. If you want to use creative methods in therapy, you will need adequate training alongside supervision from a supervisor who is experienced in working with expressive therapies (BACP, 2018).

Another important aspect to consider is that using creative methods when working with trauma can re-trigger traumatic memories including flashbacks and dissociation. Although expressive therapies provide containing structures and aesthetic distance which helps with feeling overwhelmed, it is important to work at the clients' pace and take breaks as needed. It is also important to ensure grounding at the end of the sessions and that clients are feeling safe emotionally to reconnect with the day-to-day (see also chapter 8). Using Levine's (2010) titration (sensations are introduced in small amounts) and pendulation (going back and forth to the sensations) is also helpful and allows the client to work at a steady and safe pace.

It is helpful to inform clients that following the sessions they are likely to continue to process experiences that they worked on during the sessions. Leaving space after the session for further processing will be useful. It is also beneficial to involve the body in further processing after the session so perhaps suggesting some walking, swimming, yoga, gentle movement after the session may be useful.

Collaboration is an essential part of working with trauma especially from the perspective of power dynamics as commonly clients (especially victims of domestic abuse) experienced situations where power was abused. It is very important to include clients' preferences in terms of the physical set up and themes of the sessions as well as the choice of arts modality in order to create a true sense of safety and collaboration. Therefore, the need to build strong therapeutic relationships which allows the client to trust the therapist and the therapy is paramount to working with trauma (see chapters 4 and 5). Therapists need to be aware of the importance of allowing power in the dyad to be shared, to encourage clients to find their own power within (Proctor, 2017).

The Importance of Neuroscience When Working with Trauma Using Creative Arts

Malchiodi (2020) developed expressive arts therapy for trauma based on neurobiology research. She emphasised that traumatic experiences may not always be encoded as explicit memory including thoughts and feelings and may be stored as nonverbal, sensory fragments on a bodily level (Van der Kolk, 1994). According to Malchiodi (2020) the main reason for the use of the arts in trauma work is the sensory nature of the arts. The arts are believed to access the right brain that stores sensory-based experiences, including images, sounds, and tactile experiences related to trauma (see also chapter 8). Expression and processing of these implicit memories have an important role in successful trauma intervention. The initial sensory expression may make exposure of the trauma story more tolerable, helping to overcome avoidance advancing the therapeutic process.

Van der Kolk (2014) noted that when people think of their trauma, right brain activity (that is associated with feelings and sensations) is much stronger than left brain activity. He explained that "executive functioning" associated with the left brain, which is responsible for thinking, sequencing, and organising, shuts down when somebody is distressed. When memories of trauma are re-triggered, the right brain reacts as if it is happening in the present which may lead to a shutting down of thinking. Hence the importance of working with clients in a safe, boundaried, and grounded way to keep them within their window of tolerance (Siegel, 1999) so they can continue to think. Safe use of the arts can provide this containment as therapists can co-regulate with the clients through the body including grounding, deep breathing, and posture (see also chapter 8).

Using Creative Arts When Working with Trauma

Herman's model (1992) of working with trauma is commonly used and corresponds to Steps 3–7 of working with survivors of domestic violence as outlined by Roddy (2014) (see also chapters 2 and 8). Herman's three stages are as follows:

1 Safety and stabilisation
2 Processing
3 Integration

Working with clients in an arts-based approach requires the same basic trauma work structure as in verbal approaches. Below, each stage will be discussed considering the use of the arts in the sessions.

Safety and Stabilisation

The fundamental elements of the trauma work include building relationships, finding a sense of safety, and self-regulation.

Establishing the Therapeutic Relationship Using Arts-Based Approaches

The first step in therapy with trauma is establishing a healing relationship that is empowering for the client. This is particularly important for victims of domestic abuse where interpersonal trauma could have developed (Schore, 2003). Using creative arts allows attunement and empathy which encourages developing trust and active engagement in the work. The therapist is also often a participant and a witness genuinely attending to the arts-based communications creating an environment of unconditional positive regard (Malchiodi, 2020).

Malchiodi (2020) states that creativity is often affected in people who experienced trauma as they experience self-doubt and difficulty expressing themselves fearing criticism, aggression, or violence. Finding a gradual way of engaging in expressive arts supports recovering creativity and playfulness, leading to feeling comfortable with self-expression. Often initial sessions with this client group may involve introduction to the arts to reawaken the possibility of play. However, it may take a while before clients feel comfortable and safe enough to engage in arts media. Malchiodi (2020) emphasised that unconditional positive regard is essential in this process which may come through as a genuine surprise or authentic "delight" in clients' creativity.

In order to build a relationship, clients may engage in a simple body warm-up/ stretches or music exercises. Any creative activity that actively engages participants will be helpful here and this will be ongoing throughout the therapy.

> Reflection: Play an instrumental piece of music and standing up (or sitting if standing is difficult) with some space around you close your eyes and allow your body to listen to the music. Are there any responses to the sound? Is any part of you wanting to move, tap, turn, stomp, flow? Allow any movements that want to be there and let the music and your body be your guide. Stop either when the music stops or when you feel you wish to and then gently reflect on what this was like for you and what you are left feeling.

Creating a Sense of Safety

The clients need to establish a sense of safety in their body for the healing process to take place, which is fundamental for trauma work. People need to feel subjectively safe to be able to think, feel, and attend to their needs. If they don't feel safe, they feel overwhelmed which gets in the way of therapeutic work (Van der Kolk, 2014).

As explained above, the trusting relationship with the therapist is essential for the work to take place. However, having a confined space for therapy may be very difficult for some clients so it may take time for the client to feel "safe" in the room. It is essential that the therapy room and environment seems appropriate and safe. Removing any loud or sudden noises and creating a warm and welcoming space will enhance a sense of safety. Giving clients choices where to sit and what to engage with, as well as going at the clients' pace is important. Establishing the structure of the sessions and predictability will also enhance a sense of safety.

Working within the "window of tolerance" Siegel (1999) is important for creating a sense of safety. This may include "refraction" by using a prop or figure to communicate and "projection" by using third-person narrative (Malchiodi, 2020). Creative arts therapies use the mechanism of "aesthetic distance" referring to the gap between a client's conscious reality and the fictional or imagined reality presented in a work of art which can reduce distress associated with facing reality. For example, Avetikova (2008) wrote about working with a survivor of domestic violence who made clay figures named as "Bird Monster" and "Horn Lizard," representing vulnerable parts of self that required protection. This helped the client to actively work towards managing distress and obtaining a sense of safety.

When working with trauma we don't expect clients to deal with whatever has happened head on but to find ways of dealing with it in a safe and secure way which does not retrigger the initial trauma (Levine (2010) (see also chapter 8)). We often start by creating a "safe space" clients can turn to when feeling activated or distressed. The aim of this "safe space" is to help the clients avoid feeling overwhelmed and to keep themselves connected to their mind and body.

An important point to note however is that inviting clients to create a safe space can stimulate memories about not having a safe space which can lead to feeling anxious, guilty, or ashamed (Malchiodi, 2020). Using "refraction" and working with a prop, can be helpful, for example, creating a safe environment for a toy duck, allowing for both distance and also control over what the duck might need (Malchiodi, 2015).

One of the creative activities that is often used to facilitate creating safety is a safe space exercise which can be done in imagination or physically in the space. Visualisation (or guided relaxation, Binkley 2013) can help to set a scene if the client wishes to work in this way. It is important to check if clients are willing to try this as for some clients this may be a difficult way to work and using active imagination (Jung, 1935) may stimulate responses they are not ready for. The clients can be invited to draw or make a collage of their safe space.

> Reflection: Using materials such as leaves, twigs, moss, paper including tissue paper or a small box, choose an object such as a small, cuddly toy and create a 'nest' for it. You can paint it or decorate it any way you wish. Note to yourself what it is like to build a nest for your toy. How might this relate to working with a client in a similar way?

The case study below illustrates a client discovering how to access her safe space through the sandtray (see also chapter 9) (Figure 13.1).

> *Rasheen was in her thirties when she first came for counselling, after seeking refuge with her two children due to domestic violence and abuse. She presented as very down and having trouble sleeping due to anxiety and flashbacks of her abuse. In the counselling room there were creative materials within reach. It was the sandtray that Rasheen was drawn to where she connected with the feel of the sand and would often close her eyes as she let the sand run through her fingers. After a few sessions of this sensory touch the therapist gently asked Rasheen what it was like for her to touch and feel the*

Figure 13.1 Rasheen's sandtray. Rasheen is represented by the middle Russian doll, Grandmother is the larger, and her brother the smallest doll. Rasheen's parents are represented by the grey and orange figures in the top right corner.

sand and noted that when she closed her eyes she seemed to be taken to another place. The therapist asked Rasheen if she would like to build this 'other place' in the sandtray using the miniatures. Rasheen silently choose each object for the sand scene, before sharing her completed sandtray with the therapist. She reflected how she had gone back to childhood and a memory she had forgotten, of being sent to her grandmother's one summer. In her sandtray, she showed herself and her brother with grandmother at the beach. Her parents were on the far side of the sand tray with stones representing the tall buildings of a city around them. Rasheen noted how safe and carefree she felt that summer and was surprised by the emotion that came up for her:

Rasheen took a photograph of the sandtray to keep on her phone. Throughout the therapy, she would use this photo to help ground herself and to reconnect with a sense of safety.

Self-Regulation

Learning to self-regulate to achieve stabilisation is important for working with trauma (Herman, 1992). It involves being able to control one's impulses, self-soothe and calm the body's responses to stress. Clients who struggle with self-regulation may often feel overwhelmed which can lead to developing unhelpful

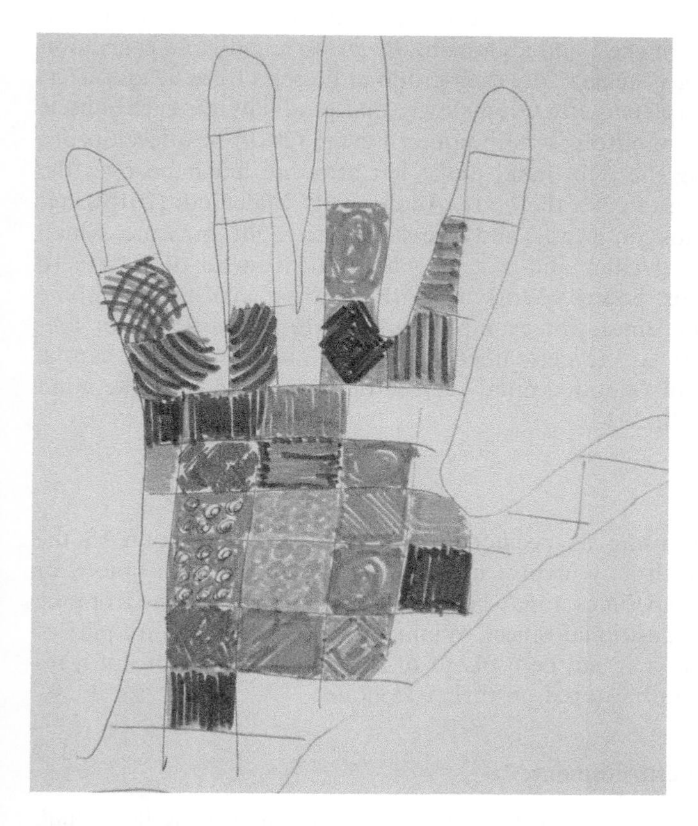

Figure 13.2 First author's drawing hand exercise during Malchiodi's Expressive Therapies and Trauma workshop in 2021. The invitation was to draw the outline of the hand and divide it with the horizontal and vertical lines. Focusing on colouring each of the boxes had a containing, regulating, and relaxing function.

ways to regulate such as substance abuse, overeating, or overworking (see also chapter 7). Active participation in the use of rhythm, movement, enactment, painting, or sound embedded in creative arts provides an opportunity to change the feeling state. This may involve simple doodling or scribbling (Winnicott, 1971), rhythmic movement, drawing hand/foot, journaling, drawing, or making objects. These activities are often pleasurable which can also help in affect regulation. At times engaging in creative arts can also offer a form of distraction which allows the body to calm and regulate (Figure 13.2).

Relaxation and Mindfulness

Learning relaxation and mindfulness are common practices in therapy aiming to develop self-regulation. See chapter 10 for exercises in controlled breathing (e.g. breathing slowly in on a count of 4 and breathing out on a count of 6 while placing hands on chest and abdomen). Progressive muscular relaxation (tensing and relaxing systematically each group of muscles from head to feet) and body scanning (placing attention slowly and gradually on each muscle group) are common mindfulness techniques. Levine (2010) has developed a "body hug" (placing the right hand under left arm and left hand over the right hand) intending to calm the body. Additionally Malchiodi (2015) suggested placing hands on heads and pressing with light pressure which can create a sense of calm and can also help clients who dissociate to reconnect with their bodies. Working with creative arts can combine relaxation and mindfulness for example by "drawing the breath" or creating a "mindfulness jar" (a glass filled with water and glitter) that can be shaken to see how an "agitated mind" can settle, helping to calm the mind and body (Malchiodi, 2020).

Anchoring

Anchoring involves using a specific object/cue to bring attention to the present moment which may involve making a sound, holding an object, or making a posture. Sometimes it may be as simple as holding a stone from the counselling room (transitional object, Winnicott, 1953) if stones are part of the creative practice or it can be a photo of their child or a photo of a favourite place that can be stored on their telephone.

Co-Regulation and Entrainment

Co-regulation invites self-regulation and can be offered via tactile, visual, and rhythm-based experiences. Examples may involve the therapist breathing or moving together with the client which has a co-regulating function and reduces the sense of embarrassment or feeling watched. Closely related to this is the idea of entrainment involving rhythmic synchronisation which Malchiodi (2020) linked with earlier life and hearing the mothers' heartbeat which is soothing and calming for babies. In therapy clients can experience this through the therapist's voice (see also chapter 8).

Mirroring

Mirroring involves reflecting movement or non-verbal communication leading to attunement or empathy and can involve mirroring gestures, stretches, and repetition of a rhythm. At times this can be overwhelming for participants so it is often helpful to invite or offer a simple specific movement (e.g. a hand wave) rather than inviting free movement.

Reflection: Think about what might be the benefits of reflecting simple movements in this 'mirroring' way with a client and also think of what the disadvantages of doing this could be.

Bilateral Movement

Malchiodi (2020) also discussed the value of bilateral movement for self-regulation by using both sides of the body at the same time for example in movement/walking or drawing/painting. This technique is particularly helpful for clients who are easily hyper-aroused or paralysed in the sessions. Suggesting to clients having a walk or swimming after the session might be a helpful way to self-regulate.

Creating a Resource Team

Creating a resource team that can help with self-regulation and can support other trauma work. This could involve imagining figures (e.g. by drawing) or using objects (e.g. in a sandtray) representing supportive people (e.g. a grandmother or a friend) or parts of self (e.g. a strong or wise part of self) (Casson, 2007; Jennings, 1986).

Using Music

Music therapy can activate memories and therefore making appropriate musical choices which can help with working on emotion regulation. Below we offer a case example where the use of music facilitated the connection with the body and initiated further trauma work.

Helena came for counselling on the recommendation of her GP. She often complained of stomach problems and headaches which had been investigated but no medical reason could be found for them, although she did have a history of bulimia. Helena lived with her partner and had recently suffered a miscarriage after what she described as a fall and insisted that she was very accident prone. She would often turn up with different bruises on her arms and occasionally on her face, which she dismissed as her 'clumsiness'.

The therapist had strong suspicions that both Helena and the baby had been endangered by the partner. Helena talked of her body as if it was a separate entity:

'My body is useless, I hate it. I knew it would never be able to have a baby'.

At session 5 of the therapy, Helena brought in some music that her sister had sent her that week. She told the therapist that it was a song they used to listen to in their shared bedroom when they were small and her parents were arguing and fighting downstairs. They would turn it up loud and dance 'until the house went quiet again'. Helena put the music on and as she listened her tears began to fall and she started to rock herself to and fro, clutching her arms around herself. When the music stopped, Helena stroked both her arms and drew a deep breath in. 'I wasn't expecting that', she said.

The music for Helena had started to loosen some deeply painful and traumatic memories. The therapist noted how Helena had stroked her arms, making a connection physically with herself. The stroking of her arm was the first sign that the therapist had noticed of Helena offering herself some self-soothing. The therapist allowed Helena to stay with what she was experiencing which helped to connect with her emotions and body much more.

Using the "Felt Sense"

Working with the "felt sense" (focusing, Gendlin, 1982) can also be helpful in affect regulation which has been developed for trauma work by Levine (2010). The client is encouraged to name body sensations when feeling safe or when looking at a beautiful picture or object and learning how they are experienced in terms of warmth, colours, or shapes. Reminding oneself of these when feeling triggered or activated can help in regulating distress (see also Chapter 8).

> Example: the therapist can ask questions such as 'what's inside for me at this moment, what can I sense, feel, what might need my attention?'. Then invite the client to try to locate where in the body that feeling is and allow any words, images to come up. Arts materials can then be used to express these words or images. This process allows the client to stay in the 'here and now' of the experience.

A more structured way of approaching the "felt sense" could be through "body mapping" (Salomon, 2007). Malchiodi (2020) used body outlines inviting people to map the different body sensations and feelings using colours, shapes, or images. For people who can get activated quite quickly, it is helpful to slow the process down, for example, by focusing only on one body part (e.g. a hand or a foot) or drawing on a smaller body outline. Starting with drawing a self-portrait might be also helpful. Having themes for the body mapping can be useful and can involve the following topics: personal history past and future, images and symbols representing challenges that have been overcome, sources of strength, supporters, and wisdom to share. When working with body sensations it is important that clients stay present in the "here and now" and are not overwhelmed. To facilitate this, distressing sensations can be seen "from above" or "from a distance."

Processing

After establishing safety, stability and self-regulation clients can decide if they want to engage in processing of memories and experiences. This process can be challenging and can lead to the client feeling overwhelmed or risk self-harming behaviours or dissociation. Some clients may decide that they don't need to continue the work as the memories are no longer disruptive for them since they have established stability and safety. This phase involves reviewing the events and their meaning and working through grief and the effects these experiences had on their life. The aim of the arts approach would be to lessen the emotional intensity of the memories and reduce flashbacks and nightmares. Using creative approaches in this phase will also help with creating new narratives and new meanings helping clients to move forward.

Clients often find talking about trauma difficult as memories may come in fragments, or they may feel overwhelmed. Talking also may not make any difference which can lead to feeling more vulnerable as well as ashamed or guilty. Van der Kolk (2000) talked about "speechless terror" that often is associated with the inability to talk about the trauma involving a sense of numbness, shock, and confusion. Therefore, creative approaches might be more beneficial in working with trauma narratives.

Lusebrink (2010) offered a helpful model of levels of processing with clients called Expressive Therapies Continuum (ETC). This model considers neurobiology of the brain in relation to processing trauma and proposes four levels of interventions including kinaesthetic/sensory, perceptual/affective, cognitive/symbolic, and creative/integrative levels. Malchiodi (2012) provided a summary of creative activities at each level depending on where clients might be at, which is illustrated in Table 13.1.

Kinesthetic and Sensory Levels

Dance and Movement Psychotherapy (DMP) enables accessing traumatic material non-directly and gradually through the kinaesthetic and sensory levels (Levy, 2005). The use of non-verbal methods supports clients to increase their capacity to articulate the trauma narrative in an embodied form, which leads to enhanced integration and well-being (Dieterich-Hartwell, 2017; Helmich, 2009). According to de Witte et al. (2021) embodiment is an important vehicle of change in DMP which includes experiencing the body and body awareness. Dieterich-Hartwell (2017) focused on interoception (sensing changing body states) which is particularly relevant to working with trauma. Engaging in movement via movement metaphors (shapes and gestures) allows access to unconscious material which can become a rich source of information.

Table 13.1 Expressive Therapies Continuum to working with trauma

Levels	*Suggested activities*	*Resulting in*
Kinaesthetic and sensory levels	Moving to a rhythm, beating a drum, chanting, scribbling, using different scents, textures.	The activities are satisfying and give sensory pleasure. The process is more important than a product. The aim of this level is sensory integration, sensory awareness, and grounding.
Perceptual/ affective level	Expressing perceptions and emotions without verbal processes. Perceptual aspects can involve creating patterns using lines and colours with art materials. Affective aspects could be expressed by using a drum, movement, sound or drawings conveying fear, anger, sadness, joy.	Ability to express emotions in a safe way and ability to reflect on their expressions. The focus is on producing a satisfying product.
Cognitive/ symbolic level	Using creative arts for problem-solving, structuring, meaning-making. The activities can focus on making a final product (e.g. collage, sandtray, clay shapes).	Clients may use symbols and metaphors to reflect on the personal meaning of expressions. There is a sense of mastery over events, empowerment and self-belief. Focus is on making a satisfying final product.
Creative level/ Integration	Rituals such as personal or group painting, singing, dancing, writing, integrating the journey of therapy, highlighting the change achieved.	There is a sense of achievement and joy in reaching wholeness of expression. Ending and acknowledging the work done in the space and time.

Perceptual/Affective Level

Art therapy including painting and drawing of colours and shapes associated with trauma memories has been helpful in processing trauma (Schouten et al., 2019). Talwar (2007) developed Art Therapy Trauma Protocol (ATTP) for processing of traumatic memories, drawing upon neurobiology. The protocol builds on client-centred and CBT approaches where the client is invited to paint the traumatic memory first followed by verbal exploration including identifying related cognitions. This is repeated by using both the dominant and the non-dominant hand (bilateral drawing) accessing the aspects of the memory clients were not aware of previously, including unconscious somatic experiences. Perceptual and affective self-expression and creating new narratives on that level can enhance emotion regulation as well as facilitate processing trauma.

Cognitive/Symbolic Level

Jennings et al. (1994) suggested that working with symbols and metaphors in creative therapies is an effective way of processing trauma as it uses "aesthetic distance." This also links with Jung's active imagination (Jung, 1997) where the content of one's unconscious is translated into images and symbols. Engaging with these linked Jung with the process of alchemy leading to transformation of trauma. Activities such as making a drawing, collage, or movement might be a helpful way of working with traumatic memories. Working on meaning is also important, gradually inviting the client to share their reflections and using movement, gesture, and sound to amplify the meaning.

Working with sandtrays (Lowenfeld, 2004) can also be helpful, for example, Kern et al. (2016) discussed using sandtrays to work with veterans with PTSD to help avoid domestic violence. Creating stories using miniatures, small figurines, or toys to represent characters in the story, allows sharing the story with some distance and containership of the distress thus allowing clients to remain within their window of tolerance.

Pennebaker and Smyth (2016) found that creative writing can be helpful when working with trauma stories. They suggested writing a couple of months after the traumatic experience (not earlier) and writing for not more than a couple of weeks. The aim of writing is to gain distance from the difficult emotions including looking at the situation more objectively and constructing new narratives.

Dramatherapy and psychodrama which utilise action methods engage with surplus reality (imagination) as a vehicle of change. Moreno (1972) discussed working with surplus reality where the client can "imagine" and "role play" a different outcome in a scenario which would be particularly relevant to working with victims of domestic abuse. For example inviting a dead parent to sit in an "empty chair" and having a conversation with them and to "hear" them say, "I love you very much and am proud of who you are" or "I've seen so much happen to you in this room and it makes me so sad to see you struggling like this" can help to gain different perspectives, empathy for self and also a sense of mastery or control over a situation.

Sometimes when talking about images and traumatic memories, it can be helpful to talk in the third person to create emotional distance. When the story is really difficult to tell it is helpful to create an opening and closing ritual for the story, for example speaking at a particular time or "putting the event in a box" before leaving the session.

Integration

The final stage of therapy includes imagining new steps in the clients' lives as painful memories are being resolved. The clients find ways of concluding the work as new meanings emerge. Malchiodi (2020) said that it is helpful for clients to complete the work with a ritual which may involve a painting, creating music/dance, or a performance. This may facilitate the closing of the painful chapter and opening to a new stage of one's life.

McNiff (2004) said that for clients who engage and actively participate in the creative approaches in therapy there is a sense of a "circulation of energy." As clients reconnect with vitality and living, new energy and hunger for life emerges in the work. Malchiodi (2020) added that through this creative work, clients can recover their own self-efficacy and confidence. She highlighted that using action-orientated creative approaches such as painting, singing, dancing, and playing instruments can recover a sense of vitality and pleasure giving clients a sense of empowerment which is essential in recovery following trauma.

Integrative Creative Therapy Approaches to Working with Trauma – Building an Evidence Base

Several authors developed integrative models for creative work with trauma. For example, Webber et al. (2021) developed a way of working based on psychodynamic and humanistic theories highlighting the interrelatedness of the arts (Knill et al., 2005). According to Knill et al. (2005) each of the arts assists the therapy in different ways and clients have an opportunity to choose a preferred style including visual, auditory, or kinaesthetic ways of working. Webber et al. (2021) illustrated this with a detailed case example where the client engaged in a range of different creative techniques to work with her trauma. For example, the client used sandtray and miniatures to externalise her images which allowed for safe distance from distress. The use of music allowed the therapist to provide empathic attunement which would not be possible with words alone. The client also used poetry which enabled her to connect with emotions and meaning related to specific words and images allowing to work at a slower pace giving a sense of agency over experience. Painting and drawing gave her the opportunity for pictorial format of emerging memories and feelings. Use of clay enabled a three-dimensional representation of a place where the client left the abuser. The use of drama and story allowed fictionalisation of the memories facilitating the emergence of new possibilities and hope.

One of the authors (Omylinska-Thurston et al., 2020) has developed with colleagues a creative, integrative, evidence-based group psychotherapy called Arts for the Blues that has been adapted to working with trauma. Arts for the Blues has pluralistic theoretical underpinnings focusing on the centrality of the therapeutic relationship and establishing individual goals that clients identify for themselves. The groupwork is structured into four parts: introduction, building strengths, addressing challenges and closure following Yalom's model of group psychotherapy (1983). It utilises multimodal creative approaches based on key ingredients present in relevant parts of the groupwork.

Table 13.2 Arts for the Blues for Trauma

	Activities
1 Introduction – safety and stabilisation	
Establishing safety	Imagine a safe space, creating a physical safe space in the room, transitional object/picture
Encouraging active engagement, including body engagement	Body scan, gestures, structured movement, using arts materials/musical instruments, creative writing
Learning skills including self-regulation skills	Doodling, scribbling, hand/foot drawing exercise, rhythmic movement, other grounding skills
2 Developing strengths and resources	
Building relationships	Mirroring, sharing drawing, verbal sharing
Expressing emotions	Free drawing/writing, authentic movement
3 Addressing challenges – processing	
Processing at a deeper level	Working with symbols, imagery
Gaining understanding	Tree of life, reflecting, receiving feedback
4. Closure – integrating	
Experimenting with new ways of being – meaning-making	Roleplay, ritual, performance
Integrating useful material	Journaling, engaging in dance/art/music activities

Arts for the Blues has been tested with clients who struggled with trauma (Parsons et al., 2020a; Parsons et al., 2020b). Participants highlighted the need for safety building which included making time to unpack feelings stirred at the initial phase and being clear and transparent about processes involved in engaging in the groupwork. The issue of containment and emotion regulation was also noted. The freedom of movement was valued but also the structure and goal orientation of the approach and the containment of the artwork was helpful. Participants wanted to continue engaging in creativity and playfulness on a regular basis which highlighted the need of using the arts for managing emotion regulation on a personal level.

Examples of activities related to each part of the groupwork and each of the key ingredients are included in Table 13.2.

Summary Points

In this chapter a creative approach to working with trauma is presented for working with adults who have experienced trauma, particularly domestic abuse. The key elements are:

1 A range of creative options are available for working with trauma such as art, music, drama, sandtray, clay, and arts-based approaches. These can be offered alongside talking and trauma-based therapies.

2 The relationship between clients and therapists needs to be collaborative so clients feel empowered and have a say in how the sessions are conducted and what creative options are being used.
3 Clients need to be willing to work with creative materials – not all clients will want to work in this way.
4 Creative arts therapies can be provided in groups as well as individually, as they offer an opportunity for hope, co-regulation, developing relationships and meaning.
5 Using creative arts offers aesthetic distance which can support clients in exploring traumatic experiences without feeling overwhelmed.
6 Creative arts therapy sessions should have a regular and planned structure, taking into account relevant models of trauma work.
7 It is important to evaluate creative therapy for trauma to improve the evidence base.

References

Avetikova.L. (2008). Healing through clay: A case study of a child witness. In S. Brooke (Eds.), *Creative therapies with survivors of domestic violence*. Illinois: Charles. C. Thomas.

Binkley. E. (2013). Creative strategies for treating victims of domestic violence. *Journal of Creativity in Mental Health*, *8*(3), 305–313

British Association for Counselling and Psychotherapy (2018). *Ethical framework for the counselling professions*. Lutterworth, BACP.10.1080/15401383.2013.821932

Casson, J. (2007). Psychodrama in miniature In C. Baim, J. Burmeister & M. Maciel (eds) (2007), *Psychodrama: Advances in theory and practice*. London: Routledge.

de Witte, M., Orkibi, H., Zarate, R., Karkou, V., Sajnani, N., Malhotra, B., Ho, R., Kaimal, G., Baker, F. A., & Koch, S. C. (2021). From therapeutic factors to mechanisms of change in the creative arts therapies: A scoping review. *Frontiers in Psychology*, *12*, 678397. 10.3389/fpsyg.2021.678397

Dieterich-Hartwell, R. (2017). Dance/movement therapy in the treatment of post-traumatic stress: A reference model. *The Arts in Psychotherapy*, *54*, 38–46. 10.1016/j.aip.2017.02.010 [accessed 2/2/2018]

Gendlin. E. (1982). *Focusing*. London: New York: Bantam Books

Helmich, J. (2009). One man's experience of accessing and transforming embodied traumatic memory: A dance therapy study. In K. Dunphy, J. Gutherie & E. Loughlin (Eds), *Dance therapy collections* No. 3, pp. 86–97. VIC: Dance therapy Association of Australia

Herman (1992). *Trauma and recovery: From domestic abuse to political terror*. (2nd edition) USA: Pandora

Jennings, S. (1986). *Creative drama in groupwork*. Bicester: Winslow Press.

Jennings, S., Cattanach, A., Mitchell. S., Chesner. A., & Meldrun. B. (1994). *The handbook of dramatherapy*. London: Routledge.

Johnson, D. R., Lahad, M., & Gray, A. (2009) Creative therapies for adults. In E. Foa, T. Keane, M. Friedman, J. Cohen (eds), *Effective treatments for PTSD:*

Practice guidelines from the international society for traumatic stress studies, pp. 479–490. New York: Guilford Press.
Jung, C. G. (1935). Modern man in search of a soul. *The Journal of Nervous and Mental Disease, 81*, 715. 10.1097/00005053-193506000-00052
Jung, C. (1997). *Jung on Active Imagination* (1997) Princeton U.
Karkou,V., & Sanderson, P. (2006). *Arts therapies: a research-based map of the field.* Edinburgh: Elsevier Churchill Livingstone
Kern, E., & Perryman, K. (2016). Leaving it in the sand: Creatively processing military combat trauma as a means for reducing risk of interpersonal violence. *Journal of Creativity in Mental Health, 11*(3–4), 446–457, DOI: 10.1080/15401383.2016.1172995
Knill, P., Levine. E., & Levine. S. (2005). *Principles and practice of expressive arts therapy. Towards a therapeutic aesthetics.* London: Jessica Kingsley Publishers.
Levine, P. A. (2010). *In an unspoken voice: How the body releases trauma and restores goodness.* California: North Atlantic Books.
Levy, F. (2005). *Dance movement therapy: A healing art.* (2nd ed). Reston, VA: National Dance Association.
Lowenfeld, M. (2004). *Understanding sandplay: Lowenfeld's world technique.* Eastbourne: Sussex Academic Press.
Lusebrink, V. (2010). Assessment and therapeutic application of the expressive therapies continuum. Implications for brain structures and functions. *Art Therapy: Journal of the American Art Therapy Association, 27*(4), 168–177.
Malchiodi, C. A. (2005). *Expressive therapies.* New York: Guildford Press.
Malchiodi, C. A. (2012). *Handbook of art therapy* (2nd ed.). New York: Guilford Press
Malchiodi, C. A. (2015). *Creative interventions with traumatized children* (2nd ed.). New York: Guilford Press.
Malchiodi, C. A. (2020). *Trauma and expressive arts therapy: Brain, body and imagination in the healing process.* New York: Guilford Press.
McNiff., S. (2004). *Art heals. How creativity cures the soul.* Colorado: Shambala Publications Ltd.
Moreno, J. L. (1932). *First book on group therapy.* Beacon House.
Moreno, J. L. (1972). *Psychodrama first volume* (Fourth Edition). Beacon House, New York, USA. (Original Publication 1946)
Murray, C. E., Moore Spencer, K., Stickl, J., & Crowe, A. (2017). See the triumph healing arts workshops for survivors of intimate partner violence and sexual assault. *Journal of Creativity in Mental Health, 12*(2), 192–202, DOI: 10.1080/15401383.2016.1238791
Omylinska-Thurston, J., Karkou, V., Parsons, A., Nair, K., Dubrow-Marshall, L., Starkey, J., & Sharma, S. (2020). Arts for the Blues: The development of a new evidence-based creative group psychotherapy for depression. *Counselling and Psychotherapy Research.* 10.1002/capr.12373
Parsons, A., Kefalogianni, M., Dubrow-Marshall, L., Turner, R., Ingleton, H., Omylinska-Thurston, J., Thurston, S., & Karkou, V. (2020a). Reflections on offering a therapeutic creative arts intervention with cult survivors: A collective biography. *International Journal of Coercion, Abuse and Manipulation.* https://drive.google.com/file/d/1r2-LIHBjE0BYWOnaxUAJuhizbOL1I5vu/view
Parsons, A., Turner, R., Ingleton, H., Dubrow-Marshall, L., Kefalogianni, M., Omylinska-Thurston, J., & Thurston, S. (2020b). Flowing towards freedom with

multimodal creative therapy: The healing power of therapeutic arts for ex cult-members. *The Arts in Psychotherapy, 72.* 10.1016/j.aip.2020.101743
Pennebaker, & Smyth (2016) *Opening up by writing it down: How expressive writing improves health and eases emotional pain.* New York: Guilford Press.
Proctor, G. (2017). *The dynamics of power in counselling and psychotherapy: ethics, politics and practice (2nd edition).* Monmouth: PCCS Books Ltd.
Roddy, J. K. (2014). *A client informed view of domestic violence counselling* [PhD, University of Leeds]. Leeds.
Salomon, J. (2007). *'Living with X': A body mapping journey in time of HIV and AIDS. Facilitator's guide.* Johannesburg. South Africa: REPSSI
Siegel, D. (1999). *The developing mind.* New York: Guilford.
Schore, A. N. (2003). *Affect regulation and the repair of the self.* W W Norton & Co.
Schouten, K. A., van Hooren, S. PhD, Knipscheer, J. W. PhD, Kleber, R. J. PhD, & Hutschemaekers, G. PhD (2019). Trauma-focused art therapy in the treatment of posttraumatic stress disorder: A pilot study. *Journal of Trauma & Dissociation (ISSD), 20*(1), 114–130. 10.1080/15299732.2018.1502712
Talwar, S. (2007). Accessing traumatic memory through art making: An art therapy trauma protocol (ATTP). *The Arts in Psychotherapy, 34*(1), 22–35. 10.1016/j.aip.2006.09.001
Van der Kolk, B. A. (1994) The body keeps the score: memory and the evolving psychobiology of posttraumatic stress. *Harvard Review of Psychiatry, 1*(5), 253–265
Van der Kolk, B. A. (2014). *The body keeps the score.* New York: Penguin.
Van der Kolk, B. (2000). Posttraumatic stress disorder and the nature of trauma. *Dialogues in Clinical Neuroscience, 2*(1), 7–22. 10.31887/dcns.2000.2.1/bvdkolk
Waller, D. (2015). *Group interactive art therapy.* London: Routledge
Webber, A., & Condaris, A. (2021). Letting go of the spider In: A. Chester & S. Lykou (Eds), *Trauma in the creative and embodied therapies.* London: Routledge
Winnicott, D. W. (1953). Transitional objects and transitional phenomena. *International Journal of Psychoanalysis, 34,* 89–97.
Winnicott, D. W. (1971). *Playing and reality.* London: Tavistock.
Yalom, I. D. (1983). *Inpatient group psychotherapy.* New York: Basic Books.

Chapter 14

Preparing Ourselves for Starting and Continuing Client Work

Jeannette Roddy and Elaine Beaumont

Learning Objectives

1 Understand the risk factors for and effects that DA client work can have on counsellors
2 Recognise the symptoms of adverse reactions in ourselves and others, and act upon them
3 Understand the importance of supervision, peer-debriefing, alternative work, and personal therapy
4 Understand the importance of self-care
5 Reflect on how you can cultivate self-compassion
6 Develop and use a self-care regime based on your own needs

Context

Working with DA is not an easy option for therapists. Whilst working in the helping professions can be rewarding, it can also be emotionally challenging and potentially lead to personal distress (Singer & Klimecki, 2014). The client can only tell their story if the counsellor is listening and has the capacity to hear what is to be shared, even when the stories are horrific and lead us to question how one human being could treat another in this way. Sometimes, when we listen to stories, we build pictures of the event as it unfolds in our mind, and then replay these images again and again. We may start to find abuse everywhere we look: the black eye of the person on the check-out becomes abuse rather than eye surgery; the friend whose partner phones more than once on a night out is now seen as at risk, rather than simply providing information urgently needed by their partner.

As we become sensitised to abuse, we need to develop the ability to judge when to react and call for support to protect the client and others, and when to support the client to make the changes they need to make on their own. Being too sensitive and reacting too quickly to a low-level concern can be very detrimental to the therapeutic relationship and to the client's likelihood of seeking support again. Alternatively, not acknowledging potential harm to

DOI: 10.4324/9781003253266-14

a client because the abuse seems less serious than for other clients could indicate minimising the client's abuse, rather than the intended work prioritisation, something to be explored in supervision. Domestic abuse work requires us to manage our own process as well as we manage our client process.

Having other people around us that we can rely on to provide perspective and to help process any unhelpful elements that we are left with in our work is essential. Having our own self-care strategies that we use and implement is also important. This chapter explores the potential impact on counsellors' mental health of working with abuse and the sort of support package you might want if you are going to do substantive work in this area.

Compassion Fatigue, Vicarious Trauma, Secondary Traumatic Stress, and Burnout

Over the last ten to fifteen years, the impact of working with trauma and abuse has been more clearly defined in four sub-categories: compassion fatigue, vicarious trauma, secondary traumatic stress, and burnout (Bush, 2009). Therapists may also experience symptoms of empathic distress fatigue, stress, secondary trauma, burnout, and self-criticism, which in turn can impact on their ability to provide compassion to both self and others (Beaumont, 2016; Beaumont et al., 2015; 2017; 2021; Beaumont & Hollins Martin, 2016; Figley, 1995, 2002; Yang & Hayes, 2020).

Although these are presented as separate categories here, they can co-exist. For example, Bush (2009) suggest empathic distress fatigue as a precursor to both compassion fatigue and burnout. Workplaces specialising in working with abuse should be monitoring for these signs within staff members. As individuals, it is also useful to know what these are, so that we can identify any warning signs either for ourselves or those we work with, as catching early signs of trauma and resolving them produces much better outcomes.

Compassion Fatigue

The nature of the work and the need for close empathic engagement means that there is a risk to one's own sense of self. At its simplest, this may be becoming aware of a growing reluctance to engage with clients at a deep level. Instead, we may try to keep sessions away from exploring difficult material as we feel we no longer have the capacity to listen or may struggle to contain the story once heard. Other symptoms are beginning to see clients as simply presenting variations of the same story, rather than their own unique one or sensing that clients are not "performing" and need to be let go. Compassion fatigue implies a lack of compassion for those we are trying to help, yet we want to be compassionate but find it difficult to do so. In some way our own bodies are saying "enough," as symptoms of tiredness, relational withdrawal, irritability, and anxiety present in the counselling room and elsewhere. It can feel like being a hamster on a wheel, with no time to stop and recharge. Supervision with someone who understands the impact of abuse on counsellors is vital so that they can notice and help to process these early signs.

Vicarious Trauma

Vicarious trauma occurs when the counsellor has heard so many stories of abuse that they lose their faith in humanity. This results in changes to thought patterns and belief systems, which can result in feelings of hopelessness and powerlessness as the waiting lists grow and the stories of abuse seem endless. Someone once said that the problem with working with abuse is that once you know what it is, you see it everywhere. You may become acutely aware of everything that is going on between people and begin wondering how often certain behaviours occurred. This may pass in due course as your own sense of what is *normal* comes back into being.

Therapists come into counselling wanting to help and support clients, and then begin to feel that there is so little that can be done given the scale and depth of the problem. Keeping a sense of balance whilst involved in the work is essential. This can be achieved in a number of ways, such as having a supportive team environment with the opportunity to debrief after a particularly challenging session or having a balanced workload with some general counselling clients alongside those who have experienced abuse. Therapy can be challenging and long-term work, particularly where the client has also suffered, for example, childhood sexual abuse, and working with a range of clients who can make recoveries over shorter time frames can be helpful. Finally, ensuring that life outside of work involves a lot of non-work activities (such as comedy programmes rather than violent crime movies on TV; or playing in the park with your family rather than reading counselling books on abuse) can provide the break required to remember that there are many positive aspects to life and many wonderful, kind and generous people in the world.

Secondary Traumatic Stress

Secondary traumatic stress is a slightly different problem. This is where the person listening to the story becomes affected by it to the extent that it impacts on their own daily life, that is, they start to experience symptoms of traumatic stress after hearing about someone else's trauma. This can happen to anyone, for example, someone transcribing counselling sessions or research interviews which explore experiences of abuse in depth. In some ways, a single session is harder to hear, as there is only the story of abuse and no process of recovery to witness over time. Counselling agencies may need to consider whether people answering the telephones, for example, are likely to hear parts of stories that could impact them and which they may need support to process.

For counsellors, the risks are potentially higher as the access to traumatic material is higher. In working with clients, many counsellors will construct their own image of what happened in their head as the client is talking. Sometimes this imagery can be so strong that it stays with the counsellor after the session and beyond. On occasion, however, this process of taking on some of the client's story can result in behavioural changes to the therapist (such as avoiding areas of town, developing a fear of something they personally had not experienced) or in havingflashbacks to the session and so on. These experiences can be brought to supervision and processed and sometimes the supervisor may recommend personal therapy where the trauma appears to have resulted from a combination of work and some personal experiences that would benefit from exploration and resolution. It can also be important to have our own routines when ending with clients. Just as we might ask a client to leave something in a box with us at the end of the session, so we may need some ritual or routine that allows us to leave our client work at the office or in our counselling room when we have finished for the day.

Burnout

Finally, there is a risk of burnout. This is the one of most concern. Foster et al. (2018) suggest that burnout is a common problem for professionals working in the field of mental health, with prevalence rates between twenty-one and sixty-seven per cent. Here, the individual enters a state of complete exhaustion and needs to take a break from the work for an extended period of time to allow them to regain their sense of self and purpose in life again. For some individuals, this will result in a career change as they feel unable to go back to counselling. It is important to address things before it gets to that stage, to be aware of our bodies and minds so that we can prioritise our needs.

The early warning symptoms of compassion fatigue, vicarious trauma, or secondary traumatic stress need to be identified and acted upon. Often these come into our awareness over time, or they are brought to us by others: family, friends, therapist, or supervisor. Much of the advice on how to prevent the adverse effects of working with abuse is centred around balance in both working and home life and having the support of compassionate individuals around us. If individuals feel isolated in the work environment, have large emotional loads to deal with and nowhere to let off steam, it is not hard to see that this could result in emotional distress for the employee or those in private practice. Of course, as counsellors, we do go to supervision and perhaps, for those with a high trauma workload in private practice, the alternative to debriefing at the workplace is to increase the rate of supervision from BACP's current recommendations of one session of 1.5 hours per month to more frequent supervision sessions to allow discussion of cases. Whilst this may result in a financial cost to the organisation or therapist, this is likely to be small when compared to a counsellor who is unable to continue in practice.

Possibility of Physical Harm

It would not be right to leave this section without making some reference to the possibility of physical harm to counsellors from working with this client group. For those individuals still in touch with their abuser, even after they have left the relationship, there is the possibility that their movements could be monitored. If movements are monitored, then the abuser will see their attendance at an agency or, if working in private practice, the counsellor's home. There have been incidents noted in the past of counsellors being attacked because the client's partner is unhappy with the changes seen because of therapy (Taylor, 2008). Whilst this will always be a risk to counsellors, it is important to note the slightly heightened risk in working with this client group due to their partners, not just the client. These are the reasons for the security surrounding the addresses of refuges and the security systems present in domestic violence agencies to allow screening of individuals prior to entry. Whilst these risks are low and should not prevent counsellors from working with clients, please do ensure that there are systems in place, wherever you work, such that an unexpected incident or guest can be managed, and support requested in an emergency.

Risk Factors and Protective Factors

The risk factors to clinicians have been researched over the years and are fairly stable in their conclusions. That is, the main risk factors are having a personal history of trauma and high case of trauma work over an extended time period (Baird & Kracen, 2006) and lack of experience, training and inability to do other non-trauma-related work (Canfield, 2005). It is worth exploring each of these in turn.

A Personal History of Trauma

At the University of Salford DA Counselling Centre, we take counsellors with and without a history of trauma and see very little difference in their ability to work with the client effectively. However, we have noticed some counsellors will be affected more by the trauma than others. Those with a history of domestic abuse are more likely to report being affected by client stories reminding them of their own abuses (either as an adult or child). These experiences trigger other memories which usually require additional sessions with their personal therapist. Those who have had more personal therapy have a higher tolerance for trauma work than those who have not, but sooner or later a client will come along to test how well they have processed their own experiences. Those who have not had traumatic experiences in the past are more likely to experience vicarious trauma as they can become overwhelmed by the different life stories of clients, compared to their own.

A High Case Load of Trauma Work

When people take on too many "complex" clients at once, this can have an adverse effect on the individual's self-esteem and self-confidence, as it can take some time to get past the initial storytelling. Having a client list with people at the beginning, middle, and end of therapy can be helpful. In services where there are short-term goals, this can be complicated as there is a quick turn-around and sometimes pressure for results. Working with complex clients and having to deliver good outcomes quickly can result in highly stressed counsellors. Having a more realistic time frame for DA clients, such as 20 sessions can help to alleviate this stress, together with agreed rather than imposed outcomes.

Unrealistic Work Expectations

Having too many clients without having time for self-care in between sessions can lead to compassion overload. Organisations need to be aware of the impact of deeply relational work on their employees and ensure that they have policies for breaks, time between sessions and holidays which they ensure work for staff. An organisation that fails to support staff in this way are likely to see large increases in staff absence and resignations which, in turn, places more stress on the staff remaining. Creating a work schedule that allows for gaps between clients and enough time to off-load if required can help to prevent this.

Lack of Counselling Experience

Being a new trainee without proper training can be very difficult. Some agencies have high rates of non-attendance, and this can undermine the counsellor's confidence. The type of experiences the clients are likely to share can be very difficult to listen to and can lead to the counsellor: questioning themselves constantly about the impact they may have had on the client through a misjudged response; realising they had taken the wrong approach during a session; being very uncertain about what had just happened in the room and what effect that had on the therapeutic relationship; or hearing something personally very difficult and struggling to stay with the client. It is not unusual for students to question their ability, experience self-critical judgement if they feel they have been unable to help a client, feel incompetent, and/or experience anxiety or stress (Beaumont & Hollins Martin, 2016; Wheeler et al., 2004). These sorts of experiences are best brought to supervision where the event can be properly explored. At the University of Salford Domestic Abuse Counselling Centre, trainees attend 2 hours of group supervision per month where they can hear from more experienced therapists about similar encounters and what they did as a result. Hearing that there are others who felt the same way in a similar situation, and learning from each other's experience, is very beneficial for all therapists.

Lack of Training

At the University of Salford, all counselling recruits undertake 42 hours of training (broadly based on this book – see chapter 15) before they can see clients. We would recommend this for all individuals seeking to work with domestic abuse. The reason for this is that a lack of training can lead to misinterpretation of a client story; lack of compassion for the client experience leading to client disruption; working constantly at the limits of capability and realising, often too late, that the response was inappropriate or upsetting to the client. This can lead to clients terminating therapy after only a few sessions. This combination of misunderstanding and always working at the edges of professional competence can have an eroding effect on the counsellor's self-esteem and confidence, leading to rumination on client sessions, and growing feelings of inadequacy. Ensuring appropriate training through CPD can help to alleviate these issues, as can having an experienced supervisor and/or placement lead who can help to mentor and coach you through the first few months of practice.

Working Only with Cases of Abuse

Working with clients who have experienced the worst of human nature on an ongoing basis can also impact negatively as counsellors can start to question whether there is humanity. This may also generate a distorted view of the risk of harm in society more generally. Working with a wider variety of clients helps to put this back in perspective, where the counsellor can see clients who have broadly healthy family environments too.

The combination of life balance, professional support, exploration professionally and personally, as well as knowledge of domestic abuse work and team relationships, provides some protection for counsellors working in this area. When recruiting into the University of Salford Domestic Abuse Counselling Service, recruits are asked to confirm that they have access to a personal therapist and to a supervisor experienced in working with abuse prior to accepting them onto the training course. Attendance at group supervision once per month is also mandatory. If you are considering starting this work, it would be useful for you to also put these professional supports in place as you begin your training, even if they are not provided by your workplace, as they might be needed.

This section may appear daunting to trainee counsellors, and it is not the intention to dissuade individuals from seeking to work in this area of counselling. This section is more about providing information about the potential risks and challenges which may occur and invite you to be clear about what you need to do to protect yourself physically and psychologically. It can be both heart-warming and uplifting in witnessing the profound changes that can take place during counselling for clients as they reclaim their lives. This witnessing also offsets the impact of the initial trauma stories as it provides hope and evidence for the counsellor that positive change can be made.

As well as the care that is gained from others through supervision, teamwork, and personal therapy, it is also important to remember that ongoing self-care is vital. Developing a strong sense of self-compassion, when we are dealing with particularly challenging material, is a valuable skill set to develop. The following section will offer some ideas and insight into what that might mean for you (see also chapter 10).

Self-Care and Managing Your Own Well-being

Counsellors' training in the counselling and psychotherapy professions experience incidents when working with people who have experienced DA that can be emotionally challenging. With the additional pressures of counselling study and personal development work, plus other personal, work, and/or family commitments it is imperative that they take care of their own well-being. Qualified therapists also juggle a variety of demands and responsibilities (Beaumont & Hollins Martin, 2016) with supervision, safeguarding, and complex client work a small part of the role. Therefore, self-care, self-practice, and self-reflection are important as these may help reduce the psychological distress that students and qualified therapists may experience from engaging in traumatic stories with clients.

Experiencing self-doubt or symptoms associated with secondary trauma or compassion fatigue can lead to therapists experiencing higher levels of self-criticism with self-compassion potentially being the antidote. According to Gilbert et al. (2004) self-criticism has various functions. For example, for some therapists it may be to improve oneself, for others they may feel their self-criticism helps them keep up standards or helps them prevent mistakes. For others their self-critical judgement may be a result of self-hatred or wanting to harm aspects of the self. In a study undertaken by Beaumont et al. (2016), using a sample (n=54) of student cognitive behavioural therapists and counsellors, high levels of self-criticism were correlated with symptoms of burnout, compassion fatigue, and reduced psychological well-being. Conversely, high levels of self-compassion were correlated with lower levels of compassion fatigue, self-criticism, and symptoms of burnout. Self-compassionate individuals feel confident in accepting new challenges, are more likely to change behaviour patterns that are unproductive, and acknowledge mistakes (Neff, 2009).

Techniques and interventions that encourage self-reflection and self-practice can help practitioners cultivate self-compassion, leading to the promotion of self-care and resilience building (Bennett-Levy & Lee, 2014; Kolts et al., 2018). Compassionate Mind Training (CMT) programmes have helped enhance well-being and levels of compassion in a variety of healthcare populations. Research suggests healthcare educators and providers (Beaumont et al., 2016; Rayner et al., 2021), teachers, and support staff in schools (Maratos et al., 2019; Matos et al., 2022), healthcare professionals enrolled on a Compassion Focused Therapy (CFT) module (Beaumont et al., 2021) and trainee therapists (Beaumont et al., 2017; Bell et al., 2016) have benefitted from cultivating compassion.

Thinking-Feeling Loops or "Our Tricky Brain"

The mind easily gets caught up in thinking-feeling loops, which can cause distress. Thinking-feeling loops are associated with reactions from the "*old brain*" *(reptilian)*, which navigates threats faced by humans, gets the body prepared for action, and pursues resources that are beneficial for survival. The "*new brain*" is linked to the prefrontal cortex and has the ability to imagine, plan, think about thinking, and reflect, ruminate, and worry (Gilbert, 2005; 2009; 2010; 2014) (see also chapter 8).

Students who believe they are not good enough, are self-critical, or compare themselves unfavourably with others, often get caught up in thinking-feeling loops associated with the "*old*" and "*new brain*." Understanding that our mind works this way can be helpful because this happens as a result of millions of years of evolution and whilst this is not our fault (we do not choose to have a brain that gets caught up in unhelpful thinking-feeling loops), it is our responsibility to try and do something about it if we want to instigate change. It might be useful to refer back to chapter 10 where we explored some of the basic principles of the compassionate mind model.

Gilbert (2009; 2014) suggests there are three flows of compassion:

- Compassion for others (*compassion flowing out*). Experiencing compassion within ourselves and directing this outward towards others.
- Compassion from others (*compassion flowing in*). Experiencing compassion from others and receiving and accepting it.
- Self-compassion (*self-to-self compassion*). Nurturing, directing, and developing compassion within ourselves and towards ourselves.

Individuals who have high levels of compassion for others, but low levels of self-compassion, can experience amplified distress (Gilbert & Choden, 2013). In order to develop compassion, it is essential that we are non-judgemental and sensitive to our own distress. Cultivating self-compassion encourages self-care, self-reflection, and self-practice and helps therapists working with DA cultivate compassion for their own struggles, feelings of sadness, worries, anxiety, and fears.

Some of the interventions and practices used in CMT include:

- **Mindfulness and focused attention**: Learning how to notice that our attention can be directed by us (e.g. when our threat system is activated our attention becomes narrow). We can learn to move our attention onto something that may be more helpful (a photograph of a loved one or a happy memory) by widening our attention. Mindfulness exercises all aim to help slow down our mind and body.
- **Soothing rhythm breathing (SRB)**: SRB aims to slow the body and mind down, help regulate the threat system, and connect with the parasympathetic nervous system.
- **Compassion-focused imagery**: Using imagery exercises to stimulate the soothing system. For example, creating a calm, peaceful place in the mind that provides affiliative feelings (see chapter 10 for the script) or using imagery to create an image of an ideal compassionate other (an image that offers compassion to you).
- **Developing the compassionate self**: Using the mind, body posture, voice tone, and facial expression to cultivate compassion – focusing on you at your compassionate best/the best version of you.
- **Our different parts**: Exploration of the different emotional parts (e.g. the angry, sad, anxious, and critical parts), and using your compassionate self to help those parts.
- **Engaging with self-criticism using the compassionate self**: Using compassionate behaviour, compassionate thinking, reasoning, and compassionate letter writing to help engage with the compassionate self and regulate the emotions experienced by the critical self.

For a comprehensive exploration of interventions see Irons & Beaumont, 2017.

Have a go at the next exercise that focuses on imaging an ideal, compassionate, supportive other.

My compassionate, supportive image

From Beaumont and Welford, The Kindness Workbook: Creative and Compassionate Ways to Boost Your Wellbeing (2020), reprinted with kind permission from Little, Brown Book Group

Find somewhere comfortable to sit where you'll not be disturbed.

Once you've settled your mind and body, gently bring your attention to your breathing, becoming mindful of it. Notice the sensations as you breathe slowly in and out. Feel your body begin to relax slightly as you breathe a little slower and deeper than usual. Let your shoulders drop and your jaw loosen. Lower your gaze and if it's comfortable to do so, close your eyes.

1 Imagine sitting in the presence of someone or something that is infinitely supportive of you.
2 Spend some time thinking about what the image looks like. If it helps think about different images and options before you settle on one.
3 Imagine this image has your best interests at heart; they are non-judgemental and have your well-being first and foremost in their mind.
4 They know how difficult life is for you and they possess the exact qualities you need, at this very moment. They're supportive, kind, encouraging, calming, and/or empowering. You may notice that they want to encourage, not judge you, and they want you to flourish.
5 Where would you like them to be in relation to you? Maybe in front of you or at your side?
6 If your image has a face, what does their facial expression look like? If your image has a voice, what does their voice sound like? What might they say to you that shows they care for you and support you?
7 Allow a slight smile to arrive on your face as you experience their warmth, compassion, and kindness. You may feel comforted or strengthened by their support.
8 Now spend a few minutes simply sitting in their presence and allow yourself to feel the care and support they're offering you.
9 Is there anything they want you to know or you want to hear?

When you're ready, with the knowledge that you can return to this exercise at any time, gently bring it to a close and widen your awareness to the chair that's supporting you and the room that you're in. If your eyes have been closed, open them: lift your gaze. Take some calming breaths and maybe have a stretch before you write about what you noticed.

Reflection: What was it like to create an image of an ideal, supportive other? What did you notice?

Three Good Things

How often do you reflect on the things that you have done well each day? Do you reflect on what has not gone well more often than the things that have gone well? If so try completing the Three Good Things Worksheet adapted from *The Kindness Workbook* (Beaumont & Welford, 2020), for at least a week with the aim of focusing on either: (1) what three things you have done well each day or (2) three things you are grateful for. For example, you may have reached out to your supervisor for support, written about how you feel, reflected on the things in your life that you are grateful for or you may have practised mindfulness or used your imagination to connect with your compassionate other.

Day of the week	*1st good thing/thing I'm grateful for*	*2nd good thing/thing I'm grateful for*	*3rd good thing/thing I'm grateful for*
Sunday			
Monday			
Tuesday			
Wednesday			
Thursday			
Friday			
Saturday			

Acts of Kindness

When you think about acts of kindness, what comes to mind? Most people will say things like: "doing a good deed for somebody," "texting a friend who is struggling," "giving someone a compliment," or "helping a colleague who needs support." Of course, all of these things are important, but can you also do something that you see as an act of kindness for yourself? Have a look at the table below for some ideas – you can also add to the list.

Self-Care

- Smile at yourself in the mirror or say something kind to your reflection
- When you notice self-criticism can you look in the mirror and say the same supportive words to yourself that you would say to a friend
- Be mindful of your body language, voice tone, and facial expression
- Send a nice text message to yourself
- Remind yourself to connect with your soothing system
- Bring your compassionate self to mind when you notice self-criticism, sadness, anger, or anxiety
- Practice mindfulness
- Connect with your calm, peaceful, relaxing place
- Look at photographs that remind you of happy memories
- Create a pre, during, and after plan when you face challenges (see chapter 10)
- Write a note to yourself about three things you are grateful for
- Say well done to yourself when you have done a good job
- Take a break from social media if that would be a kind thing to do for yourself

Summary

Working with stories of abuse can be challenging for counsellors. It is very important for therapists to ensure they take care of their physical, emotional, and professional needs to maintain a healthy work-life balance. Ensuring good supervision, access to personal therapy, a good team environment, and careful review of our response to client work can help to protect against compassion fatigue, vicarious trauma, secondary traumatic stress, and burnout. Developing self-compassion and building routines to support this can provide a strong base to work from.

Key Learning Points from Chapter 14

1. Experiencing emotional distress from working with domestic abuse clients can happen to anyone.
2. Being aware of the symptoms of secondary trauma and compassion fatigue can help to identify any issues early on and prevent the situation becoming chronic.
3. People with their own experiences of abuse should take more care to ensure they stay emotionally healthy as they are more at risk.
4. Build a network of trusted family, friends, colleagues, supervisor and personal therapist for support.
5. A good work-life balance and working with different client groups helps to maintain a realistic outlook.
6. Developing strengths in self-compassion can help counsellors boost their own well-being.

References

Baird, K., & Kracen, A. C. (2006). Vicarious traumatization and secondary traumatic stress: a research synthesis. *Counselling Psychology Quarterly, 19*(2), 181–188.

Beaumont, E. (2016). A compassionate mind model training model for healthcare practitioners and educators. *Healthcare Counselling and Psychotherapy Journal, 16*(3), 22–27.

Beaumont, E., Bell, T., McAndrew, S., & Fairhurst, H. (2021). The impact of Compassionate Mind Training on qualified health professionals undertaking a compassion focused therapy module. *Counselling and Psychotherapy Research*. doi: 10.1002/capr.12396

Beaumont, E., & Hollins Martin, C. (2016). A proposal to support student therapists to develop compassion for self and others through compassionate mind training. *The Arts in Psychotherapy 50*, 111–118. doi: 10.1016/j.aip.2016.06.005

Beaumont, E., Durkin, M., Hollins Martin, C. J., & Carson, J. (2015). Measuring relationships between self-compassion, compassion fatigue, burnout and well-being in student counsellors and student cognitive behavioural psychotherapists: A quantitative survey. *Counselling and Psychotherapy Research*. doi: 10.1002/capr.12054

Beaumont, E., Rayner, G., Durkin, M., & Bowling, G. (2017). The effects of compassionate mind training on student psychotherapists. *Journal of Mental Health Training, Education and Practice, 12*(10), 200–312.

Beaumont, E., & Welford, M. (2020). *The kindness workbook: Compassionate and creative ways to boost your wellbeing*. London: Little, Brown Book Group

Bell, T., Dixon, A., & Kolts, R. (2016). Developing a compassionate internal supervisor: Compassion-focused therapy for trainee therapists. *Clinical Psychology and Psychotherapy, 24*, 632–648.
Bennett-Levy, J., & Lee, N. (2014). Self-practice and self-reflection in cognitive behaviour therapy training: what factors influence trainees' engagement and experience of benefit? *Behavioural and Cognitive Psychotherapy, 242*(1), 48–64.
Bush, N. J. (2009). Compassion fatigue: Are you at risk? *Oncology Nursing Forum, 36*(1), 24–28. doi: 10.1188/09.onf.24-28
Canfield, J. (2005). Secondary traumatization, burnout, and vicarious traumatization: a review of the literature as it relates to therapists who treat trauma. *Smith College Studies in Social Work (Haworth), 75*(2), 81–101.
Figley, C. R. (1995). *Compassion fatigue as secondary traumatic stress disorder:* An overview. *Compassion fatigue: coping with secondary traumatic stress disorder in those who treat the traumatized.* New York:Brunner/Maze.
Figley, C. R. (2002). *Treating compassion fatigue.* New York: Brunner/Mazel.
Foster, K., Shochet, I., Wurfl, A., Roche, M., Maybery, D., Shakespeare-Finch, J., & Furness, T. (2018). On PAR: A feasibility study of the Promoting Adult Resilience programme with mental health nurses. *International Journal of Mental Health Nursing, 27*(5), 1470–1480.
Gilbert, P. (2005). Social mentalities: A biopsychosocial and evolutionary reflection on social relationships. In M. Baldwin (Ed.), *Interpersonal cognition*, pp. 299–333. New York, NY: Guilford.
Gilbert. P. (2009). *The compassionate mind.* London: Constable.
Gilbert, P. (2010). *Compassion focused therapy: Distinctive features.* Routledge.
Gilbert, P. (2014). The origins and nature of compassion focused therapy. *British Journal of Clinical Psychology, 53*(1), 6–41. doi: 10.1111/bjc.12043
Gilbert, P., & Choden. (2013). *Mindful compassion.* Robinson: London.
Gilbert, P., Clarke, M., Hemel, S., Miles, J. N. V., & Irons, C. (2004). Criticizing and reassuring oneself: An exploration of forms, style and reasons in female students. *British Journal of Clinical Psychology, 43*, 31–35.
Irons, C., & Beaumont, E. (2017). *The compassionate mind workbook. A step-by-step guide to developing your compassionate self.* London: Little, Brown Book Group.
Kolts, R., Bell, T., Bennett-Levy, J., & Irons, C. (2018) *Experiencing compassion-focused therapy from the inside out. A self-practice/self-reflection workbook for therapists.* New York; The Guilford Press.
Maratos, F. A., Montague, J., Ashra, H. *et al.* (2019). Evaluation of a compassionate mind training intervention with school teachers and support staff. *Mindfulness*, 10, 2245–2258. doi:10.1007/s12671-019-01185-9
Matos, M., Albuquerque, I., Galhardo, A., Cunha, M., Pedroso Lima, M., Palmeira, L. *et al.* (2022). Nurturing compassion in schools: A randomized controlled trial of the effectiveness of a Compassionate Mind Training program for teachers. *PLoS ONE, 17*(3), e0263480. doi: 10.1371/journal.pone.0263480
Neff, K. D. (2009). The role of self-compassion in development: A healthier way to relate to oneself. *Human Development, 52*, 211–214. doi: 10.1159/000215071
Rayner, G., Beaumont, E., McAndrew, S., & Irons, C. (2021). Exploring the impact of a compassion-focused therapy training course on healthcare educators. *Health Education Journal.* doi:10.1177/00178969211008484

Singer, T., & Klimecki, O. M. (2014). Empathy and compassion. *Current Biology, 24*(18), R875–R878.

Taylor, K. (2008). *Therapists are advised to take precautions.* The Sun, New York. Thursday 14th February, 2008. Retrieved on 25th September 2022 from https://www.nysun.com/article/new-york-therapists-are-advised-to-take-precautions

Wheeler, S., Bowl, R., & Reeves. A. (2004). Assessing risk: confrontation or avoidance—what is taught on counsellor training courses. *British Journal of Guidance & Counselling, 32*(2), 235–247.

Yang, Y., & Hayes, J. A. (2020). Causes and consequences of burnout among mental health professionals: A practice-oriented review of recent empirical literature. *Psychotherapy, 57*(3), 426.

Chapter 15

Looking Ahead

Jeannette Roddy

The creation of this book has been quite a task. To take a topic as significant, vast, and complex as the experience of domestic abuse and to condense it into 15 short and informative chapters to assist counsellors with the majority of clients they might see was perhaps over-ambitious. Nevertheless, we have identified several areas of practice that we believe are essential to working with experiences of domestic abuse. Whilst we have not always been able to write in the level of detail we would like to, we have provided signposts and a range of references to other material that we hope you find helpful, as you explore specific topics based on your client work. One of the joys of working in this area is that you are never quite sure what the next client will bring. We hope that the book will continue to be a resource for you as you see different clients at different times.

As you go through the book, you will see that we have cross-referenced many of the chapters as different aspects of client presentation appear to have multiple roots or may need an approach that encompasses several theories before finding out what works best for the client. We hope that you find these connections helpful and that you can begin to see how the topics overlap and connect. To fully understand your client work, you will often draw upon different theories and approaches to be truly effective. This is an integrative/pluralistic framework and requires knowledge, creativity, and courage to implement in full. It also requires curiosity, deep empathy, and a caring and loving nature. The competency framework talks of knowledge (in this book), skills (from additional training courses) and personal characteristics. Only you can know whether this is work that you are suitable for and whether it excites and interests you. It may be useful to reflect on the early chapters around the core conditions and the observation that the level of practice is above that required to pass most counselling practice exams. Developing those skills and allowing those caring and consistent aspects of your personality to come through in counselling will not only enhance your work with clients who have been abused, but also the other clients you will see as well.

It is important to mention at this point, that the training course that we provided at the University of Salford is different in one significant way to the

DOI: 10.4324/9781003253266-15

presentation in the book. Here, we have provided you with some theory, shared clinical experience and invited you to reflect on your own process and response to the material presented. Domestic abuse counselling is not for everyone and some of the reflections will hopefully enable you to see whether this is something you think you would enjoy or something that feels much less comfortable than you imagined. The training course that we delivered contains these aspects too, but this accounted for less than 60% of the course. The remaining 40% is made up of skills practices, case studies, role play, experiential work, and group check-ins. Whilst the theory and experience shared in this book is valuable, doing the skills practices and case study work really helps to embed the learning in a way that reflection in one's own time simply does not. It is for this reason that if, once you have read the book, you decide you would like to help people with experiences of domestic abuse, we recommend that you find a course that will allow you to practice some of what you have learned; will expose you to situations that you may not have imagined before you actually work with a client; and allows you to join a community of therapists who can provide ongoing support to each other through something like group supervision.

This training is supported by much of the current literature in the field and has also been tried in clinical practice in a university environment. It provides a snapshot of a practice for today, whilst also recognising that our knowledge of the psychology and neurology of trauma continues to expand at a rapid rate. We hope that the book supports your learning for some time but would encourage everyone to keep abreast of new developments in the field to ensure the best possible outcomes for our clients. We hope that you find the references useful today and that you add to those through your own research and reading over the next few years. Whilst research has not always been a favourite part of counselling training programmes, here we have a topic where research can help us to know more than we currently do, as it is such a new area, ripe for further exploration.

I believe it is important to share too that the team who put this project together was drawn from counselling, psychology, mental health nursing, and social work. The therapeutic contributors have core counselling training in person-centred, cognitive-behavioural, and psychodynamic theories. It is interesting to note that, despite the differences in our disciplines and preferred modalities, there is much that we have in common. In coming together and talking through our own perspectives, listening to others, and focusing on what was common between us (even if the language was sometimes different) we have produced what we believe is a unique insight into work with people who have had experiences of domestic abuse. Just as we have welcomed everyone to the table to contribute to this model of practice, so we welcome our clients from their many communities. In our practice, we focus on understanding their perspective through the language they use, so that we can share common elements of our combined understanding to identify and discuss their experience to the benefit of both.

At a time where the counselling profession is, to some extent, divided as each modality tries to show its relevance (and there have been times where that relevance has been shown at the expense of other approaches) this is one model which indicates the value in having each modality represented, with each contributing useful theories and practice. Perhaps you can see that trying to work with this range of issues would be difficult for any one discipline and that this multi-disciplinary and multi-modality approach helps us to understand the issues from numerous perspectives, which then helps us to help the client more readily. Personally, I am a great believer in teamwork. The team can become greater than the individuals when given the right opportunities. It would indeed be valuable for the field of mental health if we could adopt such a team approach in working on improving practices with other complex and challenging client groups.

Finally, it is interesting that the training programme has continued, despite people leaving the University or moving into different research areas. The enthusiasm of staff and students to participate in the training has helped us to continue the work. It is perhaps important to note that, just as we let our clients know that we are there if we are needed again, so the authors contributing to this book will still be around and contributing to the field for a while to come. There is still much to be done and space for everyone, new and old, around the table. I hope that some of you reading this book may feel inspired to do further research in the field and I look forward to hearing about your findings in due course.

As you finish this book, there is just time for you to reflect, finally, on what you see in your future when you look ahead!

Index

For Product Safety Concerns and Information please contact our EU representative GPSR@taylorandfrancis.com Taylor & Francis Verlag GmbH, Kaufingerstraße 24, 80331 München, Germany

Printed and bound by CPI Group (UK) Ltd, Croydon, CR0 4YY
08/06/2025
01896986-0009